THE HOLY WELLS OF WALES

THE HOLY WELLS OF WALES

BY

FRANCIS JONES

CARDIFF
UNIVERSITY OF WALES PRESS
1992

First Published, 1954
Paperback edition, 1992

British Library Cataloguing in Publication Data

Jones, Francis
Holy Wells of Wales. – New ed
I. Title
263. 042429

ISBN 0-7083-1145-8

First printed by the Cambrian News (Aberystwyth) Limited
Reprinted in paperback by Billings Book Plan Limited, Worcester

To

ETHEL

ELIZABETH SKEEL

and

ANNE

PREFACE

THE object of this book is to discuss the history of the well-cult, to show its influence on the people, and to try to interpret the beliefs and ritual that have been recorded or have survived to our times. The conversion of the Britons to Christianity was accomplished after a long period of missionary work. Despite the introduction of a new religion there was never a real breach of continuity in Celtic religious life. Although the greater divinities were superseded, the local gods proved more difficult to supplant. To effect this, apocryphical tales of saints and martyrs, 'pious frauds', and adaptation of primitive rites and beliefs to Christian usages, were employed to direct the faltering steps of doubting Britons on to the road of Christian salvation. Churches, wells, and megaliths were consecrated to saints, who, it was believed, could heal the sick and avert calamities. The cult of the saint united the people of a district under the patronage of an invisible head, and the older deities of well, hill, and megalith survived in a new guise.

With the passage of time and under the pressure of new attitudes of thought, traditions and legends tend to disintegrate and to become distorted echoes. Those relating to the same well often vary very considerably. However, such variations are not incompatible and the basic features can be recognised; so one need not be unduly perturbed by alternative or even conflicting versions. The ritual that has survived seems to be faithful in outline to its ancient forms, and in this case, what has been forgotten or distorted is the significance and meaning of the form of that ritual. The effect on the subject of literary influences and later borrowings renders it extremely important to find the 'earliest known reference.' I have tried as far as possible to trace the beliefs and rituals back to their earlier forms though not to their origins.

This work owes much to the co-operation and kindness of correspondents, and acknowledgments have been made to them in the body of the book. It will not be invidious if I name here those who generously placed their specialised knowledge at my disposal, namely, Professor J. Lloyd-Jones, Mr. R. J. Thomas, the Revd. Mr. A. W. Wade-Evans, the Revd. Mr. Haydn Parry, Mr. W. J. Hemp, Mr. Bob Owen of Croesor, Mr. Howell E. James; Dr. Iorwerth C. Peate for drawing my attention to Glamorgan material; my erstwhile colleagues at the National Library, to whose friendship I owe so much, namely, Dr. B. G. Charles, Mr. E. D. Jones, Mr. B. G. Owens, Mr. Myrddin Lloyd, Mr. Idwal Lewis and Mr. Isfryn Jones; Miss Janet Evans and Mr. William Griffiths (of Griffs Ltd.) who gave me the full and free enjoyment of their libraries. The practical assistance given by Mr. Ieuan T. Hughes, headmaster of Llandysul Grammar School, provides a happy example of how schoolmasters can assist research workers. Mr. Hughes gave the subject of 'Local Wells' to some of his senior pupils, and the results of the efforts of these young people (Samuel David Davies, David Gordon Griffiths, and Ednyfed Thomas) were of the greatest value to me. My debt to Mr. Alwyn D. Rees of Aberystwyth is profound. Not only did he place, unreservedly, at my disposal, evidence that he himself had collected, but he also advised me on the format and presentation of the material. I also wish to record my appreciation of the kindness and guidance that I received from Dr. Elwyn Davies and Mr. I. M. Williams during the preparation of this work for the press.

FRANCIS JONES.

The Author acknowledges with gratitude the receipt of a grant from the Thomas Ellis Memorial Fund towards the cost of this work.

CONTENTS

PART II

MAPS

BIBLIOGRAPHY AND ABBREVIATIONS

(This is a list of the most important works cited in the study. It is not a complete bibliography, and other books and manuscripts are cited in footnotes.)

AAW — *The Architectural Antiquities of Wales.* Vol 1. Pembrokeshire. No. 1. St. Davids. Charles Norris. London. 1810.

ABM — *The Ancient Burial-Mounds of England.* L. V. Grinsell. London. 1936.

AD — *Ancient Deeds.* Public Record Office publications. London. 1890—.

Add. L — *Additional Letters of the Morrises of Anglesey* (1735-1786). ed. H. Owen. 2 vols. London. 1947-49.

AHWC — *Ancient and Holy Wells of Cornwall.* M. & L. Quiller-Couch. London. 1894.

AMB — *Ancient Man in Britain.* D. A. Mackenzie. London. 1922.

Anc. Mon. — Publications of the Royal Commission on Ancient Monuments in Wales and Monmouthshire. HMSO. London. *Anglesey* (1937). *Carmarthenshire* (1917). *Denbighshire* (1914). *Flintshire* (1912). *Merioneth* (1921). *Montgomeryshire* (1911). *Pembrokeshire* (1925). *Radnorshire* (1913).

Angl. — Anglesey.

AOSC — *It's An Old Scottish Custom.* F. Drake-Carnell. London. 1939.

Arch. Cam. — *Archaeologia Cambrensis.* London. 1846—

ARR — *A History of Roman Religion.* F. Altheim. trans. H. Mattingly. London. 1938.

ARS — *Archaeology and Society.* G. Clarke. London. 2nd edn. 1947.

AS — *The Age of Saints* (in Cornwall). W. C. Borlase. Truro. 1893.

ASEG — *Antiquarian Survey of East Gower.* W. E. Ll. Morgan. London. 1899.

ATC — *Arthurian Tradition and Chrétien de Troyes.* R. S. Loomis. New York. 1949.

BBCS — *Bulletin of Board of Celtic Studies.* Oxford. 1923—

B. Britt. — *Brittany.* A. H. Brodrick. London. 1951.

BBSD — *Black Book of St. Davids* (1326). ed. W. J. Willis-Bund. London. 1902.

BCC	*British Calendar Customs.* Folk-lore Society.
BD	*Bygone Days in the March Wall of Wales.* M.N.J. London. 1926.
Benham	*The Dictionary of Religion.* W. Benham. London. 1891.
BG	*British Goblins.* Wirt Sykes. London. 1880.
BGBB	*A Book of Brittany.* S. Baring Gould. ed. I. Daniel. London. 1932.
BGBR	*A Book of the Riviera.* S. Baring Gould. London. 1905.
BGNW	*A Book of North Wales.* S. Baring Gould. London. 1903.
BGSW	*A Book of South Wales.* S. Baring Gould. London. 1905.
BHM	*History of Monmouthshire.* J. A. Bradney. London. 1904-1923.
BHS	*Historical Sociology.* V. Brelsford. London. 1943.
BK	*Baronia de Kemes.* Arch. Cam. Suppl. London. 1862.
BM	British Museum.
Brand	*Observations on Popular Antiquities.* J. Brand. London. edn. 1888.
Breck.	Brecknockshire.
BWG	*Wanderings in Greece.* F. S. Burnell. London. 1931.
Bygones	*Bygones relating to Wales and the Border Counties.* Oswestry. 1871—
CA	*Cardiganshire, its Antiquities.* G. Eyre Evans. Aberystwyth. 1903.
Caern.	Caernarvonshire.
CAL	*Antiquities of Laugharne,* etc. M. Curtis. London. 2nd. edn. 1880.
Cannwyll	*Cannwyll y Cymry.* Rees Pritchard. Caerfyrddin. edn. 1807.
Card.	Cardiganshire.
Carlisle TDW	*Topographical Dictionary of Wales.* N. Carlisle. London. 1811.
Carm.	Carmarthenshire.
CASF	*The Cistercian Abbey of Strata Florida.* S. W. Williams. London. 1889.
C Bio.	*S. Wales and Mon. Contemporary Biographies.* Cardiff. 1907.
CBPM	*Celtic Britain and the Pilgrim Movement.* G. Hartwell Jones. London. 1912.
C Brit. G	*Brittania.* W. Camden. ed. R. Gough. Vol. 2. London. 1789.

CBS *Lives of the Cambro-British Saints.* W. J. Rees. Llandovery. 1853.
CC *Coelion Cymru.* Evan Isaac. Aberystwyth. 1938.
CD *Cambria Depicta.* Edward Pugh. London. 1816.
CDG *Cywyddau Dafydd ap Gwilym a'i Gyfoeswyr.* I. Williams & T. Roberts. Bangor. 1914.
CE *Cwm Eithin.* Hugh Evans. Lerpwl. 1931.
C Fu. *Cymru Fu.* ed. I. Foulkes. Liverpool. 1862-1864.
CFV *Church Folk-lore.* J. E. Vaux. London. 1894.
CGL *Complete Guide to Llandudno.* R. Parry. Llandudno. 1864.
Chron. A *Chronicon Adae de Usk* (1377-1421). ed. E. M. Thompson. London. 1904.
CIIC *Corpus Inscriptionum Insularum Celticarum.* R. A. S. Macalister. 2 vols.
Clark GC *Glamorgan Charters.* G. T. Clark. 6 vols. Cardiff. 1910.
CLMS *The Mountains of Snowdonia.* H. R. C. Carr & G. A. Lister. London. 1935.
CMAR *Classical Mythology and Arthurian Romance.* C. B. Lewis. London. 1932.
CML *Celtic Myth and Legend.* Charles Squire. London. n.d.
CN *Carmarthen and its Neighbourhood.* W. Spurrell. Carmarthen. 1879.
COC *Cymru'r Oesau Canol.* R. Richards. Wrecsam. 1933.
Col. D *Coleman Deeds, Calendar of,* ed. F. Green. Aberystwyth. 1921.
COT *Crefydd yr Oesoedd Tywyll, neu Hynafiaethau,* etc. W. Roberts. Caerfyrddin. 1853.
CPC *Church Plate of Cardiganshire.* J. T. Evans. London. 1914.
CR *Records of the County Borough of Cardiff.* ed. J. H. Matthews. 6 vols. Cardiff. 1898-1911.
CRC *Canu Rhydd Cynnar.* T. H. Parry-Williams. Caerdydd. 1932.
C Reg. *Cambrian Register.* 3 vols. London. 1795-1818.
Cross D. *Crosswood Deeds, Calendar of.* ed. F. Green. Aberystwyth. 1927.
CSR *Celtic and Scandinavian Religions.* J. A. MacCulloch. London. 1948.
Cymm. *Y Cymmrodor.* London. 1877—.

Davies LGM 'Llen Gwerin Meirion.' W. Davies. *Transactions of National Eisteddfod of Wales,* 1894.
DCC *Dyffryn Conwy a'r Creuddyn.* E. D. Rowlands. Lerpwl. 1948.

Denb. Denbighshire.
D Hanes *Hanes Morganwg.* Dafydd Morganwg (David Jones). Aberdar. 1874.
DHPL *Hanes Plwyf Llandyssul.* W. J. Davies. Llandyssul. 1896.
Dineley *Progress of the Duke of Beaufort,* &c. (1684). T. Dineley. London. 1888.
DJNW *Diary of a Journey into North Wales in 1774* : S. Johnson. London. 1910.
DLl. *Dolgelley and Llanelltyd.* T. P. Ellis. Newtown. 1928.
DM *Diary of Montaigne's Journey to Italy in 1580 and 1581.* trans. E. J. Trechmann. London. 1929.
DNQ *The Story of New Quay.* E. B. Davies. New Quay. 1933.
DPLl *Hanes Plwyf Llangynllo.* Evan Davies, Llandyssul. 1905.
DSA *History of the Diocese of St. Asaph.* D. R. Thomas. 3. vols. Oswestry. 1908-13.
Dug. *England and Wales Delineated.* 11 vols. T. Dugdale. London. 1845.

EEE *Irish Heritage.* E. Estyn Evans. Dundalk. 1943.
EF *Ethnology in Folklore.* G. L. Gomme. London. 1892
EG *Glamorgan ; its history and topography.* C. J. O. Evans. Cardiff. 1948.
El *Elucidarium.* J. Morris-Jones & John Rhys. Oxford Anecdota. 1894.
ELM *Enwau Lleoedd yn Mon.* R. T. Williams. Bala. 1908.
ELSG *Enwau Lleoedd Sir Gaernarfon.* J. Lloyd Jones. Caerdydd. 1928.
ERE *Encyclopaedia of Religion and Ethics.* 13 vols. ed. J. Hastings. Edinburgh. 1908-1926.

Fenton TP *Historical Tour through Pembrokeshire.* R. Fenton. Brecknock. edn. 1903.
Fenton TW *Tours in Wales* (1804-1813). R. Fenton. ed. J. Fisher. London. 1917.
FFCC *The Fairy Faith in Celtic Countries.* W.Y.E. Wentz. London. 1911.
FL *Folk-Lore.* Journal of the Folk Lore Society. London. 1891—
FLBI *Folklore of the British Isles.* E. Hull. London. 1928.
Flint. Flintshire.
FLH *The Folk-Lore of Herefordshire.* E. M. Leather. London. 1912.

FLOT *Folk Lore in the Old Testament.* J. G. Frazer. London. 1907.

FPM *In Praise of Manxland.* M. Fraser. London. 1935.

FS *Funeral Sermon delivered 26 November 1576 by Richard Davies, Bishop of St. Davids, at the burial of the Earl of Essex and Ewe.* London. 1577.

GA *Geographical, Historical and Religious Account of the parish of Aberystruth in the County of Monmouth.* Edmund Jones. Trevecka. 1779.

GB *The Golden Bough.* J. G. Frazer. Abr. edn. London. 1922.

GDD *Glossary of the Dimetian Dialect.* Meredith Morris. Tonypandy. 1910.

GDE *Gwaith Dafydd ab Edmwnd.* T. Roberts. Bangor. Welsh MSS Soc. 1914.

GDNQ *New Quay.* Official Guide. Glanmor Davies. Cheltenham & London. 1934.

Geoffrey *The British History.* trans. A. Thompson. London. 1718.

GFLHS *Folk Lore as an Historical Science.* G. L. Gomme. London. 1908.

Gir. IK *Itinerarium Kambriae.* Rolls Series. London. 1868.

Glam. Glamorgan.

Gover MS. 'The Place-Names of Cornwall.' J. E. Gover. MS deposited in NLW.

HAC *History of the Ancient Church situate at Newton, Porthcawl.* D. Charles Davies. Cowbridge. 1938.

HAN *History and Antiquities of the parish of Newchurch, Carmarthenshire.* T. M. Morgan. Carmarthen. 1910.

H Carm. *A History of Carmarthen.* ed. J. E. Lloyd. 2 vols. Cardiff. 1935, 1939.

HEB *The Heritage of Early Britain.* M. Charlesworth & others. London. 1952.

Hebrides *In the Hebrides.* C. F. Gordon Cumming. London. 1883.

HEFL *English Folklore.* C. Hole. London. 1940.

HG *Hen Gwndidau Etc.* L. J. Hopkin James. Bangor. 1910.

HGC *Hen Gerddi Crefyddol.* ed. H. Lewis. Caerdydd. 1931.

HHBS *Highways and Byways in Somerset.* Edward Hutton. London. 1919.

HLG *History of Llantrisant, Glamorgan.* T. Morgan. Cardiff. 1898

HM *A Short History of Marriage.* E. A. Westermarck. London. 1926.

HMa *A History of Mathern.* E. T. Davies. Chepstow. 1950.

HMA *A History of Margam Abbey.* W. de Grey Birch. London. 1897.

HN *Northumberland.* H. L. Honeyman. London. 1949.

HNW *The Heart of Northern Wales.* W. Bezant Lowe. 2 vols. Llanfairfechan. 1912, 1927.

Hooke *The Labrynth.* ed. S. H. Hooke. London. 1935.

HPF *Hanes Plwyf Ffestiniog.* G. J. Williams. Wrexham. 1882.

HPLl *Hanes Plwyf Llandebie.* Gomer M. Roberts. Caerdydd. 1939.

HPLP *Hanes Plwyfi Llangeler a Phenboyr.* D. E. Jones. Llandyssul. 1899.

HR *Radnorshire.* W. H. Howse. Hereford. 1949.

HSM *History of St. Mary's Church. Haverfordwest.* F. J. Warren. Letchworth. 1914.

HVN *The History of the Vale of Neath.* D. Rhys Phillips. Swansea. 1925.

HWE *The Legendary Lore of the Holy Wells of England.* R. C. Hope. London. 1893.

HWG *A History of West Gower.* J. D. Davies. 4 vols. Swansea. 1877-94.

HWI *The Holy Wells of Ireland.* P. D. Hardy. Dublin. 1836.

IH *Island Heritage.* W. Cubbon. Manchester. 1952.

IRG *Illustrated Regional Guides to Ancient Monuments.* Vol. V, N. Wales, by Lord Harlech. HMSO. London. 1948.

JBG *Bedd Gelert, its Facts, Fancies, and Folk-lore.* D. E. Jenkins. Porthmadoc. 1899.

JCD *Folk-Lore of West and Mid-Wales.* J. C. Davies. Aberystwyth. 1911.

JCF *The Journeys of Celia Fiennes.* ed. C. Morris. London. 1949.

JCP *Cornwall and its People.* A. K. H. Jenkin. London. 1945.

Johnson BBA *Byways in British Archaeology.* W. Johnson.

JWHR *History of Radnorshire.* J. Williams. ed. E. Davies. Brecknock. 1905.

KSF *The Science of Folk-Lore.* A. H. Krappe. London. 1930.

LBB *The Building of Bath.* Bryan Little. London. 1947.
LBS *Lives of the British Saints.* S. Baring Gould & J. Fisher. 4 vols. London. 1913.
LCS *Churches with a Story.* George Long. London. 1932.
LEBW *Little England Beyond Wales.* E. Laws. London. 1888.
Lewis TDW *A Topographical Dictionary of Wales.* S. Lewis. London. 1843
LFH *Looking for History in British Churches.* M. D. Anderson. London. 1951.
LFLC *The Folk-Lore Calendar.* George Long. London. 1930.
Lib. Land. *Liber Landavensis.* ed. W. J. Rees. Llandovery. 1840.
Llan. 6 *Llanstephan MS* 6. ed. E. Stanton Roberts. Cardiff. 1916.
Ll. Hen *Heroic Elegies of Llywarch Hen.* ed. W. Owen. London. 1792.
LMD *Le Morte Darthur.* ed. E. Strachey.
LOC *Out with the Cambrians.* E. Lewes. London. 1934.
l.p. local pronounciation
Lhuyd Par. *Parochalia* (1695-98). E. Lhuyd. Arch. Cam. Suppl. 1909, 1910-11.
Llwyd Angl. *History of Anglesey.* Angharad Llwyd. Ruthin. 1832.
LW *The Lakes of Wales.* F. Ward. London. 1931.

Mab. G. *The Mabinogion.* trans. Lady C. Guest. London. 1909. (Everyman).
Mab. J *The Mabinogion.* trans. G. and T. Jones. London. 1949. (Everyman).
MacCulloch CF. *The Childhood of Fiction* : A. Study of Folk-Tales and Primitive Thought. J. A. MacCulloch. London. 1905.
MacCulloch MFF *Medieval Faith and Fable.* J. A. MacCulloch. London. 1932.
Mandeville *Travels of Sir John Mandeville.* ed. A. W. Pollard.
Math. *Math vab Mathonwy.* W. J. Gruffydd. Cardiff. 1928.
MC *Mynachdai Cymru.* T. Mardy Rees. Newport. 1910.
MCC *Manx Calendar Customs.* C. I. Paton.
MDeth. *Detholiad o waith Gruffudd ab Ieuan ab Llewelyn Vychan.* ed. J. C. Morrice. Bangor MSS. Society. 1910.

Men. Sac. *Menevia Sacra*. ed. F. Green. London. 1927.
Mer. Merioneth
Meyrick C. *The History and Antiquities of the County of Cardigan*. S. R. Meyrick. Brecon. 1810.
M Fardd *Llen Gwerin Sir Gaernarfon*. J. Jones (Myrddin Fardd). Caernarfon. 1908.
MMS *Migration of Symbols*. D. A. Mackenzie. London. 1926.
Mon. Monmouthshire.
Mont. Montgomeryshire.
Mont. Coll. *Powysland Club Collections*. 1867—
MONW *Memorials of Old North Wales*. ed. E. A. Jones. London. 1913.
Morgan PN *The Place Names of Wales*. T. Morgan. Newport. edn. 1912.
Morris CM *Cantref Meirionydd*. R. P. Morris. Dolgellau. 1890.
MP *Medieval Panorama*. G. G. Coulton. Cambridge. 1945.
MPFF *The Peat-Fire Flame*. A. A. MacGregor. Edinburgh & London. 1937.
MS Manuscript.
MTBM *The Minor Traditions of British Mythology*. L. Spence. London. 1948.
MT *The History of Merthyr Tydfil*. C. Wilkins. Merthyr Tydfil. 1867.

NCP *Nooks and Corners of Pembrokeshire*. H. Thornhill Timmins. London. 1895.
NCPN *Non-Celtic Place-Names in Wales*. B. G. Charles. London. 1938.
NEA 'The Story of Newcastle-Emlyn and Atpar to 1531.' Gruffydd Evans. *Y Cymmrodor*. xxxii. 1923.
Nennius *History of the Britons*. ed. A. W. Wade-Evans. London. 1938.
NLW National Library of Wales.
NM *Northern Mythology*. B. Thorpe. 3 vols. London. 1851.
NSG *The New Swansea Guide*.
NQ *Notes and Queries*. London. In progress.

OC *Old Cowbridge*. L. J. Hopkin James. Cardiff. 1922.
OCA *The Old Churches of Arllechwedd*. H. L. North. Bangor. 1906.
OCS *The Old Churches of Snowdonia*. H. H. Hughes and H. L. North. Bangor. 1924.
OHR *The Origins and History of Religions*. J. Murphy. Manchester. 1949.

OS	Ordnance Survey Maps.
OWC	*The Older Welsh Churches.* S. R. Glynne. London. 1903.
OWFL	*Welsh Folk-Lore.* Elias Owen. Oswestry & Wrexham. 1896.
O Pem.	*The Description of Pembrokeshire.* George Owen. ed. H. Owen. 4 vols. London. 1892-1936.
PAS	*Pembrokeshire Archaeological Survey.* Tenby. 1896-1907.
Pem.	Pembrokeshire.
Pem. A	*Pembrokeshire Antiquities.* Solva. 1897.
PEW	*The Parliament explained to Wales* (1646). J. Lewis. Cardiff. 1907.
PL	*Pastoral Letter of the Archbishop of Cardiff.* 6 Nov. 1948.
PR	parish register.
PRO	Public Record Office, London.
P Tours	*Tours in Wales.* T. Pennant. ed. J. Rhys. 3 vols. Caernarvon. 1883.
Rad.	Radnorshire.
RBES	*Roman Britain and the English Settlements.* R. G. Collingwood & J. N. L. Myers. Oxford. 1936.
Rees Map	*Map of South Wales and the Border in the Fourteenth Century.* W. Rees. Ordnance Survey Office, Southampton. 1932.
RGI	*Remains of Gentilisme and Judaisme.* J. Aubrey (1686-87). ed. J. Britten. London. 1881.
Rhys CF	*Celtic Folklore,* Welsh and Manx. J. Rhys. 2 vols. Oxford. 1901.
Rhys CH	*Origin and Growth of Religion as illustrated by Celtic Heathendom.* J. Rhys. London. 1888.
RJT	*Enwau Afonydd a Nentydd Cymru.* R. J. Thomas. Caerdydd. 1938.
ROD	*The Reformation in the Old Diocese of Llandaff.* L. Thomas. Cardiff. 1930.
RSD	*Diary of Richard Symonds.* ed. C. E. Long. Camden Society. 1859.
RSN	*The River Scenery of the Head of the Vale of Neath.* F. J. North. Cardiff. 1949.
RSW	*Wanderings in South Wales.* T. Roscoe. London. 1837.
RWJ	*Bywyd Cymdeithasol Cymru yn y Ddeunawfed Ganrif.* R. W. Jones. London. 1931.

SAL *Studies in the Arthurian Legend.* J. Rhys. Oxford. 1891.
SBFO *British Fairy Origins.* L. Spence. London. 1946.
SCVC *Old Stone Crosses of the Vale of Clwyd etc.* Elias Owen. London. 1886.
SF *The Science of Fairy Tales.* E. S. Hartland. London. 1925.
SFLl *Annals of St. Fagans with Llanilterne.* C. F. Shepherd. Cardiff. 1938.
SFLL *Scottish Folk-Lore and Folk-Life.* D. A. Mackenzie. London. 1935.
S Gad. *Silva Gadelica.* S. H. O'Grady. London. 1892.
SGSE *A Short History of St. George-super-Ely.* C. F. Shepherd. Cardiff. 1933.
SHW *Somerset Holy Wells.* E. Horne (Somerset Folk Series No. 12.) London. 1923.
SIM *Isle of Man.* E. H. Stenning. London. 1950.
Skinner *Ten Days Tour Through the Isle of Anglesey,* December 1802. J. Skinner. Arch. Cam. Suppl. 1908.
SMR *Myth and Ritual in Dance, Game and Rhyme.* L. Spence. London. 1947.
SN *St. Nicholas. A Historical Survey of a Glamorganshire Parish.* C. F. Shepherd. Cardiff. 1934.
SRLJ *A Short Relation of a Long Journey* (1652). John Taylor. Reprint for the Spencer Society. 1876.
SSSL *Springs, Streams, and Spas of London.* A. S. Foord. London. 1910.
SWO *A Spell of Words.* L. Eckenstein. London. 1932.

T *Traethodydd* 1893 (Quarterly Journal) Denbigh—Holywell—Caernarvon, 1845—.
TCE *History of Llangynwyd Parish.* T. C. Evans. Llanelly. 1887.
TDD *Tour.* D. Defoe.
TGJ *Welsh Folklore and Folk Custom.* T. Gwynn Jones. London. 1930.
THA *Tregaron Historical and Antiquarian.* D. C. Rees. Llandyssul. 1936.
TI *Tir Iarll.* F. Evans. Cardiff [1912]
TM Tithe Maps and Commutation Schedules (now in NLW).
TMA *Magic and Healing.* C. J. S. Thompson. London. 1947.
TNEW Llanelly *Transactions of the National Eisteddfod of Wales.* Llanelly (1895) 1898.

Trans. Cym. *Transactions of the Hon. Soc. of Cymmrodorion.* London. 1892—.
Trevelyan *Folk-Lore and Folk-Stories of Wales.* M. Trevelyan. London. 1909.
Trevelyan G *Glimpses of Welsh Life and Character.* M. Trevelyan. London. 1893.
TSW *The Tribal System in Wales.* F. Seebohm. London. edn. 1904.
TYFG *Twr-y-Felin Guide to St. Davids.* H. Evans. London. edn. 1923.

VA *The Viking Age.* P. B. du Chaillu. 2 vols. London. 1889.
View *View of the State of Religion in the Diocese of St. Davids,* 1721. E. Saunders. London. 1721.
VSH *Vitae Sanctorum Hiberniae.* 2 vols. C. Plummer. Oxford. 1910.
VW *The Verge of Wales.* W. T. Palmer. London. 1942.

WCO *Welsh Christian Origins.* A. W. Wade-Evans. Oxford. 1934.
WDSW *General View of the Agriculture and Domestic Economy of South Wales.* W. Davies. 2 vols. London. 1810, 1813.
WEL *Enwau Lleoedd.* I. Williams. Lerpwl. 1945.
WESD *Life of St. David.* A. W. Wade-Evans. London. 1923.
WEVS *Vitae Sanctorum Britanniae et Genealogiae.* A. W. Wade-Evans. Cardiff. 1944.
WFB *The Welsh Fairy Book.* W. Jenkyn Thomas. London. edn. 1908.
Willis B *Survey of Bangor.* Browne Willis. London. 1721.
Willis SD *Survey of St. Davids.* Browne Willis. London. 1717.
WMEF *Traces of the Elder Faiths of Ireland.* 2 vols. W. G. Wood-Martin. London. 1902.
WML *Welsh Medieval Law.* A. W. Wade-Evans. Oxford. 1909.
WMPI *Pagan Ireland.* W. G. Wood-Martin. London. 1895.
WWHR *West Wales Historical Records.* 14 vols. ed. F. Green. Carmarthen. 1912-29.
WWS *Where Wye and Severn Flow.* W. J. Smart. Newport. 1949.

YG *Y Geninen.* Caernarfon. 1883-1928.
YHC *Yr Hynafion Cymreig.* P. Roberts. trans. and enlarged by H. Hughes, Carmarthen. 1823.

Part I

Chapter I

INTRODUCTORY

The well—well names—distribution—value of the study.

IT cannot be stressed too often that everything relating to wells, whether in early form or in mangled survival, traces to one source—religion. There are in Wales wells which must have been sacred even in pre-Christian times, wells transformed from pagan to Christian usages, and wells that claim a purely Christian origin. Legends, practices, beliefs and folktales, the accretions of centuries, encrust them, with the result that their original significance has been obscured. The subject possesses an essential unity, and it cannot be discussed satisfactorily under separate headings such as 'saints' wells,' 'wishing wells,' 'pin wells,' 'rag wells,' etc. These categories over-lap each other in various ways and this seems to suggest the former existence of a well cult, the details of which may have varied from place to place, and variously assorted remnants of which have survived in connection with different wells. The amount of oral, manuscript, and printed material relating to the subject is almost inexhaustible, and at a certain stage of research I realised that all the information, despite its apparent diversity, dealt with facets of the central pattern. In the first part of this book an attempt has been made to interpret the evidence, showing the essential features, the development, and the decay of the well-cult. In the second part, individual wells are listed alphabetically, and, in order to facilitate reference, these are shown under counties.

(*a*) *The Well*

Most wells (n.f. *ffynnon*, pl. *ffynhonnau*) are formed in cavities in the ground, usually circular in shape. The springs (n.m. *tarddiant*, pl. *tarddiannau*) feed the well from the bottom of the cavity, but occasionally flow into the well from a little distance away. The overflow (n.m. *gofer*, pl. *goferydd, goferoedd*) sometimes forms a shallow pool which in certain districts was also considered holy. It has been stated that wells with a southern aspect were especially sacred, but the Welsh evidence of this is slight, and one writer actually states that such wells were considered to be evil [1] Wells in domestic use were improved with masonry, steps were made, and a covering raised over the whole. Christian holy wells were also, but not invariably, improved similarly, and elaborate canopies and little chapels were sometimes erected over them. In most of the canopies or well-heads were niches which held effigies of saints and vessels for oblations. Some wells were enlarged so that bodily immersion could take place. St. Winifred's Well (Flint) is the classic example of well, bath, and building. In this study we also have to consider spouts (n.m. *pistyll*, pl. *pistylloedd*) which were often accorded a sanctity. Some springs, known as *llygad, blaen*, and *codiad*, when rivers flowed from them, were held to be holy, and there are traditions of sanctuaries at river sources both in heathen areas[2] and in Biblical lands.[3] The holy well, Ffynnon Gwenlais (Carm.) is the source of the river Gwenlais, and Priest's Well (Mon.) is the source of a stream whose waters, like those of the well, were considered beneficial. The place of the holy well was taken occasionally by a pool (n.m. *pwll*, pl. *pyllau*) in a field or in a river bend. At Llanpumsaint (Carm.) five pools in the river were regarded as the pools of the saints commemorated in the place-name. Lakes (n.m/f. *llyn*, pl. *llynnoedd, llynnau*) also have to be mentioned, for the customs at both well and lake were often similar. Thus, Llyn Ffynnon Lloer (Caern.) was held in high veneration, and people assembled there on the eve of

[1] M Fardd, 167.

[2] HEB, 116. e.g. the sources of the Shannon and the Boyne.

[3] Amos VIII, 14; Judges XVIII, 29-31; I Kings XII, 29; cf. Enoch XIII, 7. The source of the Jordan—' waters of Dan '—was one of the sanctuaries of early Israel. The source of the Euphrates bestowed health—ERE, 707.

May Day, and at sunrise on May Day danced on the banks.[4] Several other Caernarvonshire lakes contain in their names the element *ffynnon*, such as Llyn Ffynhonnau, Llyn Ffynnon Gaseg, Llyn Ffynnon y Gwas, Llyn Ffynnon Llugwy, Llyn Ffynnon Llyffaint. Some lakes and pools were named after saints, such as Llyn Badrig and Llyn Maelog (Angl.), Llyn Padarn and Llyn Teyrn (Caern.), Llyn Ffynnon Fair (Flint), and St. Michael's Pool (Rad.).

References will be found below to wells in other Celtic lands, often described by their native names. In Ireland and Scotland the word used for well, fountain or spring, is *tobar* ; in the Isle of Man, *chibbyr* and *tobbyr* ; in Cornwall, *fenten, fenton, funten, fyntan* and *venton.*

(*b*) *Well-names*

Etymology is an important aid to the study of wells, but it is an established principle that no etymological explanation may be permitted without early forms. The temptation of deriving what, superficially, appears to be an obvious deduction should be resisted in cases where early forms have not been found. For example, Dr. Charles' treatment of Cresswell (Pem).[5] has destroyed the attractive fiction of ' Christ's well ' sponsored by Fenton[6] and underlined by Laws.[7] The name Ffynnon Cegin Arthur (Caern.) inspired the local legend of ' the well of Arthur's kitchen,' due to a misunderstanding of the archaic meaning of *cegin*, but Professor Lloyd-Jones has shown that *cegin* here means ' ridge,' and the local topography supports his view.[8] In anglicised parts of Wales every Ellen Well does not commemorate St. (H)Elen. It has been demonstrated that Ellenwell (Dandy parish, Glam.) is derived from the English *ellern* + *well*, i.e. elder-tree well.[9] Certain well-names have given rise to onomastic tales. Ffynnon y Barfau (Caern.) is explained as being the place where Celtic saints trimmed their beards.[10] Modern tradition states that Ffynnon Fil Feibion (Carm.) is so named because a

[4] LW, 124-5. [5] NCPN, 96. [6] TP, 150-1. [7] LEBW, 262.
[8] ELSG, 96. cf. Ffynnon Craig Arthur (Flint). [9] NCPN, 165. [10] M Fardd, 188.

thousand youths fell in battle there.[11] But the meaning of Fil Feibion (Holy Innocents) was well known to medieval Welsh Catholics.[12] In this instance, Protestantism has completely erased the Catholic version from the popular mind by calling into existence an onomastic tale to explain anew what was formerly familiar to the people. It is a significant example and shows what must have occurred often a thousand years previously when Christianity 'converted' the pagan wells of the Celts. I was told by a parishioner of Llandeloy (Pem.) that a local Ffynnon Samson was named after the Biblical hero—he had forgotten —indeed never known—that the Celtic St. Samson had laboured in Pembrokeshire.[13] Local antiquaries claim that Ffynnon Foida (Carm.) is so named because a hermit (*meudwy*) lived there, and used the mutated form *feudwy* to oust the old Celtic saint, Boida.[14] Another example of a mutilated tradition concerns Ffynnon Gurig (Caern.). The modern 'tradition,' which has forgotten St. Curig, says that the water of the well cured one 'Lady Curic,' who then built the church of Capel Curig.[15] The name Ffynnongain (Pem.) has been suggested as being the well of St. Keyne, on no evidence other than a fancied phonetic similarity, but early forms show that it belongs to the adjectival class of well-names. It is widely believed that wells containing in their names the elements—*wen* (white, blessed, holy) and *llwyd* (grey, old, holy)—possess a religious origin: similarly, it is suggested that wells bearing the name *ddu* (black, sinister) are evil. I have not found evidence to support such theories, and these names, which are numerous in all lands, may be assigned with confidence to the adjectival-name class. A further example of these

[11] TNEW, Llanelly, 36; JCD, 303.

[12] cf. 'Marwnat y vil veib', *Book of Taliesin*.

[13] Sometimes a 'twist' was given to a church legend. St. Warna was said to have sailed from Ireland to St. Agnes Isle (Scilly Is.) where a holy well is dedicated to her: since the Reformation, she is said to have brought with her the fatal gift of causing shipwrecks.

[14] M. D. Anderson improves on this by speaking of 'Llanboidy (church of the Cowshed)'!—LFH, 48.

[15] Hughes, *Hynaf. Llanllechid a Llandegai*, p. 86.

etymological dangers is found in the modern form Ffynnon Wen (Card.), which is described in 1772 as *Finnon wen alias Fenon Owen.*[16] The neighbouring Pembrokeshire farms Ffynnondridian and Llandridian are said to be memorials of St. Tridian. However, the former is described in 1326 as *Fonnan Pēdrykyaun,*[17] in 1588 as *Ffonaon pedrigion alias Fynnon Pendrigion,*[18] in 1636 as *Ffinnon Drigan,*[19] and by 1690 it had assumed its present form. Here, undoubtedly, was the well at the head (end) of the land of a man named Drigion (earlier Driciaun), and marked its boundary in the same way as Ffynnon Penarthur, which stood at the end of the land of Arthur, was a boundary mark of a manor at St. David's. Sometimes the well-name preserved a name that has passed out of currency. Thus, the present Ffynnon Nathan (Carm.) is described in 1610 as *Fabanathan's Well,*[20] and was undoubtedly the well of the son of Anathan (or Ynathan), names which occur frequently in early Welsh records, but which were discontinued before the end of the Middle Ages.

A common error is the identification of names with certain eminent personages. Arthur of the ' Round Table ' is claimed as being associated with all wells bearing his name. Llyn Llech Owen (Carm.) is said to have been formed as a result of Owen Glyndŵr's failure to replace the cover of the well after he had drunk from it. A local tradition says that Henry Tudor, on his march to Bosworth, rested at Ffynnon Dudur, near the Cardiganshire-Carmarthenshire border. Two wells bearing his name are claimed as the place where Rhys ap Tewdwr was slain. But these names were borne by many other Welshmen—princes, saints, and sinners. Lhuyd states that one Ffynnon Bedr (Ruthin parish, Denb.) was named, not after the saint, but after a rather prosaic Mr. Peter Jones,[21] while

[16] PRO, Papers of Great Sessions, Card., 1772. [17] BBSD, 87.
[18] PRO, Papers of Great Sessions, Pem., 1588. [19] *ib.*, s.d. 1636.
[20] WWHR, ii, 174.
[21] ' Lately so-called, nicknamed fr(om) one Peter Jones who found it. This is frequented in June and July '—Par. i, 147. The season of visitation suggests that it had acquired a ritualistic character.

Ffynnon Isaac (Carm.) owes its name to one Isaac Thomas on whose land a Nonconformist chapel was built in 1672.[22] Identity of name is not necessarily identity of the person whose name is most prominent in Welsh history.

However, there are certain cases, when early forms do not exist, where evidence of custom may be accepted in lieu. For instance, we may suggest with confidence that the waters of wells named Ffynnon Ymenin or Butter Well (and probably many a Ffynnon Oer) were used by the dairymaids of bygone Wales. We read that St. Docheu met women at the well at Llandaff washing butter 'after the manner of the country,'[23] and this may be the one enclosed with ancient masonry at Llandaff Court called Dairy Well. In the last century the farmers of the Penrhys district (Glam.) came during summer to Ffynnon Fair for water to make butter into pats, a process called *cwyro menyn*.[24] This practice was known in England also, and in 1684 the water of a Cumberland well was described as being 'good for dressing butter with.'[25] Analogy also offers a clue in connection with well-names. Our knowledge of the regard in which cows were held in Celtic lands in pre-Christian days, permits us to consider that the name Ffynnon y Fuwch Frech (Denb.) may retain a memory of a very early association,[26] especially as the many tales of Y Fuwch Frech show that here was an animal associated with the supernatural.[27]

The following classes of names appear:

(*i*) *Holy Names*. There are some 437 wells which bear the names of saints and such names as Ffynnon Dduw, -Fendigaid, -Saint, -Sanctaidd, -Y Drindod (Trinity), -Y Pasg, and -Y Groes, while among a further 65 wells which are associated with Christian practices we find names like Ffynnon Capel, -Ffeirad, -Y Prior, -Y Mynach, -Brodyr, -Yr Abad, Priest's Well, etc. It should be noted that wells bearing English names usually retain the title 'saint,'

[22] Morgan PN, 101. [23] Lib. Land., 378. [24] Arch. Cam., 1914, 378 n.
[25] HWE, 44. [26] Lhuyd Par., i, 105.
[27] OWFL, 129; JCD, 229; Math. 155. For enchanted cows at Irish wells see WMEF, ii, 88.

e.g. St. Mary's Well, but those bearing Welsh names rarely do so, e.g. it is Ffynnon Seiriol but never Ffynnon Sant Seiriol, Ffynnon Ddewi but never Ffynnon Ddewi Sant. Where wells are named after saints or hermits, I have found a number of cases where the personal name appears elsewhere in the locality, e.g. Ffynnon Elwad and Maes Elwad (Card.), Ffynnon Ddewi and Maen Dewi (Pem.), Ffynnon Ddewi and Cwm Dewi (Pem. and Glam.), Pistyll, Capel, and Pant Sant Fread (Pem.), Ffynnon Cawrdaf and Cader Cawrdaf (Caern.), Ffynnon Fair and Nant Mair (Breck.), Ffynnon Rhedyw and Bedd Rhedyw (Caern.), and many others. It is important to record these additional local names when they occur.

(*ii*) *Lay Names*. These are wells named after secular people, but it is possible that some of them commemorate holy men who have left no other record. Some 104 of these wells have been noticed. There can be no doubt of the secular character of names like Stradling's Well (Glam.), Ffynnon Lewis (Pem.), and Mr. Goodman's Well (Denb.). The name Gwrgan(t) may be preserved in Ffynnon Wrgan (Breck.), but the local pronounciation is Organ, and as no early forms are available, we cannot be sure of the original name. It is possible that some belong to pre-Christian divinities, such as Gwenhudw, whose name appears in Cardiganshire and Merioneth wells, while the names of giants (who always play an anti-Christian role in Welsh menology and legend) are applied to some wells. Among the latter are Llyffan Gawr, Howel Gawr, Cybi Gawr and Dilic Gawr,[28] and the matter is further complicated by the fact that Celtic saints also bore the names Howel, Cybi, and Dilic.[29] Traditions of a family of giants are connected with Ffynnon Baich y Cawr (Mont.) and Ffynnon y Cawr (Carm.). Very few feminine names appear in this class.

(*iii*) *Occupational Names*. These are named after people

[28]NLW Peniarth MS. 118, ff. 829-837, written c. 1600 by John Dafydd Rhys. In Britain and on the Continent giants are associated with pre-Christian monuments such as burial mounds, megaliths, etc. See ABM, 41.

[29] AS, 149. See also AMB, chap XVI, 'Ancient Pagan Deities'.

who used the wells or perhaps lived nearby. Some 32 wells bearing such names have been noted, such as Ffynnon y ceis, -y saer, -y gof, -y meddyg, etc.

(*iv*) *Adjectival Names.* These are common throughout the British Isles, and 93 have been listed in Wales. Among them are Ffynnon Dafolog, -lân, -deg, -wen, -felen, -ddu, -lwyd, -lâs, -goch, -oer, -berw, etc. Those bearing the descriptions, -ddrewllyd, -haearn, -chwerw, -dwym, are generally alleged to be medicinal.

(*v*) *Tree Names.* There are 25 Welsh examples, such as Ffynnon celyn, -cyll, -dderw, -ddrain, -gollen, -helyg, -onnen, -yscawen, -ywen, etc. Since the veneration of trees was a feature of pre-Christian culture, a connection with pagan religion is not to be entirely discounted, especially as sacred trees often grew at or near wells. But many of these names probably came into being because such trees chanced to grow near wells, and have no other significance. The subject is discussed in further detail in Chapter 2.

(*vi*) *Animal and bird names.* Some 61 examples have been noticed, such as Ffynnon y blaidd, -ceiliog, -y ci, -y cadno, -dwrgi, -draenog, -fuwch, -gath, -gog, -gaseg, -giach, -gwyddau, -hwch, -hydd, -llygoden, -march, -milgi, -filast, -tarw, -wiber, etc. Certain animals were sacred to the Celts, and it is possible that some of these wells were associated with them. It is equally possible, however, that the wells were so named because they were the haunts of certain animals and birds.

(*vii*) *Topographical Names.* These are self-explanatory and some 125 examples have been noticed, such as Ffynnon y ddôl, -goeg, -y grib, -y mynydd, -y rhiw, -y wern, etc.

The classes of well-names enumerated above are general throughout Wales, and, so far as I can see, there is no significance in their concentration or distribution.

(*c*) *Distribution*

In the preceding section only the names have been discussed. Now we shall note the numbers and the distribution of wells which by their names and by the associated ritual, customs, and traditions possess a significance which will be analysed later in this study. The total numbers of wells studied in connection with this work are as follows :

Anglesey	35	Radnorshire	29
Caernarvonshire	88	Brecknockshire	41
Denbighshire	76	Cardiganshire	123
Flintshire	51	Pembrokeshire	236
Montgomeryshire	77	Carmarthenshire	128
Merioneth	50	Glamorgan	180
		Monmouthshire	65

In addition to the above there are many unlocated wells. It will be observed that Pembrokeshire wells greatly outnumber those of other individual counties. Personal knowledge has enabled me to discover this large number in my native county, but similar research will undoubtedly reveal many additional wells in other counties. In view of this, it must be borne in mind that the distribution maps and statistical analysis represent the present state of our knowledge.

These wells, with the exception of a few miscellaneous ones, may be analysed according to their major attributes as follows.

1	2	3	4	5	6	7
County	Wells with saints' names	Healing Wells	Wells associated with chapels, feasts etc.	Wells associated with megaliths	Wells where pins were offered	Wells where rags were hung
Anglesey	21	19	5	3	1	
Caernarvon	37	84	9	7	11	1
Denbigh	38	20	3	1	6	
Flint ..	27	6	2	2	2	
Montgomery	23	33	1	6	3	1
Merioneth	26	23	1	1	3	
Radnor ..	9	13	3	3		
Brecknock	15	10	3	1	2	
Cardigan	42	32	4	5	1	
Pembroke	82	36	11	17	6	1
Carmarthen	35	34	12	9	5	
Glamorgan	64	50	9	6	8	7
Monmouth	19	13	4	2	5	
Totals	437	369	66	62	53	10

In a large number of cases these categories overlap. For instance, among the 437 wells bearing saints' names, some 119 are also healing wells. It may well be that originally all the wells were 'healing,' but here we are concerned only with those whose reputation in that connection has survived. Very few wells where rags were hung appear, and of the 10 listed, 7 are concentrated in Glamorgan. Either this custom was not widespread in Wales or it has been long discontinued and its memory obliterated. If it had been widespread, one would have expected to find more examples in the most 'Welsh' parts such as the counties of Caernarvon, Merioneth and Cardigan. As the 'rag-wells' are popular in England their presence in Glamorgan may be due to English influence. On the other hand, I have not found examples in Monmouthshire, a county that was subjected to English influences from early times. Research by local societies and antiquaries may produce more examples.

(*d*) *Value of the study*

It may be asked, what is the value of a study of the well-cult ? Are these beliefs and customs, after all, nothing more than superstitions, at best to be described only as 'interesting' ? Or, can something of practical use and value be derived from the study ? It will be shown that useful information relating to the past of our people, is embedded in well-history. In it are found echoes of the beliefs and ways of thought and life before written history, relics of pre-Christian beliefs. The wells indicate where the sacred sites of our pagan and Christian forebears were ; they tell us of medieval belief and practice, and they sometimes confirm and strengthen our imperfect knowledge of the areas where certain early saints laboured or where their cults, were popular. Some well-names are the sole memorials of local saints whose names figure in no martyrology and who have escaped the keen eyes of the Bollandist fathers. Dim memories of historical events, not chronicled in Bruts, are found in other well-names, while others help to interpret local history. This study touches upon religion, folk-healing, folklore, etymology and archaeology. The importance of the well-cult lies not only in its great antiquity, but in its survival to modern days. Rooted in paganism, 'converted' to Christian usage, condemned by Protestantism, 'explained' by folklorists, rationalised by modern education, the cult has survived and still wields an influence over the human mind. 'What concerns us is that we are face to face in Britain with living forms of the oldest, lowest, most primitive religion in the world—one which would seem to have been once universal, and which, crouching close to the earth, lets other creeds blow over it without effacing it, and outlives one and all of them.'[30] It is a phenomenon that calls for analysis and explanation.

[30] CML, 416

Chapter II

ANTIQUITY

Early notices—wells and megaliths—wells and trees.

THE well-cult is part of the veneration of water that characterised many early religious observances. In ancient and pre-Christian times wells, springs, lakes and rivers were worshipped as gods or regarded as the abodes of gods, and associated with them were purification ceremonies, sacrifice, divination, fertility, healing and weather charms.

Striking examples are found in the Old Testament. Israelitish kings were consecrated at the wells of En Gihon and En Rogel[1] where sacrifices were made ; pilgrimages to the wells of Beersheba were part of religious exercises ;[2] the wells of Kadesh,[3] En-haq Qoreh,[4] and the miraculous springs of Lahai Roi[5] were held in high esteem. Titles of gods were given to wells.[6] In pre-Mosaic times the Well of Judgement punished evildoers.[7] Jordan was a holy river,[8] and in much later times the waters of the pool of Bethesda were curative.[9] Similar veneration for wells, rivers, and water generally is found in Ancient Egypt,[10] among the Trojans[11] and Babylonians.[12] In Classical Greece, Zeus was associated with the wells of Aganippe and Mt Lycaeus,[13] and Hera with the well of Kanathros.[14] The well at Delphoi was associated with the oracle, that at

[1] I Kings i, 9, 38.
[2] Amos V, 5 ; viii, 14 : cf. Genesis XXI, 28-33 ; XXVI, 23-33.
[3] Genesis XIV, 7 : Num. XX, 1-13 : Exod. XVII, 1-7.
[4] Judges, XV, 18—19. [5] Genesis XVI, 7-14.
[6] *baal* and *baalath*. 2 Sam. V, 20 : 1 Chron. XIV, 11 : and Joshua XIX, 8, where we find Baalath Beer, ' the lady of the well '. See ERE, xii, 714.
[7] Genesis XIV, 7. [8] 2 Kings 5, 10. [9] John V, 2-4. [10] ERE, XII, 710.
[11] Iliad XX, 4, 47 : XXI, 130. [12] ERE XII, 706, 708, OHR, 439.
[13] ERE, XII, 705. [14]BWG, 153.

Hieron helped pregnant women, and young girls were sacrificed to river-gods.[15] In Ancient Rome the feast of Fontinalia was held in honour of sacred springs, wells such as that of Joturna, were held in great esteem,[16] and the worship of well-nymphs was widespread. Scandinavian mythology lays emphasis upon the holy well at the roots of the ash Yggdrasil.[17] There was a sacrificial spring near the sacred tree at Uppsala, and pagan baptism was also carried out at Norse wells.[18] In the Landnamabok[19] we read that Thorstein 'worshipped the waterfall.' In Germanic lands there was a belief that the gods resorted to the springs,[20] and as late as A.D. 539 the Franks were sacrificing women and children to rivers.[21] Early Anglo-Saxon belief in holy wells conformed to a similar pattern.[22]

Celtic evidence shows that wells occupied a prominent part in religion. Rivers were often named after gods,[23] and the Matronae of Gaul seem to have been connected with springs.[24] Roman writers have preserved the names of some of the deities, such as Bormo (Borvo) god of the hot springs at Aix-les-Bains, and Sul or Sulis, who presided over similar springs at Bath[25] where, it was said, a British prince had been healed in pre-Roman times. Coventina was the goddess of the sacred spring by Carrowburgh, Conditis was worshipped on the lower Wear,[26] and Latis, goddess of a pool or stream, held sway in the western parts of the Wall.[27] Sir John Rhŷs inferred the former worship of the water-god Lud on the Thames and of Nod (Nudd) on the Severn.[28] Adamnan mentions a river called Nigra Dea (i.e. Loch Lochy) in Scotland, the river itself being a deity.[29] The Irish god of medicine, Diancecht, prepared a well with healing herbs,[30] and the source of the Boyne was a holy spring.[31] The Irish rivers Cronn and Brosnach were invoked as gods by Cuchulainn and St. Ciaran.[32] There is recently discovered archaeological evidence of a Celtic

[15] ERE, XII, 708. [16] ARR, 243 : ERE, XII, 713. [17] CSR, 112, 127-9, 156. [18] *ib*, 131. [19] V, 5. [20] ERE, IX, 241. [21] *ib*, IX, 253. [22] NM, *passim*. [23] ERE, III, 748. [24] FLBI, 48. [25] COC, 375. [26] HWE, 112-115. [27] RBES, 265-6. [28] Rhys CH, 125-133. [29] *Vita St. Col.*, ii, 39. [30] FLBI, 29. [31] *ib*, 59. [32] *ib*, 55.

water-cult in Anglesey.[33] Tradition says that the wells of Dwyfan and Dwyfach (Mer.) bear the names of two men who escaped from the Deluge ; from these wells flow two streams which unite to flow through Bala Lake, without, it is said, mingling with its waters.[34] These traditions probably derive from the time when the two wells and streams bore the names of gods from which the modern name-forms Dwyfan and Dwyfach descend. In Celtic Gaul, goddesses called Alaunae and Alounae, gave name to the Breton river Alaunus, and it is possible that the same name has survived in Wales in Alun, a tributary of the Dee, in the Glamorgan stream Alun mentioned in 12th century deeds,[35] and in the Alun that flows by St. David's Cathedral. Megaliths and burials are often associated with wells.[36] Nennius states that in Ercing[37] 'is a sepulchre by a well called Licat Anir[38] and Anir was buried there. He was the son of Arthur the soldier.'[39] A mound called Bedd Samson stands near Ffynnon Garreg in Nevern parish (Pem.) ; another called Hen Domen stands near Ffynnon y Domen in Llansantffraid Deuddwr (Mont.) ; and Twmpath Garmon is a mound in the churchyard of Llanfechain (Mont.) and about 200 yards away is St. Garmon's well. A tumulus stands near Ffynnon Nonny (Carm.).[40]

Some of the stones associated with saints, and bearing the names *Cadair* (Chair), *Gwely* (Bed), *Maen*, *Carreg*, and *Coitan* (Quoit), became closely bound to the ritual at holy wells. In Ireland, St. Patrick's Chair is near St. Patrick's

[33] HEB, 75.

[34] TNEW, 1884, 226. cf. the names Dwygyfylchi (Caern.), Dwy (Angl.), and Crugiau Dwy (Pem.) which is associated with a hero named Dwy. For the elements *dwy*, *dyw*, in river-names see RJT, 13-14, 34, 139, 140-1. There are rivers named Dwyfan, and Dwyfach (now Dwyfor) in Caernarvonshire also—see TGJ, 103-4. Dwyfan is listed as a saint in LBS. [35] NLW Ewenny Deeds.

[36] See AS *passim*. For megalith worship in Celtic Britain see AMB, 146-8. For further Welsh examples see TGJ, 28-31. According to Dr. Estyn Evans the cult of holy wells is probably megalithic in origin—EEE, 163.

[37] Archenfield, Herefordshire. [38] Gamber Head in Llanwarne.

[39] Nennius, 120.

[40] For Irish evidence of mounds and cromlechau near holy wells see FLBI, 68-70, 103, 106-8, 113, 270, 272 : WMEF, i, 323 ; ii, 66, 86, 228. For Scottish evidence see BCC, Scotland, i, 144, 146-7. For Manx evidence see MCC, 113, 117.

Well,[41] and at Aughagrun a megalith called St. Patrick's Bed stands near a holy well and two ancient trees, all of which were included in the ritual.[42] A stone monument over a well is mentioned in the *Life* of the same saint, and a megalith still covers Tober Greine, Co. Clare.[43] There are cromlechau near holy wells in counties Clare and Kerry.[44] In the Isle of Man, St. Patrick's Bed and Well are near each other.[45] In Scotland there are stone 'altars' near Tobirnumbuadh in St. Kilda,[46] and near St. Ronan's Well,[47] and megaliths stand near sacred wells of Gigha Isle,[48] at Castle Bay in Barra and at Tullybelton.[49] In Cornwall, St. Madron's Bed is near his well.[50] In Brittany, the holy well of St. Cornelly and the mighty stones of Carnac were included in Christian ceremonies,[51] and there are two megaliths near the well of St. Gildas on an islet off the Breton coast.[52]

Some 62 examples occur in Wales, where there is a well-megalith association, and a further 14 cases of wells near tumuli. Sick visitors to Canna's Well (Pem.) offered a pin at the well, then drank or bathed, and afterwards tried to sleep on Canna's Chair a few yards from the well.[53] Near Llangybi Church (Card.) is the famous Ffynnon Gybi, concerning which Lhuyd wrote :

> 'On Ascension Eve they resort to Fynnon Wen ; after they have washed ymselves at ye well They go to Lhech Gybi yt is an arrows flight from ye well. There they put ye sick under ye Lhech, where, if ye sick sleeps, it is an infallible sign of recovery : if not, death ';

and he states further that Llech Gybi was 'supported by other stones,'[54] which suggests a cromlech. Writing of Ffynnon Geler (Carm.), Lhuyd says—' In ye Churchyard there is a place wch I may properly call a Caemitery (in Welsh it is call'd Lhech) where after bathing the infirm

[41] HWI, 31.
[42] *ib*, 30. For an early Irish tale where a tree, well, pillar-stone and stone circle are brought together see ERE, IV, 748. [43] FLBI, 69-70.
[44] WMEF, ii, 66. [45] FPM, 240. [46] AOSC, 229. [47] Hebrides, 207.
[48] *ib*, 36. [49] SFLL, 269. [50] AHWC, 125. [51] BGBB, 57, 158-9.
[52] B. Britt., 218. [53] JCD, 302.
[54] Lhuyd Par. iii, 66, 88. This custom was still known in 1911.

must lie down to sleep wch as many as doe are perswaded will recover, otherwise not.'[55] After bathing in the evening in Ffynnon Beuno (Caern.) feeble and epileptic children and infirm adults slept on a 'tombstone' covered with rushes in Capel Beuno, and Pennant saw on this stone 'a feather bed, on which a poor paralytic from Merionethshire had lain the whole night':[56] if they slept a certain cure was predicted. People, after bathing in Ffynnon Wtra Heilin (Mont.), proceeded to a stone circle (now destroyed) that stood in the vicinity.[57] Near Ffynnon Fair (Maenclochog, Pem.) are some stones believed to have been part of a cromlech, and tradition states that one of them, when struck, gave a loud ringing sound which did not cease until water from Ffynnon Fair had been carried into the parish church.[58] The legend is onomastic but some early well-megalith custom may be involved. Traces of a 'druidical monument' were once to be seen at Ffynnon Fair (Rad.).[59] Tradition states that 'a stone altar' stood formerly near Ffynnon Drillo (Mer.).[60] Seiriol is said to have lived as a hermit between two summits on Penmaenmawr 'where still are to be seen his *Bed* and *Well*.'[61] The well at Pencw (Pem.) is near a group of ruined cromlechau. A cross-incised capstone lay over Llangenith well in Gower (Glam.). A stone, a mound and a well were associated with the martyrdom of St. Lludd, near Slwch (Breck.). Near the Druid's Well (Pem.) is a cromlech, but as no early forms of this name are available it is not possible to accept the implication contained in it. A circle of stones once stood around Ffynnon Ffos Ana (Carm.). One tradition states that the farmer on whose land the well was, sent every new servant he hired, back to his native district to collect any curious stones (*cerrig hynod*) for him;[62] a variant says that a strange old man who lived nearby kept idols (*delwau*) around the well.[63] It is clear that we are here in the presence of no ordinary stones, but the 'traditions' seem

[55] *ib*, iii, 76. [56] See below p. 154. [57] Anc. Mon Mont. [58] NCP, 172.
[59] JWHR, 290. [60] See below p. 190. [61] Carlisle TDW. [62] Lloffwr, 427.
[63] TNEW Llanelly, 360.

to be comparatively modern efforts to explain a phenomenon the true significance of which had been long obscured. Some of these stones bore strange markings, such as the one by Penylan Well (Cardiff), which was said to have been visited by Our Lord, who left His impress on the stone.[64] Stones bearing the impress of Our Lady are found at two of her Welsh wells.[65]

Many stones that once stood near wells have disappeared. In 1483 a Maen Dewi stood near Ffynnon Ddewi in Fishguard parish, but it has long since disappeared, and another Maen Dewi at Maesymis (Breck.) was destroyed shortly before 1850. Lhuyd, in 1698, mentions an inscribed megalith 'near St. Owen's well in Arberth parish,' Pembrokeshire, which is now lost. During the last century a cromlech near the holy well of Ffynnondridian (Pem.) and another at Nine Wells (Pem.) were destroyed and a great stone called Yr Eisteddfa that stood near Ffynnon y Groes (Card.), was broken up for building purposes about 1840.[66] In 1846, a stone called Mesur y Dorth, served as a gatepost to Penarthur[67] farm near St. David's, but it had previously stood, together with two other ornamented stones, around the holy well of Penarthur.[68] Mesur y Dorth is now in St. David's Cathedral, where is it known as the 'Gurmarc stone' after the name carved on it, and the older designation is lost.[69] Another early inscribed stone was found at a holy well at Resolven (Glam.),[70] and a fragment of a Celtic wheel-cross of the 9th century was discovered at St. Teilo's

[64] Cymru Fu, 11 May 1889. [65] See below p. 46.

[66] CA, 77. The nearby farm called Steddfa commemorates the stone. The element *eisteddfa* in place-names relating to stones is often found, e.g. *Eisteddfa Arthur* (Nevern, Pem), *Eisteddfa Egwad* in Llanegwad (Carm), and *Steddfa Gurig* on Plynlymon.

[67] This personal name is found elsewhere in North Pem., in connection with pre-historic remains, e.g. *Coitan Arthur*, a cromlech on St. David's Head; *Carreg Coitan Arthur*, a cromlech near Newport; *Cerrig Meibion Arthur*, two meinihirion in Mynachlogddu parish, and *Carn Arthur* also called *Coitan Arthur* and *Bedd Arthur* in the same parish.

[68] Records of the Church in Wales, NLW: Lap. Wall. Pl 60: Arch. Cam, 1856, 50, 1886, 43 ff, illustr.

[69] There is another cross-incised stone still called Messur y Dorth in a hedge near Croesgoch, Llanrhian parish, Pem.

[70] CIIC, 2, 164: called the Bryn Cyffneithian stone, now in the National Museum of Wales—EG, 277.

Well, Llandaff.[71] There are instances where the well-name is the only indication of the existence of a former megalith. However, some of these may have been so named because an ordinary stone happened to lie, or stand, near them. Among these problematical examples we find wells named Ffynnon y Garreg (Flint, Rad., Mont., Pem., etc.), Ffynnon Maen Du (Breck.) and Ffynnon Maen y Milgi (Mer.).

In Wales, respect for megaliths seems to have died out fairly early, but in Europe some megaliths continued to be venerated as late as the latter half of the 19th century and, according to Baring Gould, such megaliths were 'most usually near fountains.'[72] Enough has been written to indicate the close connection between wells and megaliths, and many further examples will be mentioned, especially in the section dealing with belief and ritual.

Sacred trees and groves figure in many early religions. The Celtic sacred grove was called *nemeton*, plural *numidos* and *nemeta*, expressed in Old Irish by *nemed* and *firnemed*.[73] Sacred trees included the hazel,[74] rowan, ash, holly, mulberry, yew, oak, appletree, and certain types of thorn.[75] Trees growing at, or near, wells often appeared in the well ritual,[76] and in many cases bushes and briars were used as substitutes on which to hang rags and pieces of wool. A hazel tree grew over the source of the Shannon, which was said to rise in a subaqueous land. Nine hazels grew over a well in 'the Celtic Land of Promise,' and over Connla's Well (Co. Tipperary) grew a similar number whose nuts sustained the sacred salmon. Wells associated with trees are not numerous in Wales, but some 30 examples have been noted, and there are probably more. But the traditions and ritual concerning them are so much in sympathy with the tree-well association in other Celtic lands, as well as in Celtic antiquity, that it is difficult not to recognize in them a ragged remnant of what was formerly a widespread custom.

[71] EG, 277. [72] BGBR, 189. [73] SFLL, 275 ff: FLBI, ch. VI.
[74] For the hazel as a sacred tree in Gaelic lore see AMB, 150-1.
[75] The thorn may have owed its position in later lore to Christianity.
[76] AMB, ch. XV, 'Why Trees and Wells were Worshipped.'

Indeed, certain trees dedicated to saints were recognised in the Welsh Laws as being of higher value than other trees. A yew tree dedicated to a saint was worth 120 pence, but otherwise it was worth only 15 or 20 pence.[77] Yew trees grew over Ffynnon Beuno (Flint), Ffynnon Gwenlais (Carm.), Ffynnon Bedr (Caern.), Ffynnon Elias (Mont.), Llanbedr y Cennin well (Caern.), Ffynnon Capel Llanfihangel Rhosycorn (Carm.), and many others, while cattle were sprinkled with a yew bough dipped in Ffynnon Beuno (Mer.).[78] Hazels grew over Ffynhonnau Cyll and Collen (Carm.). Crutches were hung on the oak above the Llancarfan well (Glam.), and great oaks grew over Priest's Well (Mon.) and Ffynnon Dderw (Carm.). A statue of the Virgin and Child is said to have appeared miraculously in the branches of an oak near Ffynnon Fair Penrhys (Glam.).[79] Until recently, Ffynnon Wtra Heilin (Mont.) stood in an oak-grove.[80] Rags were hung on the thorn tree over Ffynnon Cae Moch (Glam.). It was believed that thunder and lightning would break out if the old hawthorn near Ffynnon Digwg (Caern.) was cut down.[81] Ash trees grew at Ffynnon Bettws Fawr (Caern.), Ashwell (Carm.) and Ffynnon Idloes (Mont.). Ffynnon Fedw (Flint) and Ffynnon Scawen (Pem.) owe their names to trees that grew by them. Ffynnon y Cyff (Carm., Card., Flint) may have been associated with a decayed tree. Although many wells are found in woods such as Bridewell (Mon.), Ffynnon y Forwyn (Carm.) and Ffynnon Lawddog (Carm.), we must not necessarily conclude that here was a sacred grove. The significance of many of these wells named after trees must not be over-emphasised, but where ritual connects well and

[77] WML, 104, 248. [78] See below p. 106.

[79] This may have been originally a pagan tree. The Clergy dedicated trees by placing statues in their branches—BGBB, 13-14. See FFCC, 434-5 for French examples of Our Lady of the Oak, and cf B. Britt.

[80] Anc. Mon. Mont. It may have been named after a holy man. Heilin was a well-known name in medieval N Wales. The name of the nearby farm is Garth Eilin which suggests 'idol', but I have found no early forms. However such a type of place-name occurs in Wales, e.g. Llain Porth y Ddelw (1737) in Llangynllo parish, Card.

[81] Similar tales are told relating to tumuli, cromlechau and wells throughout Britain, and are relics of very early beliefs.

tree it is possible that it is a relic of the belief in the sacred tree.

To summarise, we can say that well-worship was a feature of the religious life of the Ancients, being associated with gods, oracles, sacrifices, festivals, and with burials, megaliths and trees. Traces of these beliefs occur in early Celtic literature, and their singular persistence in Wales down to the present century will be discussed at length in the following chapters.

Chapter III

THE WELL-CULT IN MEDIEVAL WALES

I. Impact of Christianity—missionary policy—chapels and churches near wells—why the well-cult survived. II. Wells in the Lives of the Saints—Distribution of saints' wells—in baptism of saints—in the career of saints—in the death of saints—struggles with paganism. III. Wells dedicated to saints—to Celtic saints—to non-Celtic saints. IV. Wells in medieval Welsh life—religious—secular.

IN this chapter we shall consider material that throws light on the early struggles of the Church to dethrone the popular pagan beliefs, the methods by which this was achieved, the development of a Christian well-cult and its place and influence in medieval Welsh life.

I. The Impact of Christianity

(*a*) *Missionary Policy*

The conversion of Britain to Christianity was a gradual process in the course of which the Church re-interpreted many pre-Christian customs and beliefs and adapted them to its own purposes. The attitude of the Church is made clear in the papal instructions to St. Augustine ordering him to convert pagan customs 'into a Christian solemnity' and pagan temples into churches, while sacrifices of oxen were to continue, but as 'Christian banquets . . . to the praise of God'[1] The letter of Pope Gregory to Mellitus in 601 instructed missionaries in the way they were to overcome the recalcitrancy of their would-be flocks. Although it does not mention wells it has an important bearing on the subject. This oft-quoted letter[2] instructed that the idols in Britain were to be destroyed, but the temples that

[1] WMEF, ii, 48: AS *passim*. [2] Bede, lib 1, c 30.

housed them were to be purified with 'holy water,' altars were to be erected and then 'converted from the worship of devils to the worship of the true God.' It is important to notice here that the continuity of the *site* was ensured—the old gods were expelled, the true God installed—the *site* remained.

Ecclesiastical councils supplemented this policy. The Council of Arles (452), of Rouen and of Toledo (7th century) denounced those 'who offer vows to trees, or wells, or stones, as they would at altars.'[3] The Council of Tours (567) was equally specific in its decree that 'every priest industriously advance Christianity and extinguish heathenism, and forbid the worship of fountains.' Individual churchmen continued the pressure. Gildas (6th century) denounced the old beliefs in 'mountains, fountains, hills . . . to which the blind people paid divine honour' in former times. One of the canons of St. Cummin (died 669) proscribed the worship of wells and trees, and it was repeated in the Irish *Bobbio Penitentiale*. The secular power added to this condemnatory chorus. Charlemagne in Europe, Egbert and Edgar and Canute in England, all condemned the worship of wells. The significance of these notices is that they were repeated century after century, which clearly indicates the tenacity with which the people adhered to certain aspects of the 'elder faith.'

The 26th canon of St. Anselm is particularly significant for it decreed in 1102, 'Let no one attribute reverence or sanctity to a dead body or a fountain *without the bishop's authority*'—which shows quite clearly the extent to which the Church had compromised. In future the bishop's imprimatur was required in order to sanctify wells. Some wells had become 'authorised versions.'

The lead of Church and State was followed by the historian and literateur, and their works show how Christians were assimilating pagan material. A song on Our Lord by Eilif Gudrunarson shows that He had supplanted the god Mimir, and it was He who now sat on a rock 'South at the

[3] MMS, 180.

well of Urd.'[4] Striking examples, in which the name of Christ and the Irish deity Goibniu appear together, occur in early Irish incantations.[5] During this long period of conversion the well-cult became so assimilated that it became almost an article of faith in Christian lands. The saint ousted the older deity, but many of the earlier customs survived. 'A new myth for an old rite has often been a device of priests and potentates.'[6] The writings of Mandeville show how firmly the cult remained in those very lands where Christianity had its origin. Outside Cairo there was a field containing seven wells 'that our Lord Jesus Christ made with one of his feet, when he went to play with other children.'[7] Inside St. Anne's Church at Jerusalem was a well and 'into that well angels were wont to come from heaven and bathe them therein. And what man, that first bathed him after the moving of the water, was made whole of what manner of sickness that he had.'[8]

(*b*) *Chapels and Churches near Wells*

Evidence relating to the conversion in Wales is meagre. The main source of information is contained in the written *Lives of the Saints*, which will be considered in detail below. It is sufficient to say here that the saints are represented as overcoming opposition and establishing chapels, churches and holy wells, and in some cases actually converting pagan wells to Christian usage. There is, however, another aspect which tends to throw light on the methods employed by the Welsh missionaries. This concerns the location of chapels and churches near holy wells and monuments of a recognised pagan character.

It has been noted that the Church decreed that pagan sites were to be converted to Christian solemnities, and this the missionaries did by rededicating the well, megalith and tree, and by erecting churches or chapels near them. Many churches were built over wells, such as Lanmaur and Notre

[4] VA, i, 473. [5] FLBI, 168, where other examples are also noted.
[6] H. J. Fleure, *A Natural History of Man in Britain*, 1951, 98.
[7] Mandeville, 34 (A.D. 1322+). [8] *ib*, 59.

Dame de Folgoët in Brittany, and Carlisle, Glasgow and Winchester Cathedrals and York Minster in Britain.[9] Conclusive evidence of this continuity is found in Man where many of its 180 keeills were built on pre-Christian sites, which is proved by the Bronze Age finds in their foundations, and of these it is recorded, 'almost invariably there was a spring or gentle stream near by every keeill.'[10] Walter Johnson[11] and A. H. Allcroft[12] have collected a great deal of evidence (some of it, admittedly, questionable) which strongly supports the intentional adaptation of pagan sites to Christian usage, and this view is also accepted by Plummer[13] and other authorities.[14]

I have found nearly 200 examples of chapels and churches built at or near holy wells in Wales. They are distributed as follows in Welsh counties :—Anglesey 9, Caernarvon 22, Denbigh 15, Flint 10, Montgomery 8, Merioneth 14, Brecknock 8, Radnor 4, Cardigan 14, Pembroke 33, Carmarthen 14, Glamorgan 24, Monmouth 7. Although it is impossible to prove that all of these owe their location to a holy well of pre-Christian antiquity, the tradition of this siting is too consistent and widespread to be set aside lightly, particularly as it is in sympathy with the facts known elsewhere in Britain and on the Continent. It is possible that in some cases saints and hermits built cells near wells for no other reason than the necessity to procure water for human sustenance, or the equally practical reason that wells were necessary for Christian baptisms. But there is certainly much more to it than this.

Let us consider the co-incidence of churches and wells at sites with strong pre-Christian connections. In a sequestered district in the Precelly hills is Llandilo Llwydiarth,[15]

[9] Dom Ethelbert Horne, who has discussed holy wells near Somerset churches, goes so far as to say, 'We can be quite certain, however, that the spring of water must always be older than the oldest church.'—SWH, 10.
[10] IH, 19, 22-25. [11] Johnson BBA, chapters 1 and 2.
[12] *The Circle and the Cross, passim.* [13] VSH, p. cxlix.
[14] e.g. AS *passim* ; SWH *passim* ; FLBI, 108 ; MacCulloch MFF, 11 ; Hebrides 240 ; HWI, 29, 31 ; WMEF, 1, 323 ; ii, 86 ; LFH, 16ff.
[15] So-named to distinguish it from nearby Llandilo Gronwy, and not from Llandilo (Carm.) as is often stated. The name Llandilo Gronwy appears in deeds as late as 1570 (NLW Bronwydd Deeds) but is now lost.

today a parish of over a thousand acres of mountain land. It must always have been sparsely populated and in 1670 there were only five houses there. The ruined church lies at the extreme southern end of the parish. But we are dealing with times when there was no parish and when the Celtic population, given as it was to transhumance, was not static. The soil of the district is not rich, the area remote, and in some ways unattractive. However, it contained a famous well concerning which significant traditions and ritual have survived. The church was built near to it, and in the churchyard are two megaliths bearing inscriptions in Ogham and Roman characters. Rhŷs wrote :

> ' . . . I would now only point out that we have here an instance of a well which was probably sacred before the time of St. Teilo : in fact, one would possibly be right in supposing that the sanctity of the well and its immediate surroundings was one of the causes why its site was chosen by a Christian missionary.[16]

The topographical disadvantages of the St. David's district have been the theme of most tourists since Giraldus. Archaeology shows it to have been inhabited for centuries before the advent of Christianity. There were at least nine earth forts there which establish that its population was not inconsiderable, in addition to which are the remains of six cromlechau, two tumuli, and at least four monoliths. Here also was the prophetic stone Llechllafar bridging the stream Alun, whose waters in later times contained unusual fish. There are in the district twelve holy wells, seven of which are concentrated in the immediate vicinity of St. David's, as also are most of the cromlechau. It is probable that some of these wells were there in pre-Christian days. In St. David's time, a powerful pagan family lived there. Yet it was here in the heart of the pagan camp that the missionaries settled, and it was here that Dewi built his church, and twelve chapels were erected in the same district. It is possible that in this remote headland, with its rugged cairns

[16] Rhŷs CF, 400.

looking westward over the waves towards the setting sun, lay the sacred mysteries of our ancient pagan stock.

The same remarks apply to the church of St. Elvis to the east of Solva, in a poor parish that never contained more that two farms. But at its ruined church are two broken cromlechau and a holy well. The evidence, of course, is slight, but it cannot be ignored. A tradition in the same district, although it does not involve a church, indicates a remarkable continuity of local religious history. It concerns Nine Wells, a spot between Solva and St. David's. By these wells stood a cromlech which was destroyed in the last century, and where a mound still exists. The tradition states—that in pagan times twelve maidens each under twelve years of age were burnt alive as a sacrifice on the stone altar (*allor*) there; that in Catholic times (*amser pabyddiaeth*) mass was celebrated at the wells, priests dipped their rosaries there, and water was carried thence to St. David's Cathedral to wash the sepulchre (*beddrod*)[17] ; that sick pilgrims came from Tregroes via Dwrhyd by Llwybir Pererindod[18] to bathe at Nine Wells, and were then conveyed in a cart[19] to Non's Well where the cure was completed, and were finally carried to the Cathedral where they were blessed by a priest.

The majority of the old well-chapels have disappeared. Some fell into decay and were abandoned, and a large number were deliberately destroyed during the Reformation such as Capel Pistyll Meugan (Pem.)[20] while many of those that survived the fury of the Reformers subsequently became ruins whose stone-work was used by farmers and masons for building purposes. It is said that the oldest Baptist chapel in Wales, at Ilston (Glam.), was built about 1649-1650 with stones from a pre-Reformation well-chapel dedicated to St. Cenydd, and later, when the Baptist chapel itself became a ruin and was enclosed with railings, the holy well (which cured sore eyes) was destroyed[21]—the only known example of that denomination's hostility to water.

[17] The shrine of St. David ? [18] The path and name are lost.
[19] My informant called it 'gambo'. [20] See below p. 59. [21] EG, 264-5.

The demolition of St. Non's Chapel (St. David's) was completed in the spring of 1810, 'and many of the neighbouring stone fences had then risen from the ruins.'[22] Some have disappeared so completely as to leave no trace whatsoever apart from names like Ffynnon y Capel, Park y Capel, Cae Capel Ffynnon, etc.[23]. Others are known through stray references in early deeds and records, such as the chapel of St. Gwynlliw (father of Cadoc) in Llanelly parish, described in 1553 as *capellam Gunlliw,* in 1592 as *Capel Gwnlliw,* and in 1605 as *Capell Gwnlliw.*[24] In 1593 and 1622 we find that a *Chappell Tylo* was near Pistyll Teilo in the parish of Kidwelly.[25] The chapel of *Pistyllsawil* in Llansawel parish (Carm.) was functioning in 1331. In some cases these chapels were built over the well itself such as St. Trillo's Chapel (Caern.), Wigfair (Denb.), Capel Ddeuno (Denb.), Capel y Pistyll (Pem.).[26] Others were built alongside or near the well. Despite the decay and destruction that has removed these interesting and intimate little edifices from the Welsh countryside, sufficient has been preserved for us to learn what manner of buildings they were.

Among those in a good state of preservation are the well-chapels at Ffynnon Gybi (Caern.) and Ffynnon Seiriol (Angl.). The former, one furlong NE. of Llangybi parish church, consists of a small rectangular building within which the well flows, and adjoining it on the south side is a larger building of drywalling and corbelled vaulting similar to early Irish cells; in this larger building is a pool, a paved walk, and a series of niches in the walls.[27] At St. Seiriol's Well (200 yards NE. of Penmon Priory Church) is a similar building, the structure now enclosing the well representing the nave and chancel of the old chapel, and the adjoining foundations of a raised oval hut representing the dwelling of the saint.[28] The Penmon well structure has been

[22] AAW. [23] See below Part II, *passim.* [24] NLW Cilymaenllwyd deeds.
[25] NLW Muddlescomb Deeds.
[26] It is possible that some of the structures we now recognise as well-chambers may have been in the first instance well-chapels. [27] IRG, 14, 31.
[28] *ib,* 15, 28.

assigned to the time of Seiriol himself (6th century) while that at Llangybi may be almost as early.[29] If the dating of these primitive structures is correct, then they are the oldest surviving examples of Christian building in Wales. It is from such primitive simplicity that St. Winifred's impressive well-chapel evolved.

There are several ruined well-chapels in South Wales. In Llanddarog parish (Carm.) the little Capel Begewdin, 28 feet by 15½ feet, is built over a fine well which still flows abundantly, though the small well-chamber within which it rose is choked by debris of fallen roof and walls. The east and west walls are standing and the water of Ffynnon Capel Begewdin is still in repute for sprains.[30] The ruined Capel Herbach (or Erbach) in Llanarthney parish (Carm.) is possibly of the early 14th century; the well rises within the chapel, and its overflow runs along the side of the chapel, passing out by a small orifice and exterior spout to form a rill: the chamber measured 16 feet by 12 feet. The water of Ffynnon Capel Herbach is still regarded as curative and especially so in the case of spasms.[31]

It seems likely that many parish churches, particularly those with wells within the churchyard, such as Cerrigceinwen (Angl.), Llanfair Caereinion (Mont.), Pilleth (Rad.), Halkyn (Flint), Llandeloy (Pem.), Oxwich (Glam.), and others, may have evolved from similar beginnings. Owing to restoration and rebuilding most, if not all, the earlier features have disappeared from Welsh churches.

(*c*) *Why the well-cult survived*

As we have seen, the survival of the well-cult was partly due to Christianity itself. During the Middle Ages and later, wells appeared in the religion of the people, in their songs, in folk-tales, in primitive medicine. Wells were visible, and what is seen perpetuates local legend and ancient belief. Where a well rose and fell (this is not uncommon in limestone tracts), where a well was warm or

[29] *ib.* [30] Anc. Mon. Carm. The l.p. is 'Begowdin.'
[31] Arch. Cam, 1894, 19: Anc. Mon. Carm.

occasionally steamed, or never froze, people desired some explanation. Where a phenomenon could not be explained, the supernatural was invoked. There is no doubt that the survival of the respect for wells is largely due to their actual or supposed healing qualities. The wells were the doctors of the peasantry. However, this will not explain the survival of the rites and customs, particularly those governing divination and commination. These belong to the pagan and Christian religions, and what we call 'superstition' in the modern Welshman, is, in reality, a survival of the religious convictions of his earlier ancestors. The pagan gods did not die: they were not allowed to.

II. Wells in the Lives of The Saints

Welsh legends and poems were not recorded until the Middle Ages. They present distorted memories of historical events, often bringing together personages from different centuries, and, who, before their biographies were chronicled, had lived a changing life in the repertoire of the story-tellers and bards. The saints are intimately connected with the wells and it is clear that the legends and cults of Dewi, Beuno, Cybi, and Gwenfrewi, for example, have had a greater influence on the Welsh mind than the actual historical figures themselves. It is important to remember this. When we dismiss the fictitious tales and romantic inventions as unhistorical, we must accept the fact that such tales and such inventions influenced the ways of thought of our ancestors. So it is with the well-cult. We are not concerned so much in this study with the element of truth in the traditions as we are with the undisputed effect the well-cult had on the human mind.

Charles Plummer was the first to bring analytical scholarship to bear on the Lives in his masterly introduction to *Vitae Sanctorum Hiberniae*, and since his work appeared, over forty years ago, further research has served only to emphasize and support the conclusions he had then drawn and so brilliantly presented. The Lives are sacred fiction. The surviving manuscripts relating to Welsh saints were compiled between 1100 and 1400, but numbers of them are copies and redactions of much earlier manuscripts now missing. Many have been 'edited' by the copyists, and part of the material contained in them reflects the thought and conventions of the period of those copyists. The earlier Christian missionaries and priests, who altered the older material, also introduced to Britain new types of legends, mainly from Mediterranean lands, and these were incorporated into the Lives. Many of the attributes of the old Celtic kings, heroes, and pagan priests have also been assigned to the saints.

No writer discussing foundations and dedications by Celtic saints can evade the formidable difficulties involved in their study. The crux of the whole matter depends on dating, i.e. whether the church sites do in fact extend back to the Age of the Saints. Since the Lives were written at a much later period to popularise certain saints, not only is it possible, but likely, that many churches, chapels, and wells owe their association not to the saint himself but to the much later clerical propagandists. Archaeology may determine that the sites are indeed much earlier than the time of the written Lives, but whether they were associated initially with, or dedicated to, the saints commemorated in the Lives is difficult to decide. The question is further complicated by the fact that much re-dedication has taken place, particularly during the Norman period. The fact that the name of a saint is found in a church or well dedication does not necessarily imply that the saint ever visited such places. The dedication may have been due to the *cult* of the saint which may have been genuinely early or a much later manifestation connected with the propaganda period of the Lives. The point at issue is—do these dedications extend back to the Age of the Saints or to the Age of the Lives of the Saints? Or, indeed (in some cases) even to the latter? The information that we possess at the moment is inconclusive, and so we must approach the question of dedications with caution. The most we can do is to apply to the problem the principles of historical probability, and, assisted by archaeology and hagiology, draw conclusions which at the best can be only of a tentative nature.

This is not the place to discuss re-dedication, but an observation must be made where it involves the names of wells. One attitude, and a popular one, is that when the name of the local holy well differs from the dedication name of the church, it indicates that the latter has been changed. This, sometimes, may have been the case, especially where there is only one holy well near the church or in the parish, although too much weight must not be given to parish boundaries as we know them today. However, I have been struck with the fact that numbers of parishes contain not one, but several, wells dedicated to different saints, and this complicates the view quoted above. For instance, what are we to do with Llanreithan (Pem. ded. St. Rheithan) where there are wells dedicated to St. David and to St. Aaron ? Who was the original saint of the church here ? Dewi, Aaron or Rheithan ? Or Mathry (Pem. ded. The Holy Martyrs), where there is a Ffynnon Fair and a Ffynnon Ddewi ?[32]

(*a*) *Distribution of Saints' Wells in Wales*

The list of saints' names given to wells and their distribution is given below. Where the saint had only one well, the name of the county alone is given : where the saints had more than one well, the figure is given in brackets after his name followed by the counties in which they were located, and where more than one well occurs in any one county a figure is given in brackets after that county.

Aaron—Pem. *Aelhaiarn*—Caern. *Aelrhiw*—Caern. *Afan* (2)—Breck., Card. *Allgo*—Angl. *Anne* (3)—Glam., Mon., Rad. *Asa* (3)—Denb. (2), Flint. *Anthony*—Carm. *Annun*—Angl.

Baglan (2)—Caern., Glam. *Barruc*—Glam. *Bennion* (3)—Mont.

[32] There are no traditions, place-names, or archaeological remains, in Llanreithan or Mathry parishes to suggest former well-chapels which would otherwise clear up the difficulty.

Berwyn—Carm. *Beuno* (6)—Angl., Mer. (2) Caern., Flint (2). *Bleiddan*—Glam. *Boida*—Carm. *Brothen*—Mer. *Brynach* (5)—Pem. (4), Carm.

Cadfan (2)—Mont. Mer. *Cadfarch* (2)—Caern, Mont. *Caffo*—Angl. *Canna*—Pem. *Caron*—Card. *Cathen*—Carm. *Cattwg* (6)—Glam. (5), Breck. *Cawrdaf*—Caern. *Caradog* (3)—Card., Pem., Glam. *Ceinwen*—Angl. *Ceitho*—Card. *Celer*—Carm. *Celynin*—Caern. *Chad* (2)—Flint, Rad. *Collen*—Denb. *Curig* (4)—Caern, Pem., Glam. (2). *Cwyfan*—(2) Caern., Flint. *Cybi* (5)—Angl. (2), Caern., Card., Mon. *Cynfelyn*—Card. *Cynfran*—Caern. *Cyngar* (2)—Flint, Breck. *Cynhafal*—Denb. *Cynllo* (2)—Card. Rad. *Cynog* (2)—Breck., Carm. *Cynon*—Glam. *Cynwyd*—Glam. *Cynydd*—Rad. *Cynydr*—Breck.

Daniel (5)—Denb., Flint, Caern., Mer., Card. *Decuman*—Pem. *Degfel*—Pem. *Degwel*—Pem. *Deifer*—Flint. *Deiniolen*—Caern. *Dene* (*Denis*)—Glam. *Derfel* (2)—Mer., Glam. *Deuno*—Denb. *Dewi* (32)—Rad., Breck. (2), Card. (6), Pem. (18), Carm. (2), Glam. (3). *Digain*—Denb. *Doged*—Denb. *Dogfan*—Mont. *Dogmael*—Pem. *Dunawd*—Caern. *Dwyfan*—Mont. *Dwynwen*—Angl. *Dwrdan*—Caern. *Dyfnog*—Denb. *Dyfrig* (2)—Glam. (2). *Dygfael*—Angl.

Edren—Pem. *Edward*—Rad. *Eigion*—Breck. *Eilian* (2)—Angl., Mont. *Elaeth*—Angl. *Elen* (*Helen*) (6)—Caern., Mer., Pem. (2), Carm., Glam. *Elfodd*—Denb. *Elicquid*—Mon. *Elli*—Carm. *Elian*—Denb. *Enddwyn*—Mer. *Erfyl*—Mont.

Fagan—Glam. *Ffraid* (8)—Angl., Denb., Flint, Mer., Card., Pem., Mon. (2). *Fidalis*—Card.

Garmon (6)—Caern., Denb. (2), Mont. (2), Carm. *Geneu*—Breck. *George* (2)—Denb., Glam. *Gofan*—Pem. *Gofor*—Mon. *Gower* (*Cywair*)—Mer. *Grallo*—Glam. *Gredifael*—Angl. *Gwas Patrick*—Denb. *Gwenfaen*—Angl. *Gwenfil*—Denb. *Gwenlais*—Carm. *Gwennog* (2)—Card., Mon. *Gwerfil*—Card. *Gweslan*—Pem. *Gwladys* (2)—Card., Mon. *Gwnda* (2)—Card., Pem. *Gwnno*—Glam. *Gwnnod*—Denb. *Gwnnws*—Card. *Gwyddelan*—Caern. *Gwyddfaen*—Carm. *Gwynhael*—Mon. *Gwynwy*—Caern.

Howel (4)—Card., Pem. (2), Glam.

Iago (6)—Pem., Carm. (3), Glam. (2). *Iase*—Pem. *Idloes*—Mont. *Iestyn*—Angl. *Illog*—Mont. *Illtud* (4)—Glam. (4). *Isho*—Breck. *Ithel*—Denb. *Iwan*—Mont.

John (4)—Pem., Glam. (2), Mon. *Jose*—Glam. *Justinian*—Pem.

Leonard (2)—Pem. (2). *Llawddog* (3)—Card., Pem., Carm. *Llechid*—Caern. *Lleucu* (2)—Flint, Card. *Lleuddad*—Caern.

Madoc (5)—Denb., Mont., Card. (2), Pem. *Maeddog*—Pem. *Mael*—Flint. *Maelog*—Angl. *Mebwyn* (?-*wen*)—Card. *Marchell* —Denb. *Margaret* (3)—Pem., Glam., Mon. *Maughan*—Mon. *Mair* (75)—Angl. Caern. (5), Denb. (6) Flint, (9), Mont. (4), Mer. (8), Rad., Breck., Card. (7), Pem. (15), Carm. (4), Glam. (13), Mon. *Mair Fadlen* (2)—Denb., Carm. *Melyd* (2)—Flint (2). *Meugan*—Pem. *Meuric*—Mon. *Mihangel* (12)—Flint. (4), Mer., Mont., Card., Pem., Carm., Glam. (2), Mon. *Mil Feibion* (2)—Carm., Glam. *Milo*—Breck. *Mordeyrn*—Denb. *Myllin*—Mont.

Nefydd—Denb. *Nicholas* (5)—Breck., Pem. (2), Glam. (2). *Noe*—Mon. *Non* (2)—Pem., Carm.

Oswald—Flint. *Owen* (5)—Caern., Card. (3), Pem.

Padarn (3)—Mer., Card. (2). *Patrick* (3)—Angl., Mer., Mon. *Pedr* (17)—Caern., Denb. (2), Rad., Card. (2), Pem. (2), Carm. (2), Glam. (6), Mon. *Pedrog*—Caern. *Peris*—Caern. *Petrox* (? *Pedrog*)—Pem.

Rhedyw—Caern.

Sadwrn—Denb. *Salmon*—Pem. *Samson* (3)—Pem. (3). *Sannan* —Mon. *Sawyl*—Carm. *Seiriol* (4)—Angl. (3), Caern. *Silin*—Denb. *Stephan*—Carm. *Sulien* (2)—Flint, Mer. *Sul*—Carm.

Tecwyn—Mer. *Tegan*—Pem. *Tegid*—Mer. *Tegla*—Denb. *Teilo* (6), Pem. (2), Carm. (2), Glam. (2). *Telau*—Mer. *Tewdric*—Mon. *Trillo* (3)—Caern., Denb., Mer. *Trinity* (10)—Denb., Mont. (5), Card. (2), Glam. (2). *Tudno*—Caern. *Tudur* (3)—Denb., Card., Carm. *Tudwen*—Caern. *Tybie*—Carm. *Tydfil*—Glam. *Tydecho* —Mont. *Tydwal*—Caern. *Tyssilio* (2)—Denb., Mont. *Tyssul* (2) —Card., Carm.

Winifred (Gwenfrewi)—Flint.

Duw (3)—Caern., Mont., Breck. *God*—Mont.

(*b*) *Wells in the baptism of saints*

In the Lives, wells associated with a saint's baptism were either already in existence and became hallowed by the baptism of the infant, or, on the other hand, suddenly flowed to provide water for the ceremony.[33] When Cadoc was to be baptised, a large fountain arose at the prayer of the priest, whereupon the enterprising babe leaped into it 'and dipped himself thrice in the water in the name of the Holy Trinity.'[34] The same Providence caused a well to punish a man who was indifferent to the needs of the child Cadoc. This man refused to give fire to warm the infant, whereupon he was consumed by fire, and on his threshing floor arose 'an unseemly fountain.'[35] A miraculous spring arose at Porthclais (Pem.) at the baptism of Dewi, who was immersed three times in it, and its waters restored the sight of a blind man who held the babe, a circumstance that inspired a medieval bard to write :

> dyw wrth vedyddiaw dewi
> y wnaeth ffons oddyfwr yni
> roes y dad bedydd medd rai
> y olwc gynt ny welai[36]

(At the baptism of Dewi, God made a well for us, which, some say, gave sight to Dewi's blind godfather.)

During the early centuries people were baptised at wells, and, later, water from holy wells was carried to the fonts of churches for baptism, a practice that continued in some parts of Wales to the end of the 19th century.

(*c*) *Wells in the careers of saints*

The medieval Christian demanded and expected that saints should perform miracles. 'What was said of one saint might be said of many—it was a miracle when he did not perform miracles.'[37] In the Lives we find the saint initiating new wells, sanctifying existing ones, and Providence producing wells to meet a special want of the saint.

Wells rose to mark miracles performed by saints, such as the Ffynnon Ddewi within a Cardiganshire cottage where

[33] For other Celtic parallels from the Lives see VSH, i, introd.
[34] CBS, 315 : WEVS, 30-1. [35] *ib.* [36] NLW Llanst. 6, f. 185.
[37] MacCulloch MFF, 133.

St. David raised a youth from the dead. Wells within houses were not uncommon in Wales.[38] The Life of St. Samson relates that the saint found near the Severn 'a cottage, in which was a most delightful fountain.'[39] Many appeared as the result of the prayers of the saints, such as Pistyll Dewi and the wells of Gweslan and Eliud in St. David's parish,[40] and Ffynnon Elian (Denb.).[41] They also rose where the tears of saints had fallen such as the Ffynnon Ddewi, Brawdy (Pem.)[42] and an unlocated well of St. Samson in South Wales.[43] Others rose after the saint had struck or pierced the ground with his staff, such as Gwynllyw's Well (Glam.),[44] and a second Ffynnon Ddewi in Brawdy,[45] and several others. Some wells assumed sanctity and healing properties as a result of saints bathing in them. Thus Ffynnon Enddwyn (Mer.) became famous after St. Enddwyn had been cured of a sore disease after bathing in it;[46] and Ffynnon Goch (Pem.), where Brynach washed his wounds.[47] The tradition concerning Illtud's Well (Gower) relates that when the saint's lands were being inundated, an angel instructed him to order the sea to withdraw. Illtud did so, and the sea obeyed 'as if it were a sensible animal.'[48] He then struck the ground with his staff and a clear well arose.[49] Holy wells are also found at or near places where saints lived, such as Ffynnon Geneu (Breck.), Ffynnon Gybi (Card.), Ffynnon Seiriol (Caern.) and Ffynnon Degan (Pem.). Ffynnon Ddyfnog (Denb.) is said to owe its healing properties to the action of St. Dyfnog, who did penance there by standing under the cold water as it issued from the *pistyll*.[50] Wells acquired a sanctity after a saint had drunk from them, such as Ffynnon Non (Carm.) and Ffynnon Ddegfel (Pem.) Others like Ffynhonnau Gybi and Seiriol (Angl.) became holy and curative because

[38] Wells were found in Siamber Wen (Flint), Pennantwrch (Mont.), Pontllefrith farm (Breck.), Pwllheli (Caern.), St. David's and Fishguard (Pem.), and Ffynnon Fihangel flows in an old ruined house in Merioneth. In 1365, Richard de Wolley undertook 'to mend the common well beneath his chamber' in Caernarvon town. [39] Lib Land, 297. [40] El, 18. [41] TGJ, 108.
[42] Giraldus, Op iii, 390. [43] CBS, 480. [44] WEVS, 181. [45] WESD, 16.
[46] LBS, ii, 452. [47] CBS, 7-8, 293. [48] *ib*, 478. [49] *ib*, 478.
[50] LBS, ii, s.n. Dyfnog.

they were the venue of saints.[51] God looked after SS David and Teilo, and He 'caused fountains to arise for the thirsty saints .... and they who drank of those fountains asserted that they did not drink water but wine, so pleasant was its taste.'[52] God also gave a well to St. Cynog when he lived on top of a remote hill in Brecknockshire.[53] St. Cyngar Virgin made a habitation at the foot of a Brecknockshire mountain, 'and by her prayers to God obtained a spring there to flow out of the Earth; which by the merits of the Holy Virgin afforded health to divers Infirmities.'[54] On one occasion, in order to provide hospitality for visitors to St. David's, our patron saint caused the water from a well to turn into wine.[55] This is a development of a Biblical theme. Such parallels are numerous in the Lives, and are sometimes found also in secular tales, such as the three wells in the kingdom of Prester John, one of which ran with wine, another with honey, and the third with milk, 'at his list.'[56] It was believed that an addition to a well of water drawn from the Jordan increased its virtues. The Welsh St. Cadoc, who had caused a well to flow in Cornwall, returned with a bottle of water from the Jordan, which he poured into the well, 'and it became more holy by this position and mixture; for previously it restored only some to health, but afterwards it cured more than a hundred fold.'[57] Saints also used wells for baptising members of their flock, and Myllin is said to have baptised converts in Ffynnon Myllin (Mont.).

(*d*) *Wells at the death of saints*

The emergence of a well is characteristic of the martyrdom of many saints, and locomotion after death and the carrying of a severed head is sometimes present also. Where St. Justinian's head fell on Ramsey Island[58] a well arose, and the saint then picked up his head, walked over the sea to the mainland where he was buried at St. Justinian's

[51] LBS, ii, 209. [52] Lib. Land, 338. [53] BM Harl MS. 4181, f. 71.
[54] *ib*, f. 74. [55] El, 113. [56] Mandeville, 184. [57] CBS, 359-361.
[58] There were two early chapels on Ramsey, and 'each of these Chapels has a fine Spring of pure Water running by it.'—Willis SD, 59.

chapel near which is another of his holy wells. The Ramsey Island well became famous for healing, and John of Tynemouth (d. 1350) wrote that its waters 'quaffed by sick folk, conveys health of body to all.'[59] A man suffering from a swelling in his stomach, drank from it, became very sick, then threw up a frog, and was cured immediately.[60] After St. Decuman was beheaded in Somerset, he washed the head in a well, then tucked it underneath his arm, crossed the Bristol Channel to South Pembrokeshire, where St. Decuman's Well still flows.[61] Wells emerged at the place of execution of SS. Tybie and Eilwedd. These wells, indeed all such saints' wells, became famed for healing and represent miracles of a life-giving character caused by the saints in their last moments. There is one example of a well disappearing when a saint was martyred, probably as a punishment to his executioners. When St. Cynog was beheaded while at prayers on a Sunday morning in Merthyr Cynog (Breck.), his head fell into a well which immediately dried up, whereupon Cynog picked up the head and carried it down the hillside—' those who saw him being amazed.'[62]

Sometimes milk and oil figure after the death of saints. It must be appreciated that milk was regarded as a sacred elixir in Celtic lands in pre-Christian times,[63] and these legends together with certain well-names, such as Ffynnon Lefrith may reflect dim memories of early beliefs. For three days after St. Winifred's death her famous well gave forth milk,[64] and milk flowed from St. Illtud's well leaving fatty substance on the edges of the well.[65] The Welsh *Life of St. Catherine* states that four streams of oil flowed through the grave from her breasts 'giving health to innumerable multitude of sufferers.'[66] We also learn, '*y ffynnawn o olew adardawd or dayar yw ffynnyawn ydrugared alithrawd or wyry veir*' (the well of oil that sprang from the earth is the well of mercy that flowed from the Virgin Mary).[67] On Bardsey Island, St. Llawddog

59 WESD, 51. 60 BGSW, 221. 61 HHBS, 377. 62 BM Harl MS. 4181, f.71.
63 See AMB, 151 ff, where this is discussed, together with examples of milk place-and-river-names in Ireland and Scotland. 64 CBS 527.
65 Arch Cam, I, iii, 264. 66 CBS, 218. 67 El, 18.

milked a cow over a well whose waters turned into milk for his visitors, and in a cywydd, Howel ap Dafydd ap Ieuan ap Rhys mentions this feat by 'Lewdad lwydwyn.'[68]

Wells of beheaded virgins appear frequently in the Lives. The pattern is constant—(i) The virgin flees from a would-be lover; (ii) He catches and beheads her; (iii) A well appears where the head or blood fell; (iv) The virgin is sometimes restored to life and lives for many years after the experience. St. Lludd was beheaded by a pursuer on Slwch hill (Breck.) and 'her head rowling a little down the hill, a Cleare Spring of Water Issued out of the Rock where it rested.'[69] A similar circumstance attended the origin of St. Winifred's Well (Flint), and in this case, St. Beuno restored the stricken virgin to life.

This type of tale was also assigned to secular persons. An Anglesey workman so ingratiated himself at the court of King Ynyr of Gwent that he was given the king's daughter, Digwg, in marriage. On the homeward journey the boor became increasingly alarmed at the prospect when his royal wife discovered his true social position. He decided the question by beheading her as she lay asleep at Pennarth (Caern.), whereupon a spring, which ever after bore her name, issued forth at the spot where her blood fell. St. Beuno, however, happened to be passing and restored her to life.[70] It seems likely that here was an old secular tale, into which Beuno was, later, introduced, in order to magnify his stature as a saint. An interesting example of modern manipulation of old material is the tradition relating to Priest's Well (Mon.). At this curative well there were stones which bore red marks, which were explained as the bloodstains of 'a Catholic priest' who was beheaded there during Elizabethan days.[71] This class of tale was popular in the Lives, and stones bearing the

[68] CBPM, 357. A variant says that Llawddog 'came where there was a well and he took a bowlful of milk and he threw it into the well, and then Llawddog parted the milk from the water freely and others failed to part it.' —NLW Llanst. MS. 34.

[69] BM Harl MS. 4181, f 76a. See p. 146 below. [70] CBS, 306: WEVS, 20.

[71] BD, 81-2.

bloodstains of martyred saints were also found, e.g. at St. Winifred's Well, and St. Michael's Well (Mon.), and elsewhere. The red stain of iron found at chalybeate wells helped to give rise to these tales.

(*e*) *Struggles with paganism*

Pagan opposition is clearly revealed in the Lives. Sometimes the opponents appear as chieftains, women, giants, demons. They are introduced to increase the prestige of the saints who conquer them, but it is likely that some of them represent memories of actual opposition. That wells figure in this struggle is an indication of their importance in both the pagan and early Christian religions. Adamnan's *Life of St. Columba* (written 7th century) describes a poisonous well which the Picts ' worshipped as a god,' which was ' converted by the saint into a blessed well.'[72] St. David acted similarly at Glastonbury—' and he came to a place where the water was full of poison, and he blessed it, and he caused it to become warm until the day of judgement ; and it was called the Hot Baths.'[73] St. Collen is said to have fought at Bwlch Rhiwfelen (Denb.) a giantess called Cawres y Bwlch, who devoured human beings. After a hard fight the saint slew her and washed his bloodstains in a well still called Ffynnon Gollen.[74] There is a tradition that near Ffynnon Baich y Cawr (Mont.) lived a giant and giantess and their servant, and these perhaps represent the ancient gods. St. Brynach had to overcome hostility in Pembrokeshire. His wells are in remote valleys and beside hillside ways, confirming what his medieval biographers tell us about the districts of his labours—Ffynnon Buarth Brynach and Pistyll Brynach (Nevern), Ffynnon Fyrnach (Llanfyrnach), Ffynnon Brynach (Henry's Moat), Ffynnon Fyrnach (Llanfair Nantgwyn), and Ffynnon Goch in the last-named parish, which is probably the Fons Rubens of the Lives, and whose location has caused much speculation. All those wells are in North Pembrokeshire where we find churches dedicated to Brynach—Dinas, Nevern, Pontfaen,

72 BCC, Scotland, i, 128. 73 CBS, 402 ff. 74 LBS, ii, 160.

Llanfyrnach and Henrysmoat. In the same district, just over the Carmarthenshire border, is Ffynnon Frynach (Llanboidy) and near it was Pant Brynach. This saint married Corth, daughter of Brychan Brycheiniog,[75] and her dower lands were in Emlyn. On one occasion she was not enthusiastic about her husband's return from a missionary tour, and hired men to kill him. He escaped, badly wounded, and washed his wounds in a well afterwards called the Red Spring or Well (Fons Rubens).[76] According to Gould and Fisher,[77] this well is identical with Bernard's Well in Henrysmoat, but they produce no evidence to support the assertion. It has been suggested that it was near the river Cleddy and probably at Haverfordwest, where there is a Red Gate and a Red Hill—but where there is no Red Well. The Life, supported by church and well dedications and by place-names, makes it clear that Brynach's sphere of activity was North Pembrokeshire, and his wife's lands were on its northern border. This was his home and it was here that he would return from missionary work. So, it is in the north of the county that we must look for the Red Well (Ffynnon Goch) for that was the actual name of the well we seek, as we are told by Brynach's own biographer. Near an earthwork called Castell Coch, in Llanfair Nantgwyn parish, there is a Ffynnon Goch. There is evidence that Brynach was connected with this very parish, for a record, dated 1665, mentions a field near Trefach called *Park y ffynnon vernach*.[78] Immediately south of the parish is Waun Cleddy where the Eastern Cleddy rises. It would appear that this Ffynnon Goch has a strong claim to be the Fons Rubens of the Lives.[79] The Lives relate that after his unfortunate experience the saint went to Pontfaen where he quelled evil spirits. This Pontfaen is said to be the church of that name in the nearby

[75] A famous figure in Welsh hagiological and genealogical literature. In the 17-18th centuries there was a *Brychanswell* which was either in Glamorgan or Brecknockshire (Golden Grove MS.).

[76] CBS, 7-8, 293 : LBS, i, 321-7. [77] LBS, ii, 219.

[78] PRO. Court of Great Sessions, Pem, 1665.

[79] The only other Ffynnon Goch in Pembrokeshire known to me is in Jordanston parish, Dewsland. I know of no Red Well in the county.

Gwaun valley, but it should be noted that just over the western boundary of Llanfair Nantgwyn parish, there is a place called Pontfaen. It is not unlikely that the hostility to Brynach is another way of expressing opposition to his religion.

The opposition to St. David is well known. Its mainspring was the family of Boia of Clegyr, whose wife[80] was particularly offensive. In Rhygyfarch's Life, Boia is called a druid. The wife invited her step-daughter, Dunawd, to go with her to the wood of Glyn Hodnant to gather nuts.[81] Presently she sat down and asked the girl to lay her head in her lap so that she could dress (*trin*) her hair. When the girl did so, the stepmother cut her throat, and 'a clear fountain arose in the place where her blood flowed to the ground, which abundantly cured many diseases of mankind, which place the common people call the Martyrium of Dunawd to this day.'[82] The primitive elements are all here—the woodland with hazel trees, the ceremonial dressing of the hair, the sacrifice of a girl, and a well. Here was a relic of a very early legend which the biographers could not ignore, and so it was conditioned and introduced to show the kind of opposition with which David had to contend and which he overcame. Maen Cetti, on Cefn-y-Bryn, Gower, was worshipped by Welsh pagans until David split it with a sword and then commanded a holy well to flow there.[83]

III. Wells Dedicated to Saints

We will consider now wells which do not appear in the surviving Lives. We have to rely on later evidence concerning these, evidence that has been influenced by alien and comparatively modern beliefs. Like those of the major

[80] Note that women were the main opponents of Collen, Brynach and Dewi. This may have been due to the prejudice of medieval churchmen against women. The pagan was not a menace when the Lives were written, but woman was.

[81] This suggests that it was a hazel grove, and most certainly that there were hazel trees there.

[82] El, 109. CBS, 126. WESD, 12, 91. [83] Mont. Coll., 269 ff.

Celtic saints, these wells possess the same attributes, being holy and healing, while similar practices attach to them. It is possible that certain saints were personally associated with some of these wells, but others were doubtless posthumous dedications, such as those of the non-Celtic saints, in the same way as churches were dedicated to saints with whom they had no personal connection.

(*a*) *Wells dedicated to Celtic Saints*

Within the see of St. David's there are many wells dedicated to the national saint, whose total number of wells in the Principality greatly exceeds those of any other Celtic saint. Many of these are in the districts where he is known to have laboured, and it may well be that they were associated with him during his lifetime, although not mentioned in his Lives. I have not found a single well dedicated to Dewi in North Wales. The wells of Dewi and his mother Non are often found near each other such as in St. David's parish (Pem.), in Cornwall[84] and in Brittany.[85] The ability of Dewi's wells to relieve disease is mentioned by Gwynfardd Brycheiniog (c. 1175-80).

> Dichones rhag gormes gormant greireu
> A phynnawn Dewi a'i phynnhonneu llawn
> Llawer un radlawn frwythlawn frydeu[86].

The phrase, '*mor laned a ffynnon Ddewi*' (as pure as Dewi's well) is still current in North Pembrokeshire.[87]

The cult of St. Patrick seems to have been more popular in North Wales than in the south. Two of his wells are located in Anglesey and Merioneth and there is a Ffynnon Gwaspatrick in Denbighshire.[88] His sole well in South

[84] St. David's Well in Davidstowe, and St. Non's Well in the neighbouring parish of Altarnon.
[85] In the Plougastel district. cf. the suggestions by Canon G. H. Doble that Non is identical with the male St. Nonna, who may have been a companion to Dewi —Doble, *St. Nonna*, Cornish Saint Ser, No. 16.
[86] HGC, poem xviii. [87] See GDD, 294, n.
[88] In Cerrig y Druidion parish, where the church is dedicated to Ieuan Gwas Badrig with Mary Magdalene. cf. the hamlet of Trefwaspatryk in Anglesey, AD 1294—TSW, App Aa, p. 6.

Wales is in Monmouthshire. Giraldus states that the holy man, Caradog, lived near Portfield, Haverfordwest, where there is a St. Caradog's Well. He died in 1124 and is said to have been canonised by Innocent III at the instance of Giraldus.[89] This is an example of a late canonisation, and is confirmed by a deed, dated 1315, which gives the location of ' the common well, enclosed with stone and lime, called the well of St. Caradoc near the well of St. David,' at Haverfordwest, and which further states that its water was then used for domestic purposes.[90] The Cardiganshire Ffynnon Garadog may be connected with this saint.

A Pembrokeshire tradition shows that saints were cantankerous and violent on occasions. It is said that SS Aedan and Gwynda, on their way to St. David's, stopped to drink at Ffynnon Tregroes in Whitchurch parish. Each wished to bestow his name on the well, tempers became uncontrollable, with the unsaintly sequel that poor Gwynda received a good hiding. Aedan then calmly dedicated the well to himself and, pleased with the turn of affairs, went on his way to St. Davids. Gwynda took a different direction and hurried via Caerfarchell, Llanbedr y Moch by Mathry, Llangloffan Cross, Tremarchog, Rhiw Cnwc y Llygod, Trefelgarn, Cargowil, and so to Llanwnda. Having put this distance between himself and his muscular conqueror, he felt a little safer, and proceeded to establish a church (Llanwnda) and to sanctify a well (Ffynnon Wnda).

The distribution of wells indicates the area of a saint's cult, and sometimes confirms the Lives in a striking fashion —unless the well-names had been inspired by those Lives. A period of St. Samson's Life concerns Pembrokeshire, and in that county there are three of his wells,[91] while archaeological remains further indicate his popularity in the

[89] *Itin*, Bk 1, cap xi.
[90] Haverfordwest Corporation Deeds. This is the only early record I have seen, to confirm Giraldus' statement that Caradog was canonised, and is thus important.
[91] I have been unable to locate a fourth Ffynnon Samson said to be in Mynachlogddu parish in *Arch. Cam.*, 1903, 319.

same districts.[92] Some local saints,[93] whose piety caused their memory to be revered in remote districts, but whose names never figure in menologies, are, nevertheless, remembered in the names of wells and chapel sites. The Cardiganshire Ebwen (perhaps Mebwen,—wyn) is one of these forgotten saints. A royal confirmation to Strata Florida in 1426 recites a charter from Rhys ap Tewdwr in 1184, and among the boundary marks is *Finan Mebwyn*, between Castell Flemys and Coet Mawr, and it also mentions 'the part of the nuns[94] of *Fennaun Vebwynn*.'[95] A deed,[96] dated 1704, describing properties in Lampeter parish, as *Tyr Capell ffynnon Ebwen*, proves conclusively that here we are in the undoubted presence of a holy well with its attached chapel, named after a local saint. It is possible that Elin, whose name is recorded in Professor Rees' map in Ffynnon Elin, south of Llanilar (Card.), is another example, and also Govan and Degan (Pem.), and perhaps Gwenno (Carm.) and Mymbyr (Caern.)—all of whom had wells bearing their names. Perhaps the monk, Gynaid, was also an uncanonised saint: he spent his life in a cave on Bardsey 'and his sustenance was a drop of water to drink, which after that continues to heal the sick.'[97] It is for consideration whether Ffynnon Gwenlais (Carm.), source of the river Gwenlais, owes its name to an obscure saint. Lhuyd says that *Cappel Gwenlais* stood there, and Fenton saw a large yew growing over it. The latter adds:

> 'The tradition is of this Spring, as that of Holywell, that a Virgin was there murdered, and that on the Spot a spring gushed out. The Spring has two eyes, they say, of a very

[92] e.g. in North Pembrokeshire. A tumulus on an islet off the Dewsland coast is called *Bys Samson*. The Longhouse and Trellys cromlechau are called *Carreg* and *Ffyst Samson* respectively. The Garn Wnda cromlech is called *Carreg Samson*, and the saint is said to have thrown a large stone which landed near Rhosycaerau at a place called Coitan. The Pentre Ifan cromlech stands in a field called *Corlan Samson*. A tumulus in Nevern parish is called *Bedd Samson*. A few yards from Cefnygarth tumulus, Cilgerran parish, is a boulder called *Marbl Samson*. A boulder-throwing legend concerns the monolith Maengwynhir in Llanfyrnach parish, which is said to have been thrown from the summit of Frenni Fawr by St. Samson.

[93] For the early significance of the Welsh *sant* see CBPM, 345-6.

[94] Of Llanllur. [95] Williams, *Strata Florida*, Appx, lvii.

[96] NLW Conwil Gaeo Deeds. [97] NLW Llanst. MS. 34.

different nature . . They shew a Cavity, about the size of a Grave, near the Well, on very dry ground, of which it is said that, fill it as often as you please to the surface . . it will always sink to the same depth, that is about a foot or 15 Inches from the surface.'[98]

However, we have to consider also whether the name Gwenlais is the older, and that the element *gwen*—gave rise to the tradition of a slain virgin.

It is not clear whether some wells are named after saints or princes or heroes or ordinary laymen. Such are the wells of Arthur, Llewelyn, and Gollwyn. The question is complicated by the fact that some wells which came to be considered holy were initially connected with layfolk such as Ffynnon Dunawd (Pem.) and Ffynnon Digiwc (Caern.) mentioned above.

(*b*) *Wells dedicated to non-Celtic saints*

By far the most popular of these saints was Our Lady whose wells are found in all parts of Europe. Her name appears in connection with Welsh wells in the following forms—Mair (Fair), Mary, Our Lady, and Lady. In a great number of cases where the name Lady Well occurs, the parish church is dedicated to Mary, and there can be no doubt at all that she is the patron of those parish Lady Wells.[99] It is important to grasp this point, since during the post-Reformation period she has been confused with the 'Ladi Wen' (see p. 126 below) who is sometimes regarded as a spirit or guardian of the well. Her wells are distributed through Wales (see Map 4) as also are the churches dedicated to her. She was a favourite saint of the Normans and the map shows that the majority of her wells are in districts where the Anglo-Norman influence was strongest. However, we must be careful about drawing from this what would appear to be the obvious deduction, because the cult of Our Lady came into being in the 4th

[98] Fenton TW, 60-1

[99] For English examples see HWE, *passim*, and for Scottish examples see *Proc. of the Society of Antiquaries of Scotland*, 1883, pp. 197-199.

century and became extremely popular and widespread in a short time. Further there was always a considerable Welsh population in those areas that later came under the Norman influence.

Some seventy-six of her wells are found in Wales, and there are traditions that she actually visited the country. It is said that she came to the shores of Kidwelly (where there is a Ffynnon Fair) and asked a man to throw her back into the sea. He slew her instead. According to local tradition the man and his family became accursed, and his descendants are marked out to this day as people who never succeed in their undertakings.[100] The other tradition is more felicitous. It relates that Mary landed at Llanfair (Mer.) where a church was dedicated to her. She walked towards Hafod-y-llyn, a small lake near Bryn Llynau farm, two miles south-east from Harlech, and knelt at the roadside to drink from a stream. When she had done this, marks remained on the rock on which she knelt, and at its side there arose a spring of pure water which possessed miraculous healing powers. On reaching the lake, she and the maidens with her, bathed, and ever after 'water lilies grew there.'[101] The image of Our Lady of Cardigan was supposed to have been found at the mouth of the Teifi, with the Child in her lap and a burning taper in her hand. The legend says that she was removed to 'Christ Church,' Cardigan, but returned four times of her own accord to the place where she was first found. Finally St. Mary's, Cardigan, was built, and now content, she stayed there. The taper she held in her hand continued to burn steadily for nine years, until a Welshman forswearing himself, it went out and could never be relighted.[102] There was also a cult of Mair o Fynyw (St. Davids) and it is as such that she is addressed in a poem by Howel Swrdwal

[100] NEW Llanelly, 363. There are similar traditions in Europe, and she is said to have visited Brittany and Spain.
[101] LW, 144. By 1931 this tradition was almost forgotten, and it has been suggested that the story related to another Hafod-y-llyn near Llyn Mair, a few miles away at Tan-y-bwlch.
[102] H. Maynard Smith, *Pre-Reformation England*, London, 1938.

(1430-1460).[103] Her well was at the east end of the Cathedral, and nearby stood St. Mary's College.

The popularity of the Virgin is reflected in medieval literature, and I have shown elsewhere how Welsh families actually traced their pedigrees to the Holy Family and were satirized for so doing.[104] This respect continued in Protestant Wales, and the Vicar of Llanilar (Card.) said in 1911 that he had heard from an old woman that when she was a girl it was customary for women to curtsey to an 'oil painting' of Our Lady when entering Llanilar church.[105] Ffynnon Fair, near Aberdaron (Caern.), is reached by a dangerous path called Grisiau Mair and Ysgol Fair, and the folktale concerning the origin of this well mentions a 'beautiful lady' and a 'strange lady,' which no doubt represents the Virgin of Catholic days. On a rock beside this well are two impressions, one said to be that of Mary's hand, the other of her horse's hoof. Perhaps her most famous well was at Penrhys (Glam.), which had a tremendous reputation for healing. The bard Gwilym Tew went there in 1460 to be cured of the ague and fever, and wrote a poem on the event. Lewis Morgannwg (1500-1540) mentioned in one of his poems some of the cures that had been wrought at Ffynnon Fair Penrhys. He says that the Virgin brought the dead to life, mad people were baptised, if the blind had faith they recovered their sight, cripples came and afterwards ran, and the deaf obtained hearing. It was one of the most famous shrines in South Wales and pilgrimages to it were frequent. Prior to the Dissolution, Penrhys was valued at £6 per annum.

It has been suggested that Ffynnon y Forwyn (Carm.) is also one of her wells, and the Simmery Well (Mon.) retains her name in corrupted form. The only Ffynnon Fair in Wales, known to me, which is dedicated to another Mary,

[103] BM Add MS. 31072, f. 45.
[104] Trans. Cymm, 1948, 325-6, 332, 361. It is a singular fact that I have not found in a single Welsh pedigree or record prior to the Reformation, the name Mary (Mair) borne by a Welsh woman. There were a number of women named Morwyn Fair, but that is another matter.
[105] JCD, 327.

is that in Cerrig-y-Druidion (Denb.) (where the church is dedicated to St Mary Magdalene) described by Lhuyd as *Ffynnon Vair vagdalen*: it is probable that Ffynnon Fair, near St. Clears (Carm.), was also under the same patronage as the old Cluniac priory and the parish church of St. Clears are dedicated to Mary Magdalene.

Non-Christian elements impinging on a well dedicated to the Virgin are found in Pembrokeshire. At Cresswell Hill, near Lady's Well, grew a row of tall beeches, on one of which a pentacle or pentalpha[106] was carved about 1811. A local tradition says that many years ago 'white ladies' were charmed away from the vicinity of this Lady's Well by means of several pentacles being cut into the bark of the neighbouring trees.[107] It is likely that the holy name of the well suggested in more modern times the 'white ladies' of Welsh folklore.

St. Peter (17 wells) enjoyed a high popularity. Some of his wells were difficult to locate, and Lhuyd wrote, under Cilymaenllwyd (Carm.), 'I was informed by an old man who was then aged about four score and ten yt he had heard or was told yt one had prophesied that there is a spring in Cwm fynnon Beder springing towards the south & if discovered it would cure the blind, the deaf, dumb & criple.'[108] Michael (12 wells) and John (4 wells) were also highly regarded. Tradition has been corrupted in some cases, such as that concerning St. John's Well alias Ffynnon Iwan (Mont.), which states that a man named Iwan or Ifan bathed the wounded warriors with water from this well after the battle of Cadnant, and that it was thereafter known by his name. But in the same locality are Carreg Ifan and Mynwent or Corlan Ifan,[109] which suggest a religious origin. Elen (Helen) was popular throughout Christendom, but she was especially remembered in Wales,

[106] This design was regarded in South Pem. as a physical charm and the repository of talismanic power.
[107] JCD, 285.
[108] For a Scottish example of difficulty in finding a virtuous well see BBC, Scotland, i, 164.
[109] *Bygones*, 3 Aug. 1910.

for apart from her purely religious associations (she has 6 wells) she appeared as an ancestress in the dynastic Welsh pedigrees. Margaret has three wells, and in the late 12th century the chapel of St. Margaret, Coed Ffranc (Glam.), was built close to Margaret's Well.[110] Over St. Anne's Well, near Llanmihangel church (Glam.), was a bust of the saint so constructed that the water flowed through her breasts. Trinity Wells (10) were usually visited on Trinity Sunday.

IV. Wells in Medieval Welsh Life

(*a*) *Religious*

The life of the medieval Welshman was intimately concerned with wells and well-chapels. Pilgrimages to these were made at all times of the year especially during the *gwyl mabsant* or wakes. Some of the chapels were elaborate such as that of Gwenfrewi (Winifred)[111] at Holywell, perhaps the most famous well-shrine in medieval Britain. The prestige of St. Winifred was very high, yet it is a remarkable fact that no other single well or church in Wales was dedicated to her. The well and chapel of Holywell had been granted in 1093 by the Countess of Chester to the monastery of St. Werburg, and in 1115 her son, Earl Richard, made a pilgrimage to the well. Its possession reverted to the Welsh lords, and in 1240 Dafydd ap Llewelyn granted it to Basingwerk Abbey, which held it until 1537. In 1189 Richard I sheltered in Basingwerk when attacked by the Welsh while he was on a pilgrimage to

[110] A deed of 1705 mentions this 'St Margaretts Well'. It is marked as Ffynnon Verad on Kitchen's map (1754) and Walpoole's map (1784). It is now called Ffynnon Farged. Mared, merred, frequently occurs in medieval pedigrees as the Welsh form of Margaret. Lhuyd mentions a Fynnon Varred in Mer. (Par. ii, 64).

[111] Her name was Brewi to which *Gwen* was prefixed to indicate her holy status. This adjective was used both as prefix and suffix. The following occur in connection with Welsh wells—Gwenfaen, Gwenfil, Gwenfrewi, Gwenhudw, Gwenlais, Gwenno, Gwennog, Ceinwen, Dwynwen, Gedwen, Mebwen (Mebwyn), Mynwen, Tudwen, Gwynda, Gwynhael, Gwynlliw, Gwynno, Gwynwy, Berwyn, Gollwyn, Tecwyn.

St. Winifred's well.[112] In 1416, 'the King with great reverence went on foot in pilgrimage from Shrewsbury to St. Winifred's Well in North Wales.'[113]. In 1439 the Countess of Warwick presented her russet velvet gown to the chapel, and Edward IV (1461-83) is said to have made a pilgrimage to it. Richard III conferred an annuity of 10 marks upon the Abbot of Basingwerk for maintaining a priest at the well. The offerings at St. Winifred's were worth £10 per annum in 1535. The Lives record many stories of miraculous cures at this well. Bards like Iolo Goch (1326-1402),[114] Ieuan Brydydd Hir (1440-70),[115] and Tudur Aled (1480-1500),[116] sang the praises of Winifred and her well.

In Anglesey much of the wealth of Llanddwyn was derived from the offerings of the numerous pilgrims to the shrine and well of Dwynwen, who came there 'from diverse countries' carrying candles and offerings hoping to be cured of their afflictions.[117] A further example of the material benefits of a local well-cult is found at Llanrhaiadr (Denb.) where a fine Jesse window was erected in 1535, being paid for from the contributions of pilgrims who sought cure of skin diseases at the nearby Ffynnon Ddyfnog.[118] Two farms in Anglesey were purchased from the offerings made at Ffynnon Eilian and the rents were were applied towards keeping the parish church and well-chapel in repair.[119]

When making pilgrimages abroad, Welshmen often visited the three wells in Rome, that had gushed forth when St. Paul's head had rebounded thrice after his execution. Dafydd ap Gwilym, Lewis Glyn Cothi, Lewis Morgannwg, Lewis Trefnant and other poets refer to them.

(*b*) *Secular*

Secular literature has preserved the names and history of many wells ignored in sacred literature, together with much

112 OPem, iv, 562. 113 Chron. A, 313.
114 *Gweithiau Iolo Goch.* ed. C. Ashton, Oswestry 1896, pp. 600-603.
115 CBPM, 401-2. 116 *ib*, 402-405. 117 LBS, ii, 389-91 : Carlisle TDW.
118 LOC, 88-9. 119 LBS, ii, 439 : Carlisle TDW.

early pre-Christian material that has been disguised or edited out of existence from the religious works. In Manawydan fab Llyr, Pryderi came to a *caer* where there was a fountain with marble around it and a golden bowl attached to four chains.[120] In the tale of Taliesin we learn that the dwelling of Tegid Voel, 'a man of gentle lineage,' was in the middle of Llyn Tegid.[121] Several folk-tales have survived concerning Llyn Tegid which is said to have been formed by an overflowing well which its negligent guardian had forgotten to cover.[122]

The Arthurian cycle is full of references to magical wells, but it should be remembered that they derive in essence from Classical Mythology, and modern scholars have shown that there are very few native or 'Celtic' elements in them.[123] Sir Accolon of Gaul, who hunted with Arthur, found himself by a deep well, 'and there came out of that fountain a pipe of silver, and out of that pipe ran water all on high in a stone of marble.'[124] Trees invariably grew over these wells. A pine tree that never shed its needles grew over one.[125] The 10th century Irish text, *Navigatio Sancti Brendani*, describes how voyagers came to an island and found a well overshadowed by a tree whose branches were covered with birds which sang the canonical hours on holy days. At wells, usually in forests, beautiful damsels or fays waited for human lovers whom they entertained.[126] The *Eluicidatum* (ed. A. W. Thompson, 1931) describes how King Amangon violated one of the female well attendants, with the result that the land became unfruitful and the well-maidens retired to their underground abode. A parallel is found in the legend about the Shee or Shew Well (Glam.)[127] Three streams united at the Shee Well,

[120] Mab. J, 46. [121] Mab. G, 263. [122] See below p. 133.
[123] e.g. see CMAR, *passim*. [124] LMD, 80. [125] ATC, 289.
[126] e.g. the tale of Gauwain, ATC, 95, 224.
[127] Also called Ogmore Spring, near the W boundary of St. Bride's Major, a little to the SW of Ewenny—Lewis TDW. I have been unable to find any earlier forms of the name Shee or Shew. It is well, perhaps, to note that the Gower word for stye is 'she'. and certain glass beads, called locally 'she stones', are used to cure styes. Did the Shee Well specialise in the cure of styes? Wells that cured sore eyes are common.

and it was believed that at their sources dwelt water-ogres who captured girls and kept them. One maiden who escaped became dumb so could not relate her experiences. Some lawless men who lived on the banks of the Ewenny and Ogmore, so offended the Shee Well, that the well dried up and gave vent to moans and groans, while snakes and toads were found instead of fish in the stream that flowed from the well and in the Ewenny and Ogmore. The wild men were penitent and visited a cavern in the hills to which the Shee Well had receded. They promised to reform if the ogre of the well caused the waters to return to their normal condition. The ogre agreed, and furthermore it planted trees so that the place looked cool and inviting. The people danced and rejoiced in honour of the return of the Shee Well, and it was said that old folk grew young again for joy.[128]

Combats often took place between a knight and the guardian of the well.[129] Several tales describe storm-producing wells, a typical example being the Breton well in the forest of Broceliande,[130] but this has been shown to be derived from the rain-making ritual so clearly marked in classical mythology.[131] Wells were also entrances to the underworld,[132] and such tales contain some of the Celtic religious belief in Elysian lands below wells and lakes.[133]. Similar wells sustained people, such as the food-giving well on an island of immortal youth amid 'the streams of the ocean' (*Book of Taliesin*, No. XIV). Stones and great megaliths alongside wells occur frequently in these secular, or 'secularised' tales.

Wells appear in those popular features of medieval literature, 'Prophecies' and 'Marvels.' The prophecies of Merlin, as given by Geoffrey, state that the fountains of Armorica will break forth, the fountain of a river will turn to blood, the waters of Bath will grow cold and cause

[128] Trevelyan, 19. [129] ATC, 264, 274.
[130] Mab. G, 390 : Giraldus, Op. V, ed. J. F. Dimock, 1867, 89 ff.
[131] CMAR, *passim*. [132] cf. ATC, 306-7.
[133] Rhŷs CH, 187 ff : Joyce, *Old Celtic Romances*, 246-59.

death.[134] Of the twenty marvels mentioned by Nennius,[135] thirteen were associated with water. The Severn bore is represented as the clash of the two water-kings of Severn. In the land of Cinlipiuc (between Wye and Severn) was Finnaun Guur Helic, twenty feet in diameter, its water knee-deep, and surrounded by high banks, no water flowed into or from it ; those who fished from the north, south, east and west banks, caught entirely different kinds of fish. The well at Pwll Meuric, near Chepstow, contained a magical log on which people stood when washing their faces. The Severn bore used to flood this well and the ebb took the log out to sea, but on the fourth day it was returned miraculously to the well. To test this, a rustic buried the log, but on the fourth day it was back in the well, and within a month the bold rustic was dead. In Anglesey an inland ford was said to ebb and flow with the sea-tides, a claim common to many Welsh wells. Wells possessing any unusual feature were noticed with enthusiasm by medieval writers. Giraldus describes ebb and flow wells near Dinefor and in Tegeingl, and a well on Arthur's Seat in Breconshire, square in shape, which contained trout, and from which no water flowed. Malory writes of Galahad's well which seems to have been near the Welsh border.

> Galahad came into a perilous forest, where he found the well which boiled with great waves, as the tale telleth before. And as soon as Galahad set his hand thereto it ceased, so that it burnt no more . . . And this was taken in the country for a miracle, and so ever after was it called Galahad's well.[136]

Geoffrey had written of a well called Fons Galabes (to which Merlin frequently resorted) which was *in natione Gewisseorum*,[137] and it is probably identical with that of Galahad. Dafydd ap Edmwnd mentioned it :

> gwlyb ywr grvdd a glybvr gwres
> gwlybwr ffynnon galabes.[138]

A 16th century *De Mirabilibus Cambriae*, an adaptation of

[134] Geoffrey, 212-215. [135] Nennius, 116-121. [136] LMD, 406.
[137] Geoffrey, 245. [138] GDE, 8.

earlier material, contains a description of St. Winifred's well and its wonders.

Some were so well-known that it was necessary only to mention their names without giving information as to their location. One of the Llywarch Hen poems states simply that Cadwallon's army camped by *Fynnawn Vedwyr*, and his contemporaries knew exactly where this was and also knew a lot about Bedwyr. We can only conjecture that it was in the northern part of Gwentllwg.[139] Wells were also associated with calamitous events. There is a tradition that Ffynnon Sul (Kidwelly) gushed forth at the spot where 'the prince Benisel' was slain.[140] In the little valley of Nant Llewelyn just south-west of Cefn y Bedd, Ffynnon Llewelyn still flows, and, according to Adam of Usk, 'The spring wherein the head of Llewellyn ap Griffith, last prince of Wales, was washed after it was cut off, and which is in the village of Builth, throughout a livelong day did flow in an unmixed stream of blood.'[141] There is a tradition that Ffynnon Pen Sir Rhys (Breck.) flowed with blood when Rhys ap Tewdwr was beheaded.[142].

Redlake (Rad.) is said to have run with blood for three days after a great battle. Similar stories are related of a well near the churchyard wall of Llanyblodwell parish, of a well on Bryn y fedwen farm,[143] and Blood Well (Mont.) Ffynnon y Gwaed near Maes Garmon, Ffynnon Iwan (Mont.), Ffynnon Gwaed near Mynydd Islwyn and Ffynnon Gwaed in Upper Bedwas (Mon.), Ffynnon Grog (Card.). Tradition says that the waters of Ffynnon y Gwylliaid (Mer.) were red after murderers had washed their hands in it.[144] It is said that combats were fought by Welsh warriors near Llanunwas well (Pem.), and, that after blood had been drawn, the 'spears' were washed in that well. This seems to imply some ceremonial washing of weapons.

Medieval deeds and records have preserved the names and locations of some wells (religious as well as secular),

[139] Ll. Hen, 112. [140] NEW Llanelly, 361. [141] Chron. A, 218.
[142] Carlisle TDW: Fenton TW, 352. [143] *Bygones*, 1 Feb. 1911.
[144] Davies LGM, 227.

because they were used extensively as boundary marks. They persist until the 17th century when enclosures made it possible to identify property with precision. Owen Cyfeiliog's charter to Strata Marcella in 1170 mentions *Fons Tessiliau* (Mont.), and the charter of Llewelyn ap Iorwerth to Aberconway in 1198 names *Ffynnon y Meyirch*. The *Liber Landavensis* contains many early examples, such as *Finnaun Dioci* (Mon.),[145] *Finnaun Diguinid Aruen* (Mon.),[146] and *Ffynnon y cleiuon* near Dingestow (Mon.)[147] *Ffynnaun Elichguid* occurs in a grant of Mathern by Meurig ab Tewdrig in the time of Bishop Oudoceus, and was probably named after the Monmouthshire saint, Elicguid, who witnessed three charters in the *Liber*.[148] Examples are also found in Clark's *Glamorgan Charters*. An undated grant by King Morgan to Llandaff, of what is now Bishopston church, describes one boundary as *finnaun Canthed*, and a grant by Cadwallon to Llandaff mentions *Finnaun Liss*: a grant by Hywel ap Rhys of what is now Merthyr Mawr mentions *aperfinnaun Uanon*.[149] The story of how Ffynnon Oer became a boundary mark contains some typical medieval elements. Rhiwallon ap Tudfwlch, riding away after he had plundered the churchgoers of Lannmocha (St. Maughan, Mon.), was 'exceedingly amazed' at seeing a great fish leap out of Ffynnon Oer, which so startled his horse that the rider fell in great pain and broke his arm. He then surrendered the booty and granted lands to Llandaff, the well becoming one of the boundaries.[150] The fish represented the pagan spirit of the well, and here, under clerical influence, it has been metamorphosed into a guardian of the Church.

The boundary of a Brecknockshire property was the influx from the Spring of the Twelve Saints into the Lake of Syfaddon (Llangorse).[151] A grant in 1233 by the Earl of

[145] Lib. Land, 231. RJT, 141. It was near Monmouth.
[146] Ffynnon Dywynydd Arfon: the stream is still called Dywynydd. See Lib. Land, 221: RJT, 140-1.
[147] Lib. Land, 218. [148] Lib. Land, 142. OPem, iv, 455.
[149] See below p. 187. [150] Lib. Land, 253. [151] Lib. Land, 389.

Pembroke to Tintern mentions the well of Angedy,[152] and *Fynnon a Burrough* occurs in a royal grant of lands in Raglan to Sir William Herbert in 1485. Margam Abbey deeds mention *St. Yelthut's Well* circa 1200. *Fennaun Arthur* and *Pistillcoleu* in 1203, and *Fynon gattuke* in 1518.[153] A holy well in Burton parish (Denb.), now only a faint depression in a meadow, is of special interest since it was one of the fixed boundary marks between England and Wales, being described as such in a Minister's Account for 1448.[154] The Three Counties Well near Llanymynech (Mont.) is so named because the borders of Shropshire, Denbighshire and Montgomeryshire meet at that spot. A few examples are found in deeds after the close of the Middle Ages, such as *Fynnon Sevte* a boundary of Ystradvellte parish (Breck.) in 1502,[155] and in 1667 *Ffynnon Ryddwern* and *Ffynnon Varred* occur as boundaries of the manor of Neath Citra (Glam.)[156] One such record shows the extension of the cult of Derfel Gadarn to South Wales. A survey in 1597-8, describes *Dervel's Well* as a boundary mark of the manor of Landimor in Gower.[157] There was some argument about Moor Well on the boundary of Gresford parish (Denb.). In 1642, the curate of Gresford and some parishioners came to the Moor Well as they had done for many years before, to claim the well to be in Gresford parish. However they saw some soldiers by the well, 'which wanted to see their fashions', whereupon the curate and his company departed and never came to claim the well again.[158]

Some of these wells which did duty as boundary marks or were near boundaries, may not have been so secular as we are led to believe. Writing about Manx holy wells, Mr. William Cubbon says, 'So much were they treasured that even parish boundaries have been so formed as to capture the blessing that they shed, and saints' names were

[152] This well is at Higga. The stream called Angedy joins the Wye at Tintern.
[153] Deeds in NLW. [154] Anc. Mon. Denb. [155] BM Harl. Ch III, B 22.
[156] HVN, 201. [157] HWG, 189.
[158] VW, 75. It was to the financial advantage of the parish church to possess the holy well.

given to them. The boundary between Begoade in Conchan and Cooilroi in Lonan is a stream. In order to secure a much-desired well on the Conchan side of the stream, Lonan has taken a small bite from her neighbours.'[159] He gives other examples and one striking plan of a well 'captured' within a parish boundary.[160] A close investigation of Welsh parish boundaries in relation to holy wells may reveal some significant examples of the influence of the well-cult on the mind and behaviour of bygone Celtic parishioners.

[159] IH, *22*. [160] *ib*, p. *23*.

Chapter IV

THE WELL-CULT IN POST-MEDIEVAL WALES

The Reformation period—the seventeenth century—the eighteenth century—' old simple people '—' smells much like gunpowder'—antiquaries and wells—the nineteenth century and later.

(*a*) *The Reformation Period* 1535-1600

JUST before the hammer blow of the reformers fell, two monarchs of Welsh ancestry carried out devotional exercises at holy wells to the accompaniment of the prayers and hymns of the Catholic church. In England, Henry VIII made a pilgrimage to the well of Our Lady of Walsingham in Norfolk, walking the last two miles in his bare feet. A queen of equally ancient British descent, Anne of France, Duchess of Brittany, made a pilgrimage to the holy well at Morlaix in which she bathed her eyes and gave money to erect a building over it. But within a few years King Henry had inaugurated a new era in British religious life and the ancient shrines fell before the determined onslaughts of the Protestants.

The Reformation struck heavily at wells, and, together with relics and pilgrimages, they were denounced as superstitions. Although not enthusiastically received in Wales, there was no considerable resistance to the Reformation. It was supported by the leading clergy and the great landowning families, while the majority of the countryfolk whose untutored minds were unversed in the subtleties of theological and political controversy, remained loyal in their hearts to the observances of the medieval Church, and were bewildered when effigies were removed, church wall-paintings obliterated, rood-lofts and shrines destroyed, pilgrimages to wells and sacred sites prohibited. All they knew was that the visible and outward symbols of their faith were removed. They remained bewildered, and afterwards apathetic, until Welsh Nonconformity provided a spiritual leadership such as had not been known in Wales since the Age of the Saints. Grants of church property to leading Welsh laymen and to Englishmen planted in Wales, secured the co-operation of the ruling class, while the appointment of English officials, some of whom, like Rowland Lee, heartily detested the Welsh, and iconoclastic prelates like Bishop Barlow, ensured that the edicts of government reached all parts of the Principality. Although some cathedral chapters and parish priests opposed the extremists, it was in vain, and the effigies of Our Lady of Penrhys which had presided at the lonely well in the mountain fastnesses, and Derfel Gadarn the pride of many generations of Welshmen, were removed to London and burnt. But their wells remained.

The chapel of Gwenfrewi was too notable for destruction, and the reformers had their eyes on its monetary possibilities. In 1535 it was leased to a William Holcroft who was not long before he complained that some 'bold Catholics' had entered the well-chapel with boxes in their hands crying 'Put your money here where it shall do good to your souls; if you put it into the regular stock of alms, it will go to the king and shall not advantage you.'[1] During the short Marian reaction, Bishop Goldwell obtained from the Pope a renewal of the indulgences for pilgrims to St. Winifred's Well. A manuscript[2] written about 1550, discusses the value of pilgrimages from the Catholic standpoint, and the writer illustrates his views by quoting the miracles performed at the well of St. Winifred. Towards the end of 16th century Welshmen continued to refer to the potency of this well despite what the new teaching laid down for the good of their souls.[3]

Capel Meugan (Pem.) was not so fortunate. On 14 July, 1592 men were ordered

> 'to repaire to the place called St Meigans where somtyme offringes & superstitious pilgrimages have been used, and there to cause to be pulled downe and utterlie defaced all reliques and monuments of that chappell, not leaving one stone

[1] *Flintshire Hist. Soc. Journ.*, 1919-20. [2] CBPM, 19-21, 406.

[3] For an account of the secreting, and the ultimate discovery, of a relic from St. Winifred's Chapel, see BD, 39.

> thereof upon an other, & from tyme to tyme to cause to be apprehended all such persone and persones of what sexe kinde or sorte whatsoever that shall presume herafter contrarie to the tenor and p'rporte of the said honorable commission, to repair either by night or daie to the said chappell or *well* in superstitious maner & to bringe or send before us or enie of us . . .'[4]

So thoroughly was the work carried out that no traces of the chapel now remain, but the waters of Pistyll Meugan continue to bear testimony to the saint. The priory of Whitewell at St. Davids was destroyed completely, but two of its holy wells remain to remind us of its existence. One is the holy well still flowing at the site of the priory: the other is mentioned in a survey of the manor of Whitewell in 1616 as Ffynnon y Prior.[5]

Ffynnon Fair Penrhys, a centre of South Welsh Catholic devotion, suffered similarly. In 1537, Llantarnam Abbey, to which Penrhys belonged, was surrendered to the Crown, and in the following year both were granted to John Parker of the Royal Stables. The famous effigy was still in the well-chapel. On 23 August, 1538, Thomas Cromwell instructed William Herbert to remove the effigy 'as secretly as might be,' since it was feared that such action would provoke a local rising. On 26 September, 'the Image and her apparel' were removed and sent to London where they were burnt. Ffynnon Fair could not be obliterated and it remained an ordinary healing well throughout the centuries until the restoration of its significance on Sunday within the octave of the Feast of the Nativity of Our Lady, 12 September, 1947, when some four thousand Roman Catholics made a pilgrimage, paid their devotions, and used again the waters of Ffynnon Fair Penrhys.

Some of the ancient aristocratic families, whose sympathies were with the common people, tried to temper the wind to the shorn lamb. This is shown by what took place in 37 Elizabeth (1594-5) at Ffynnon Gwyddfaen in Carmarthenshire. In their Bill of Complaint in the Star

[4] NLW, Vairdre Book. [5] PRO, Rentals and Surveys, SC, 11. Roll 790.

Chamber against Morgan Jones of Tregib (a squire descended from Urien Rheged), Griffith Gillam and Rice Morgan, averred that two years previously a commission had been issued to John Gwyn Williams by the Council of the Marches, for the suppression of pilgrimages and 'idolatrous places,' and especially a well, known in the Llandilo-fawr district as *Fynnon Gwiddvaen.* At this well, Williams apprehended a large number of persons whom he brought before Mr. Jones, who, not only refused to imprison, but even to examine them. In his Answer, Morgan Jones admitted that 'some poor sickly persons' who had gone to the well to wash 'hoping by the help of God thereby to have their health,' had been brought before him by Williams, but he thought them harmless and discharged them. He also admitted that Williams had told him that there were some two hundred or more people still left unapprehended at the well.[6] This evidence is significant, not only because of the attitude of the magistrate, but also on account of the fact that such a large number of people continued to arrive at the well at the same time. There is no doubt that this was a pilgrimage pure and simple, made under the excuse of healing. Mr. Jones knew very well what was afoot.

The writings of the period show that the Protestantism of the people lagged behind that of their leaders. In the course of a funeral sermon in 1576, the Bishop of St. Davids condemned those who 'defende papistrie, supersticion and Idolatrie, pilgrimages to *Welles* and blind Chappelles, procure the wardens of Churches in tyme of visitacion to periure, to conceale images, roode loftes and aulters. This is lamentable . . . .'[7]

David Powell, in 1583, came out equally boldly on the side of Protestantism and he included wells among the superstitions that he denounced—

> 'Loca quaedam peregrinationibus assulta, in hac euangelii luce, vsque in hodiernum diem, ingenti peregrinantium multitudine

[6] PRO, Star Chamber Proc. G. 45/3, 37 Eliz. I am indebted to the kindness of Mr. Glanmor Williams, M.A., for this reference. [7] FS.

singulis annis superstitiose frequententur : *vt fons diuae Venefredae sacer* : *fons Dyfnoci in strata cludensi* : fanum Aenoe[8] regis in aruonis : fanum Davidis in Demetia.'[9]

A letter written about 1590 said of Welsh people,

> 'They doe still goe in heapes one pilgrimage to the wonted *welles* and places of superstition ; and in the nightes after the feastes when the ould offringes were used to be kept at anie chappell, albeit the church be pulled down, yet doe they come to the place where the church or chappell was, by great journeys barefoots.'[10]

The transition to Protestantism is reflected in contemporary poetry. The bard Gruffydd ap Ieuan ap Llewelyn Fychan addressed a poem to St. Cynhafal asking for help to cure his leg at Ffynnon Gynhafal, and wrote,

> Ffynnon iti hoff ennaint oedd
> Ffrwd nod a ffardwn ydoedd
> Aml yn hon ymlaen henaint
> Ydd oedd help i ddioedde haint.

Later, he was converted to Protestantism, and then wrote a poem roundly condemning the old practices,

> Rhoi urddoliant ar ddeulin
> A ddylai Grist i Ddelw grin
> ffyniant Gwenfrewi ffynon
> ffiaidd a ƚyll fu'r ffydd hon.
> Elian offrymwyd eilwaith
> Ar Grog o Gaer gorwag waith.[11]

Another example is provided by the verses of Dafydd Benwyn, who was cured after visiting Ffynnon Gollwyn (Glam.) in 1580.[12] Dafydd, later on, accepted Protestantism, and the quill that had praised Ffynnon Gollwyn now produced a denunciation against the veneration of effigies.[13] An anonymous bard, however, came out stoutly for the old faith, its images, wells, and devotion, as his poem addressed to St. Dyfnog shows.[14] He says that he reveres Dyfnog's effigy, accepts his miracles, praises his miracle-working well

[8] There was a Ffynnon Owen in Llysfaen parish (Caern.), mentioned by Lhuyd (Par. i, 40).
[9] Giraldus, *Itin*, ed. Powel, 85. [10] Arch. Cam. 1901, 113. [11] M. Deth, 60.
[12] *Yr Oes*, 1826, p. 178. [13] BM. Add MS. 31086, f. 180.
[14] NLW Llanst. MS. 167, pr. in CBPM, 390-1.

which gives grace to all nations and cures all ills—dumbness, deafness, 'y frech wenwynig',[15]—indeed there was none other like it.

(*b*) *The seventeenth century*

During this century the religious diehards of Elizabethan days passed away and Roman Catholicism ceased to be a force in Wales. But Protestantism as interpreted by the Church of England did not make any initial appeal to the Welsh. However there is evidence that many found solace in those superstitions that the reformers had so vigorously attacked in the previous century. The Cardiganshire author John Lewis of Glascrug had grave doubts about his countrymen when he wrote in 1646,

> 'I must tell you [Welsh people] abating gentry and a few others, that by the benefit of education may be otherwise; generally (I dare bouldly say) we can be but Papists, or worse in Wales. I need not remind thee of that swarm of blinde, superstitious ceremonies that are among us, passing under the name of old harmless custom; their frequent calling upon saints in their prayers and blessings, their peregrinations to *wells* and chappels.'[16]

The same story is found in other Celtic lands. Bishop William Foster, appointed to Sodor and Man in 1633, was strict in suppressing popish practices in the Isle of Man. One of the most famous of the island wells was Chibbyr Undin in Kirk Malew, and the wardens in answer to the bishop's questions on the matter reported that 'we heare that many other parishes doe repaire and resorte unto a well, to what intent we know not.'[17] The Scottish kirk was equally active in its attempt to purge the land of its ancient customs and in 1638 the General Assembly enacted penalties against those making pilgrimages to holy wells.[18]

Generally speaking, a conscious adherence to Catholicism as such was waning among Welsh well-visitors, apart from

[15] Probably pox. Lhuyd says about this well, 'some say twould cure ye Pox' (Par, i, 110).
[16] *Parliament explained to Wales*, 1646 (ed. 1907), 30.
[17] IH, 159. [18] AOSC, 2.

avowed Roman Catholics. The main purposes of the visits were for health reasons or as pleasant holidays as distinct from holy days and wakes. Catholic, and even pagan, beliefs and ritual continued their firm grip, but it is doubtful whether the people were fully aware of their true significance. Another interest in the well-cult appeared, namely the antiquarian interest, which was shown by the English Camden at the beginning and the Welsh Lhuyd at the close of the century.

St. Winifred's remained queen among Welsh wells. Visited by Catholic and Protestant alike, both in search of health, the former alone carried out the ritual with any appreciation of religious association. Early in 1605, Sir Everard Digby, one of the Gunpowder Plot party, accompanied by thirty horsemen, made a pilgrimage there. In 1606 Doctor Siôn Dafydd Rhys advised Sir Richard Bodenham, who suffered from a skin disease, to bathe at St. Winifred's well, and as a result of his visit we are told that 'his skin became as sound as that of a newly born infant.'[19] A document in the Public Record Office, headed 'Papists and priests assembled at St. Winefred's Well on St. Winefred's Day 1629,' contains their names and addresses, and also of 'divers other knights, ladies and gentlemen and gentlewomen of divers countries to ye number of fourteen or fifteen hundredth; and the general estimation of about 150 more priestes, the most of whom well-known who they were.'[20] In obedience to instructions from the Privy Council, Sir John Bridgeman, Chief Justice of Chester, attempted to stop all pilgrimages, and in 1637 the churchwardens of Holywell were ordered 'to take away the iron posts around the fountain, and disfigure the image of the Saint.'[21] Despite this, an attempt was made about 1642-3 by Jesuits to build a large house for pilgrims at Holywell but this was stopped by the authorities. In 1652, the Water Poet wrote that 'the fair Chappell over the well is now much defaced owing to the injury of these late wars

[19] *The Life of Saint Winefride.* ed. Thos Swift, London, 1888, 71.
[20] *ib,* 70-1. [21] *ib,* 71. It is noteworthy that her image was still there.

. . . . it is frequented daily by many people of Rich and Poore, of all Diseases . . .'[22] People came there from long distances, and among them, in 1674, a Cardiganshire yeoman, Cornelius Nicholas of Tremaen, who had failed to be cured by the apothecaries and the local wells. A royal visit was made on 29 August, 1686, when James II and his queen arrived to crave the prayers of Winifred that they might be blessed with a son. The king presented the chapel with part of a dress worn by Mary Queen of Scots at her execution, and the queen gave £30 towards the chapel fabric.[23] Is it to this Welsh well that history owes the Old Pretender, born in June 1688 ? The lively Celia Fiennes had much to say about what she saw at Holywell in 1698. Describing the bathers she wrote :

> ' . . . and so they walke along the streame to the other end and then came out, but there is nothing to shelter them but are exposed to all the Company that are walking about the Well . . . but the Religeuse are not to mind that . . . they tell of many lameness's and aches that are cured . . . I saw abundance of the devout papists on their knees all round the Well . . .'[24]

The voices of seventeenth century Welsh bards are again heard, some in praise and some in condemnation of saint and well. William Burchinshaw of Llansannan was a devotee of St. Winifred, and in a poem he praised her, and her well, which he says was in a delightful spot,

> Ffynnon mewn gorhoff annedd
> Gwn fry mai Gwenfrewy ai medd.[25]

Another, Robert Miltwn, composed four neat verses to the same well, and in one of them he says :

> Kael enaint a braint berwiach—gwiw nowsaidd
> Gan Iessu yn gynnesach
> Ffynnon Gwenvrewy ffeiniach
> A na'r enaid yn iach.[26]

[22] SRLJ, 11. Here is an example of the hostility of the Parliamentary army to well-chapels, cf. Aubrey's statement about a holy well at Oxford, 'stopt up since the warres' (RGI, 34).
[23] It is interesting to note that in 1663, Charles II had taken his queen, Catherine of Braganza, to the wells of Bath, hoping thereby to cure her sterility (LBB).
[24] JCF, 180-1. [25] CBPM, 400. [26] *ib*, 400.

William Mydleton, on the other hand, employed the muse to denounce Roman Catholicism and everything connected with it. He condemned the effigies of Dewi of Mynyw and Mair of Penrhys, and had no time at all for the bells of St. Anthony and St. Elian. He mentions the wells of Winifred, Dyfnog, Anne of Buxton, Mary Magdalene and Einion,

> Ffynnon Gwenfrewy ae chyffunydh
> Ffynnon i Dhyfnog ffein iawn dhefnydh
> Ffynnon Ann bwcston dan hoff winwydh
> Ffynnon fair fadlen awen newydh
> A ffynnon Einion eunydh y brenhin
> Yn y gorllewin min mynydh.[27]

Wells were noticed in South Wales. Richard Symonds, who was at St. Fagans with King Charles in 1645, wrote :

> ' In the orchard of this howse under an old ewe tree, is a spring or well within the rock called Saint Faggin's Well : many resort from all parts to drink it for the falling sichness[28] which cures them at all seasons. Many come a yeare after they have drank of [it] and relate there health ever since.'[29]

Towards the end of the century, Anthony Thomas of Baglan Hall noted another Glamorgan well, and wrote, ' Under the north w part of the said Mynidd dinas is a small spring, in former ages they say of much vertue, & now of late much frequented being found something beneficiall in curing children that have the rickets. 'Tis resorted unto for Three thursdayes in May, Ascension day to be one w'thout faile.'[30] Here, the dates of visitation confirm the former religious character of the well. In June 1662, John Ray, the naturalist, came to Pembrokeshire where he saw ' St. Gobin's Well by the sea side, where under the cliff stands a little chapel sacred to that saint, and a little below it a well, famous for the cure of all diseases.'[31] At the end of the century Lhuyd's correspondent wrote, ' Within the Chappell [St. Govans] ther's a spring & another below the Chappell toward the sea. The watter of these springs is found to be good for many distempers.'[32]

[27]BBCS, Nov 1936, 243.
[28] epilepsy. [29] RSD, 215. [30] Lhuyd Par. iii, 29. [31]Pem A, 77.
[32] Lhuyd Par. iii, 74.

These writers do little more than state that the wells were curative, and that they were visited by people in search of health, and the same tendency is found in English writers of the same period.[33] The main value of the references is that they show that the well-cult was still virile. Our debt to Edward Lhuyd is very much greater. During the years 1695-98, he collected, mainly by correspondence, materials for a history of Welsh antiquities. He was a scholar, he knew exactly what he wanted, and he realised the significance of the material he handled. This material often contains information as to the exact location of the wells, and the beliefs and customs and ritual associated with them.[34] Legal records also helped to preserve the memory of many old wells. An account of the beating of the bounds of Church-Stoke parish (Mont.) in 1702, mentions twelve wells as boundary marks.[35]

(*c*) *The eighteenth century*

In this century a distinct change of attitude occurs in literary and historical references to the wells. We have already noted that at the inception, or change, of a religion, wells were always condemned. The early Church, having initially condemned wells, later adapted and assimilated them to Christian rule. During the Reformation the authorities proscribed well-pilgrimages and practices as unbridled popery and tried to suppress them. Puritans continued the assault. The approach had invariably been a religious one. However, the eighteenth century was inclined to regard wells from standpoints other than religious. There were several reasons for this change:

1. The complete eclipse of Roman Catholicism.
2. The growth of Nonconformity.
3. The wave of antiquarian learning initiated by Lhuyd and developed by the Morris brothers,

[33]cf. Fuller's 'Worthies', where in his brief notes on English counties, he only includes wells specifically described as medicinal in the modern sense.
[34] See Chapters 5 and 6 below, and Part II, *passim*.
[35] *Bygones*, 22 Nov 1911.

Pennant, Dr. Owen-Pughe, Iolo Morganwg and Gwallter Mechain.

4. The spread of scientific knowledge and the advance of medicine.

With the eclipse of Catholicism and the general apathy towards established religion, the Welsh saints became *demode*, and the religious association was greatly weakened. With the rise of Nonconformity, the use of the word 'superstition' received greater emphasis. However, Protestantism and Nonconformity quite unwittingly helped to perpetuate the earlier paganism. In many cases where they erased the saint's memory, and where the saints' wells lost their religious significance, they became 'wishing' wells—that is, the 'wish' replaced faith. The spirit that actuates 'wishing' at wells is not Christian however worthy the 'wish.' It is pagan. The antiquaries taught observers to regard well practices as part of folk-learning, as 'interesting' and as 'curious survivals.' Methods of scientific analysis of water became general, and it was shown that chalybeate wells, for example, were curative because of the particular content of the water and not because of any saintly intervention that had taken place a millenium previously. The discovery of the healing properties of Llanwrtyd Wells illustrates the changed attitude. The Revd. Theophilus Evans, who suffered from a scorbutic complaint, espied an extremely healthy-looking frog emerging from Ffynnon Ddrewllyd. It occurred to him that water which could produce such vitality in a frog might do similarly for a priest of the Established Church. Where the frog had gambolled the vicar now quaffed, with the result that within a few weeks he was cured. This was in 1732, and before long Llanwrtyd acquired the reputation it has never since lost. The vicar did not attribute his good fortune to any saint or sprite of the well and he did not observe any of the traditional practices. He knew that the water had cured him because of its mineral content. In the Middle Ages such an event would have been hailed as a miracle, and the vicar might have had difficulty in avoiding canonization.[36]

New buildings, bath-houses, and residences were built for the convenience of the visitors to the wells, and the hotel took the place of what would have been a well-chapel in pre-Reformation times. Such building had commenced at the end of the previous century and Lhuyd refers to a Flintshire landowner erecting pillars around Ffynnon Asa,[37] but that may have been due partly to an antiquarian interest. Mr. W. J. Hemp informs me that bath-houses were built around some wells by the landed gentry of Wales for bathing, in the modern sense.

(*i*) '*Old Simple People*'. Reviewing religion in the diocese of St. Davids in 1721, Erasmus Saunders complained that the people still clung to many customs of the proscribed religion, and invoked not only Almighty God:

> 'but the Holy Virgin, and other Saints, for Mair-wen, Iago, Teilaw-mawr, Celer, Celynog, and others are often thus remember'd, as if they had hardly yet forgotten the use of Praying to them. And there being not only Churches and Chappels, but Springs and Fountains dedicated to those Saints, they do at certain times go and Bath themselves in them, and sometimes leave some small oblations behind them, either to the Keepers of the Place, or in a Charity Box prepar'd for that Purpose, by way of Acknowledgment, for the Benefit they have, or hope to have thereby.'[38]

John Lewis of Manorowen (c. 1700-1720), writing about Pembrokeshire, says, '... sainted wells do every where occur, to the waters of which rare and salutary qualities are found inherent.'[39] About the same time, Browne Willis wrote of St. Non's chapel near St. Davids,

> 'There is a fine Well beside it, cover'd with a Stone-Roof, and inclos'd within a Wall, with Benches to sit upon round the Well. Some old simple People go still to visit this Saint at some particular Times, especially upon St. *Nun*'s Day (March 2) which they keep holy, and offer Pins, Pebbles, Ec at this well.'[40]

It was not only 'old simple People' who cherished Non's

[36] The discovery of the curative wells of Llangammarch is attributed to a similar circumstance in which a sick pig was the central character.
[37] Lhuyd Par. i, 64. [38] View, 35. [39] Cam. Reg. ii, 119.
[40] Willis SD, 52-3.

well on the windswept cliffs above Caerfai, as the following note, written between 1739 and 1761, shows—' Beside which [Non's chapel] a little house is lately built. Here is a celebrated spring over which is an arched stone roof, which Dr. Davies,[41] late Chantor of St. Davids, not long since improved.'[42]

In Denbighshire, Willis noticed ' the famous well of S. Dyfnog much resorted to, and on that account provided with all conveniences of rooms, etc., for bathing, built around it.'[43] At Holywell, St. Winifred continued to receive pilgrims, but under difficulties. Daniel Defoe recounts the legend of Winifred, adding dryly, ' of which I believe as much as comes my share,' and he states that the priests there ' were very numerous ' but had to ' appear in disguise.'[44] In May 1719, the authorities hearing that Catholics intended to celebrate St. Winifred's feast, sent dragoons to Holywell, who seized the priest as he was officiating, the plate and effigies, ' and also found a parcel of writings, which discovered several estates settled to superstitious uses.'[45] In 1722 the chapel was used as a secular day school ; ' however to supply the loss of this chapel, the Roman Catholics have chapels erected in almost every Inn, for the devotion of the Pilgrims that flock hither from all the Popish parts of England.'[46]

Towards the end of the century, reprehensible conduct was noted. Pennant, in 1796, showed that Protestants as well as Catholics flocked to St. Winifred's Well. He stated that the first Sunday after St. James' Day was kept there in honour of certain saints, but

> ' not with prayers or with holy masses, but in every species of frolick and excess. It [the custom] originated in the *Romish* church : but I clear that congregation from being concerned in any part of the orgies ; which are, I fear, celebrated by persons of our own religion only, who flock here on that day for most unsaintly ends. The day is called *Dydd Sul y Saint* or the Sunday of the Saints.'[47]

[41] John Davies, collated precentor in 1717, was of the family of Llannerch and Gwysanney, Flints.
[42] Men. Sac, 2. [43] Willis B, 327. [44] TDD, ii, 66. [45] *Gent. Mag.* 1809.
[46] Pemberton, *Journey through England,* 1722. [47] HWH, 227.

The ultimate fate of Ffynnon Gwyddfaen at Llandyfaen, near Llandilo, is of peculiar interest. We have seen that in 1594-5 this well figured in a law-suit (p. 60 supra). A building, probably a chapel, had been erected at the well in medieval times and it survived until the end of the eighteenth century. The spot was frequented on Sundays by people who indulged in ball-games and dancing—relics of the old wakes. After Lord Mansel of Margam had suppressed these Sunday gatherings at Ffynnon Gwyddfaen, Peter Williams of 'Beibl Mawr' fame came there to preach in 1748. Later it became a centre of Baptist activity. It was in the well during the period 1771-1787 that the local Baptists first baptised their converts, a circumstance that caused a great sensation at the time. In 1808 a chapel was erected there and named Soar. The sanctity of this site has been perpetuated despite all the vicissitudes in our religious history.

The comminatory well of St. Elian (Denb.) became prominent during this period. Ffynnon Elian flowed in response to the prayers of the 6th century saint whose name it bears.[48] When Lhuyd wrote it was still an ordinary healing well,[49] and in 1723 its reputation was still unsullied. Before the end of the century its powers for evil had become a terror in the countryside. It was believed that if a person was cursed at the well he was doomed to suffer and, finally, to die. In Pennant's time its evil power was paramount. He wrote that the soil near Mostyn was favourable for turnip growing, but

> 'the farmer is obliged to give up the cultivation, by reason of the depredations the poor made on his crops. They will steal the turnips before his face, laugh at him when he fumes at them ; and ask him how he can be in such a rage about a few turnips ? As a magistrate I never had a complaint made before me against a turnip-stealer. Our farmers . . incredible as it may appear, numbers of them are in fear of being cursed at St. Ælian's Well, and suffer the due penalty of their superstition.'[50]

He stated further, 'I was threatened by a fellow (who

[48] TGJ, 108. [49] Lhuyd Par. i, 37. [50] HWH.

imagined I had injured him) with the vengeance of St. Ælian, and a journey to the well to curse me with effect.'[51]

Wells were still a source of income to some churches. Money was put in the poor box and also handed to the parish clerk in connection with Ffynnon Degla (Denb.) during the period 1699-1743. Two Anglesey farms, Tan-y-Fynwent (Llanelian) and Gwenithfryn (Llanfechell), were purchased from the offerings at Ffynnon Eilian, and their rents were applied to church repairs : the offerings there in the 18th and 19th centuries, which were considerable, were applied to poor relief.[52] The parish clerk of Llanberis was paid 6s. 4d. annually, the money being derived from offerings of the visitors to its famous well. The parish records show that he was paid from that source during 1776-1816, but the offerings in 1816 were described as 'very trifling.'[53]

It is to be stressed that while the holy wells were still being visited and religious practices observed, the main reason for the visits was for healing purposes. A poem, written about 1723, denouncing well visitations, shows that purely pagan practices still co-existed with the Christian ones.

> Rhoi gröt wen o arian i offrymu'n Llanelian
> A diysbydd y ffynnon rhag bob trallodion
> Os llysywen a welaint, neu frithyll neu lyffant
> Mae eu coelion a'u cred yn damweinio rhyw dynged,
> Rhai obobtu Gwyl Ifan yn y mor a ymdrochan
> Rhai o bell aneiri A an i ffynnon Gwenfrewi.[54]

(At Llanelian they offered a groat and emptied the well to protect them from disasters : if they saw an eel, trout, or frog, they divined that some fate was in store : about the Feast of Ifan some folk bathed in the sea : folk from a great distance came to St. Winifred's well.)

(*ii*) '*Smells much like gunpowder*'. We have seen that the observation of the habits of a frog occasioned the rise to fame of Llanwrtyd Wells. Towards the middle of the century more scientific methods were employed, and doctors were

[51] P Tours, iii, 150. [52] LBS, ii, 439. [53] *ib*, iv, 92-3. [54] RWJ, 97.

busy analysing samples of well-water. Dr. D. W. Linden published *A Treatise on the Medicinal Mineral Waters of Llandrindod Wells* in 1758, and seven years later appeared *An Experimental and Practical Enquiry* of the waters of Llangybi (Caern.).[55] Such pamphlets were to become more numerous during the next century. The wells of Llandrindod, Llanwrtyd, Llangammarch, Builth, Aberystwyth, Trefriw, and Llandudno, and others in England,[56] popularised new terms in the language—'watering place' and 'spa'.

Lewis Morris had much to say about curative wells. In 1748 he wrote, concerning Builth Wells,

> 'Here is a Well of mineral water at ye Sign of ye Black Lyon noted for curing Cutaneous distempers by washing, and taken Inwardly is good for asthmas and diseases of ye Lungs, consumptions, &c. It tastes strong of sulpher & smells much like gunpowder.[57] About a Quarter of a mile out of Town there is a Salt Spring called ffynnon y park which produces common salt but not white ; about 3 pints of ye water will purge briskly. It tastes a little brackish.'[58]

In 1760 he visited the 'chalybeate purgative spring' of Graig Fawr (Card.), which was 'good for certain diseases if drank with judgement,' and he expressed his intention of visiting Llanwrtyd Wells during the following summer.[59] The same writer described the waters of Llandrindod[60] in 1760. In 1764, when he suffered from dropsy, he sent 'for Dwfr Ffynnon Cwm y Gôf,' and as a result of this and other medicines, the swelling in his legs was reduced.[61]

The origin of the fame of Ffynnon Ddefaid (Caern.) as a curative well is known. One Richard Lewis, gardener at Plas Hen, discovered its virtues when bathing his sore eyes there about 1772. It became a famous healing well, but has been destroyed.[62] A charity school at Llangynog

[55] *Gent. Mag.* July 1766, 328.
[56] For excellent material on holy wells and watering places in England see *English Spas* by W. Addison, London, 1951.
[57] Readers of Dickens will recall that in the waters of Bath, Sam Weller detected 'a wery strong flavour o' warm flat irons.' This disagreeable smell and taste of mineral waters gave rise in Wales to the names Ffynnon Ddrewllyd Ffynnon Ddrewi, and Ffynnon Chwerw.
[58] Add. L, i, 188. [59] *ib*, ii, 493. [60] *ib*, ii, 480. [61] *ib*, ii, 618.
[62] M Fardd, 171.

(Carm.) was said to have been founded in 1705 as the result of a cure effected by Ffynnon Newydd on one of the Vaughans of Derllys.[63] In Llanbister parish (Rad.) were three 'black sulphurous mineral springs' which cured sufferers from skin diseases.[64] At Fishguard (Pem.) there was a 'fine mineral spring' good for the cure of numbness, and, when enclosed in 1793, a stone bearing a Greek inscription was discovered at the well. The wells of Trelleck (Mon.) were in Lhuyd's time 'much frequented and reputed to cure the scurvy, colic, and other distempers.'[65] Nathan Rogers wrote in 1708, 'Treleg wells of late years have been found very Medicinal and of the Nature of Tunbridge waters, flowing from an iron-ore mineral.'[66] About 1779 chalybeate springs were discovered at Plas Crug, Aberystwyth, and a small square building was erected around them, and a sulphurous well was discovered at nearby Penglais some time before 1845.[67]

On analysis, some of the saints' wells were proved to be medicinal. In 1767, Dr. Linden's report on Ffynnon Gybi (Caern.) showed that it possessed mineral properties. Its owner, William Price of Rhiwlas, built a bath and a bath-house at the well. Its use as an oracle continued to co-exist with its more prosaic virtues, and Dafydd Ddu Eryri wrote that some sick men resorted there hoping that it was 'old Cybi' who ruled its waters.

Ambell ddyn, gwaelddyn a gyrch
I bant goris Moel Bentyrch
Mewn gobaith mai hen Gybi
Glodfawr sydd yn llwyddaw'r lli.[68]

A register of cures at Ffynnon Gybi made in 1766 states that Shôn Rhydderch, who had been blind for about thirty years, recovered his sight after bathing his eyes in the well for a consecutive three weeks: William Shôn Thomas, a Llangybi tailor, was relieved of 'a sharp pain in the nose' after using the water.[69] An amusing story is told of a party

[63] Carlisle TDW. [64] JWHR, 230. [65] Lhuyd Par. iii, 20.
[66] N. Rogers, *Memoirs of Monmouth-shire*, 1708, p. 34 [67] Lewis TDW.
[68] M Fardd. 176. [69] Arch. Camb. 1904, 113-4.

of smugglers, who, when returning with casks of spirits from Porthdinllaen, were challenged by an excise officer. The smugglers said that the casks contained water from Ffynnon Gybi which they were taking to the well-known landowner, Mr. Price of Rhiwlas.[70]

Certain traditional rites and customs were observed at most of the medicinal wells, and these were identical with the earlier pagan and later Catholic counterparts. The questions that now arise are these—were these wells visited for centuries prior to the time they became purely curative, and were the ceremonies inherited from that earlier period? Or, did these curative wells, after their discovery in comparatively modern times, acquire such ceremonies from the general customs associated with wells ? The names of some, and the location of others, suggest answers. Now, there are in Wales several wells bearing the names Ffynnon y claf or y cleifion, which are purely curative. It is said that they are the ' wells of the sick,' which is a correct translation of the present meaning of the word *claf*, pl. *cleifion*. The word is found in Ffynnon Claf and Dŵr y Cleifion (Pem.), Ffynnon y Cleifion and Pont y Cleifion (Mon.), Ffynnon y Clwyf (Glam.), Pont y Cleifion (Cardigan town), Rhyd y Cleifion (Flint), ' Werglodh y Kleivion ' in which stood a megalith, in Llanrwst parish (Denb.), and many others. Mr. Phillimore has established that as *clwyf* and *clwyf mawr* meant leprosy in medieval Wales, it is probable that *claf* and *cleifion* indicated the same disease.[71] The name was applied to wells in early times, e.g. Ffynnon y Cleifion near Dingestow (Mon.).[72] There can be no doubt that wells so named were used when leprosy was general, and what ritual is attached to them in modern times must have been inherited.

Like the holy wells, the healing wells had their poets. Dafydd Ionawr wrote ten verses to Ffynnon y Gro Gwynion near Dolgelley, in 1796. He stresses the healing qualities

[70] *ib*, 113. [71] Arch. Cam. 1920, 229. [72] Lib. Land, 486.

of this well, which he claims to be superior to that at Holywell. One verse runs :

> Ffynnon Gwlad Feirion glodforaf—heddiw ;
> Mae'n haeddu'r glod bennaf :
> Ei chroyw ddwfr gloyw a wna glaf
> Ddynyn yn iach ddianaf.[73]

The words of a Monmouthshire man, Edmund Jones, indicate the attitude of the man in the parish towards the eighteenth century development now under discussion. Writing of the many springs and streams of his native Aberystruth he says,

> 'This is one of the great mercies of GOD to the Inhabitants, especially as the water is for the most part clear and wholesome for Man and Beast. An addition to this mercy is the medicinal Well called Ffynnon y Rhiw Newith, in the Church Valley, and on the East side of the *Beacon* Mountain : It was said to have performed many cures in times past, and it had stones put about it by some virtuous benevolent person ; But it was demolished by a malevolent drunken man, as some have said ; but by order of a Physician who lived in the Parish, as others have said. The allshewing light of eternity will discover who did this unkind action, to his shame and sorrow. The Well is now deserted, as if it had lost its virtues, which yet I am not sure it hath, if people tried it in faith and sobriety.'[74]

(*iii*) *Antiquaries and the wells.* Browne Willis, whose main interests were church architecture and ichnography, noted the well-cult. In 1715, he was told about the Cwmwdig well-chapel (Pem.),

> 'There is a gentleman now living of the age of ninety, who saw the west end doorway of this chapel up, and that he remembered a gentlewoman of the name of Butler lodging at his father's house, who would be at her devotion often in the chapel, and come every Thursday night to bathe in the chapel well which was firmly arched over ; and on Wednesday night she went down to Nun's chapel and bathed in the well adjoining it.'[75]

Archdeacon Yardley of St. Davids, with interests similar to those of Willis, has preserved useful data in regard to several wells.[76] Bishop Maddox of St. Asaph, who compiled

[73] NLW MS. 7942. [74] GA, 18. [75] Fenton TP, 65. [76] Men. Sac.

historical notes in 1736-1743 noted many examples of well-veneration and described the ritual and ceremonies practised at them.[77] Pennant, who made tours in North Wales, and the English baronet Sir Thomas Gery Cullum in South Wales, noted the customs of the wells and refer to architectural details. Dr. Johnson, passing through Holywell in 1774, noted the wells of Winifred and Asa,[78] while his friend Mrs. Thrale notes them in her *Journal.* Gough's edition of Camden's *Brittannia* contains much useful evidence. Tourists rarely failed to note Welsh wells, and descriptions are found in the published tours of Mrs. Morgan (1795), Skrine (1798), John Evans (1803), Malkin (1807) and many others who wrote at the end of the eighteenth and the beginning of the nineteenth century.

Artists painted or sketched the more picturesque wells. St. Winifred's figures prominently in their works. Speed was the first to publish a view of her well and chapel in the early 17th century, and he was followed by Thomas Dinely in 1684. Francis Place etched a north view of the well and chapel, which was published by P. Tempest, and in 1742 another view was published by the Bucks. Mr. Pether exhibited in London a picture of the same well in 1770. Godfrey engraved it for Grose in 1772, and Mazel (after Moses Griffith) engraved it for Pennant's *Tour* (i. 6). In South Wales, a country gentleman, Mr. Campbell of Stackpole Court, made a fine etching of St. Govan's well in 1755.

(*d*) *The Nineteenth Century and Later*

By the end of the eighteenth century the pattern of the well-history had been stamped with the impress that has lasted to this day. The nineteenth century saw only a development of the tendencies of the previous centuries, modified by the continued onslaught of the church on the practices and ceremonies. The rationalisation of well-belief was continued by the application of medical science and by the spread of education. Until the middle of the century

[77] Quoted in LBS *passim*. [78] DJNW, 77.

well customs were regarded by educated people either as gross superstition or as quaint survivals, depending on the background and outlook of the observer. After 1850 a further change came over this attitude. A new term had been coined in 1846, 'folklore', and the well-cult was placed in this new and convenient category. Gradually the stigma of 'superstition' waned. That wells became significant was due mainly to two writers, a clergyman and a layman. The researches of the Revd. Elias Owen in the latter half of the century showed that the study of holy wells threw light on the spiritual development of the people and on a bygone way of life. It was left to Sir John Rhŷs to raise the study to the status of scholarship. He was the first to use folklore as a weapon to assault the grey walls that had stood hitherto between Welshmen and their early history. In the light of further information we know that Sir John Rhŷs made several mistakes (some of which he revised during his lifetime) and today the evidence he collected is more important than some of his opinions. Nevertheless, it was he who blazed the trail for others, it was he who realized the significance of what had been so long neglected, condemned or ignored.

The literature of the wells since 1800 is tremendous. It is beyond the scope of this work to enumerate the works, and we must content ourselves with a brief survey of the material and to indicate its salient characteristics. The evidence of historians, biographers, tourists, and dictionary-makers, proves that the cult of the wells, despite the rationalisation, remained firmly entrenched in 19th century Wales. In 1810 Meyrick wrote, 'The lower order of people in Cardiganshire are uncommonly superstitious, nor has the light of reformation overcome those bigotted prejudices originally received from the Druids, and afterwards with equal zeal cherished by the Roman Catholics.'[79] But not only among the 'lower order', for a Pembrokeshire writer of good family informed his readers in 1811, that, in accordance with 'the general usage' he 'was often dipped'

[79] Meyrick C, p. cxxii.

when a child in St. Non's well, St. Davids, a parish that was 'thick sown with chapels, crosses, and sainted wells; and many of the latter are to this day held in great repute.'[80] In 1860 we learn from Murray's *Handbook of South Wales* that St. Govan's well still attracted 'patients even of the upper classes' (p. 34), some of them from far afield. In the early part of the century, John Cain Jones wrote from North Wales to the Revd. Mr. Rowlands, Carmarthen, as follows,

> 'Minau ydwyf yn Proffesu fy mod yn un o'r gwehilion, y mhell om gwlad gwedi cael afiechyd, ac Ewyllys genyf i fyned i Fynnon Saint govins swydd Benfro I ymgais am feddeginiaeth, ac yn gyfing a chwerw arnaf yn fy ymgylchiad yn y Byd.'[81]

(I profess that I am one of the outcasts, far from my native part, having had illness, and in straightened circumstances, but possessing the will to go to the well of St. Govans, Pembrokeshire, to seek a cure.)

We owe much of our information about the first half of the 19th century to the *Topographical Dictionaries* of Nicholas Carlisle (1811) and S. Lewis (1843), T. Dugdale's *England and Wales Delineated* (1845), and T. Rees' *Beauties of Wales* (1815). There are numerous well-references in these works. Some customs are described as 'now discontinued,' 'of late years much abandoned,' and so on, but others are shewn to have survived in strength. Later in the century numbers of parish and local histories were published and these often contain valuable evidence. Some works regarded the interpretation of the evidence of wells as of primary importance. Foremost among them are the essays of Elias Owen in *Arch. Cam.* 1891, *Mont. Coll.* 1893, and his book *Welsh Folk-Lore* 1896. Superior in scholarship are Sir John Rhŷs' essay in *Traethodydd* 1893, and his book *Celtic Folklore, Welsh and Manx* 1901, Gould and Fisher's *Lives of the British Saints* 1913, and Professor T. Gwynn Jones' *Welsh Folklore and Folk Custom* 1930. Other works of less erudition, but nevertheless extremely useful, are W. Sykes' *British Goblins* 1880, T. E. Morris essay 'Sacred Wells in Wales' in *Folk-lore* 1893, Myrddin Fardd's *Llen Gwerin*

[80] Fenton TP, 63-4, 227. [81] NLW MS. 1891.

Sir Gaernarfon 1908, M. Trevelyan's *Folk-Lore and Folk-Stories of Wales* 1909, and J. C. Davies, *Folk-Lore of West and Mid-Wales* 1911.

The medicinal wells received considerable attention. Gwallter Mechain's valuable report on agriculture contains information about chalybeate, sulphurous and alum wells. Analysis established many new wells. In 1811, Carlisle called Rebecca's Well (Carm.), a mineral spring 'lately discovered.' A prospectus was issued in 1825 concerning the Llanarthney wells (Carm.), whose waters were analysed by Doctors Saunders and Babington under the direction of Sir William Paxton. Towards the middle of the century the eminent Dr. Herapath analysed the water of many Welsh wells. Dr. A. Wynn Williams published an account of Ffynnon Cegin Arthur (Caern.) in 1858, to which he directed his patients.[82] Confidence in the potency of such wells was so strong in Glamorgan that 19th century prize-fighters drank the sulphurous water of Ffynnon Ddrewllyd, Gilfach Goch, believing that it increased their strength and ferocity.[83] This well is still visited by sufferers from rheumatism and sore eyes. An old Glamorgan saying is 'Tri dwr wellws lawer o bôn, y cryd a'r mwyth, y llygaid tost a'r manwynio—Ffynnon Fforchdon, Ffynnon Gwynno a Nant y fro.'

Parson, minister and magistrate still had occasion to fulminate against certain pagan ceremonies, details of which will be considered in the next chapter. In 1823 it was stated that due to the increase in education and scriptural knowledge, the wells were being neglected, and 'within a generation or two' they would be completely forgotten in Wales.[84] Doubtless, that prophecy had been made in previous centuries. It remains unfulfilled. Examples of how the religious association had been transformed into seemingly secular customs are found in numerous references to rustic games, competitions, dancing and jollity at wells. Such holidays were held at wells throughout Wales.[85]

[82] *King Arthur's Well.* [83] ex inf. Mr. Joseph Griffiths, Gilfach Goch.
[84] YHC, 177. [85] see Part II *passim*.

Although the drinking of sweetened water and the eating of cakes on such occasions were regarded in the nature of a picnic, there is no doubt whatsoever that they are the degraded forms of the old wakes held at wells and the pilgrimages once made to them on the saints' days. The dates of the visitations clearly show this connection. To this category, too, belong the fairs held at certain wells on the feasts of the saints. All this junketing was not merely idle play. In essence it was the real thing.

Belief in the efficacy of the wells survived all buffets. This was not confined to healing wells alone but was extended to theurgical wells, oracular and mystical wells. At the beginning of the 20th century the people of Rhaeadr (Rad.) district bathed the eyes of babies in Ffynnon Fair, and I have had the pleasure of speaking to many people who were bathed in that well as children. Rhaeadr children were also dipped in a small rill called Bwci's Wave, which was believed to possess a mysterious virtue, and the local couplet proudly states :

> The fairest children Wales can have
> Are those that dip in Bwci's Wave.[86]

Significance is given to the Rhaeadr practice when we recall that Aristotle (*Politica*, VII, [xv. xvii] 2) records that the Celts had a custom of 'plunging their newborn children into a cold river.'

During the 1914-18 war people visited Ffynnon Deilo (Pem.) to drink water from the skull of the saint, hoping thereby to secure a speedy end to hostilities. We are very many centuries removed from the 20th century here.

Another ancient custom was the use of water drawn from holy wells for baptism. The water was carried to the font, sometimes hymns were sung while it was being carried. Gwallter Mechain was baptised with water drawn from Ffynnon Armon (Mont.). Elias Owen was told by the parish

[86]ex inf. Mrs. R. M. Morgan. Cf., W. H. Howse, *Old-Time Rhayader*, (Llandrindod Wells, 1951), p. 20, where it is called 'Bwgey.'

clerk of Abererch (Caern.) that when ordinary water was substituted 'some years ago' for that of Ffynnon Gadfarch for baptism in the church font, the congregation watched the event 'with considerable dread and misgivings.'[87] Old people, living in 1908, remembered the survival of an ancient lustration ceremony in Caernarvonshire. The water of Ffynnon Sanctaidd (Carnguwch) was kept in a vessel behind the church door together with a little brush with which the water was sprinkled over each person on entering the church: the brush was called 'ysgub y cwhwfan.'[88] Modern survivals will be discussed at length in the next chapter.

I end this section by drawing attention to the unbroken poetic tradition relating to the wells.[89] In 1823 an anonymous writer published a poem[90] on 'The Marvels of Wales,' which describes the ebb and flow well near Rhuddlan and St. Winifred's at Holywell. Of the latter he says:

> . . . Ar ei banciau gellir gweled
> Amryw gannoedd o glaf weiniaid,
> Gwedi dyfod ar ffyn-baglau,
> Ond yn gallu rhedeg adre'
> Ar y ceryg, yn y ffynnon
> Mae y gwaed yn amlwg ddigon,
> Rhwn a gollodd Winiffreda
> Pan ga'dd ei phen ei dori yma . .

(On the banks are hundreds of sick folk who have arrived on crutches, but who can run back home: on the stones[91] in the well may be seen clearly the blood of Winifred which fell when she was beheaded here.)

In the same year, David Morris (Bardd Einion) composed

[87] Mont. Coll, 1893, 269. [88] M Fardd, 191.

[89] Several poems on Welsh Wells were also written by English people, such as Mrs. Hemans, who wrote on 'Our Lady 's Well' (Wigfair), and Mathew Arnold's sonnet 'East and West' (the wells of Seiriol and Cybi, Angl.). Some featured in novels such as St. John's Well (Glam.) in Blackmore's 'Maid of Sker.'

[90] YHC, 10-13.

[91] The medieval biographers refer to three stones in the well spotted with red, being Winifred's blood. These were constantly in motion and were regarded with great awe.

a verse[92] to Ffynnon Fadog in Llanfair Caereinion parish (Mont.) :

> O tyred fy mrawd tirion—o ddifrif
> I ddyfroedd Caer-einion ;
> Pwy a wyr nad llwyr a llon
> Iach wellir dy archollion.

(Come, seriously, my gentle brother, to the waters of Caer-einion ; who knows but that all your wounds will be cured.) In 1836, Mr. Williams of Aberpergwm (Glam.) gave a prize for an englyn on Ffynnon Pergwm, which was won by Tegid, and afterwards carved on a large stone at the back of the well.[93] Thus :

> O ddaioni Duw i ddynion—llawn wyf
> Lloned sychedigion ;
> Hoff y rhed o hyd ffrwd hon
> Gwiw liviant ! mae gloew afon.

(I appreciate the goodness of God towards men : let thirsty ones be thankful : fondly does this rill run always, like a clear stream).

Gwynionydd wrote a poem in 1867 on the ancient Ffynnon Geitho (Card.).[94] Ceiriog wrote five verses[95] on Ffynnon Dwynwen (Angl.), the well that cured the ravages of love. The second and third verses read as follows :

> Mi eis i Landdwynwen ar ddiwrnod o hâf,
> Yn isel fy meddwl, o gariad yn glâf :
> Mi yfais o'r ffynon, on trois yn ddioed,
> I garu fy nghariad yn well nag erioed.
>
> Gofynais am gynghor, a d'wedai hen ŵr,
> Y dylwn ymdrochi yn nghanol y dŵr ;
> Mi neidiais i'r ffynnon a suddais fel maen,
> Ond codais mewn cariad dau fwy nag o'r blaen.

(I went to Llanddwynwen on a summer's day, melancholy and lovesick : I drank from the well, and, immediately, I loved my sweetheart more than ever. I asked for advice, and an old man told me to bathe in the water : I leaped

[92] *Bygones*, 21 March, 1894. [93] HVN, 199. [94] *Caniadau*, 1867, 94.
[95] *Cymru Fu*, 1862, 423.

into the well, sank like a stone, but arose twice as much in love as ever before).

Several verses were carved on the walls of the building at Clawdd Llesg Well (Mont.) by those who had benefitted from the waters. They included the following:

> Yn y lle hwn ni chewch wellhad—oni
> Wnewch uniawn ddefnyddiad,
> Ac erfyn ar Dduw cariad
> Heb rith am ei fendith fad.[96]

(In this place you will receive no cure, unless you make proper use, and to crave the blessing of the God of love, without hypocrisy.)

And :

> Dwr y Pistyll Bychan
> Rheda i'n sirioli
> Dwr y Pistyll Bychan
> Daw pob dydd i'm lloni, 1856.[97]

(The water of the little spout runs to gladden me, and makes me happy each day.)

And, in English,

> Lord grant us from this little brook
> Thy crystal water clear
> To wash our souls and heal our wounds
> While we are lingering here.

> I wrote this verse for the first time in the year 1873, but I now again visit the place and I find it vanished and I write it again. G.G. 1873, Nov. 1899.[98]

In some places initials alone were carved, and there were once hundreds of initials carved on the trees near the healing well, Ffynnon y Gwaunydd (Caern.).[99]

In 1874, Ioan Glan Crewi wrote an *englyn* to Ffynnon y Llynlloedd, Machynlleth, and in 1888 Gwilym Cynwyd wrote on Ffynnon y Pandy. In 1889 Gwilym Ardudwy wrote on the well of Abermaw, and one line has a most modern ring,

> Hon yw *barmaid* Abermaw.

In 1891 Gwydderig wrote two verses on the healing well of

[96] *Bygones*, 21 March, 1894. [97] *ib*, 26 July, 1899. [98] *ib*, 26 July, 1899.
[99] M Fardd, 176. In 16th century Europe it was the custom of the nobility to leave at the wells a painting or carving of their coat of arms 'as a pledge of the obligation they are under to those waters'—DM, 220.

Cwmtwrch, and in 1909 'Can Ffynon Llanharan,' by Lewis Hopkin the Third, was published.[100]

It will be remembered that the poems of the medieval Catholic bards referred to great miracles as well as to physical cures. The verses we have just examined were written by Protestants, and it will be noted that they make no extravagant claims, and for what benefit they have received they, very properly and humbly, thank Almighty God. We shall now turn to an entirely different kind of poetry, namely that of the *gwerin* (folk), and the contrast is remarkable. Apart from the fact that the language is unpolished, it is noteworthy that the lines contain Catholic, and even pre-Christian, material, and furthermore the verses go into a certain amount of detail as to *why* and *how* the cure was effected, while certain ritual features are clearly indicated. I do not know how old these verses are, but it is clear that they have been repeated by generations of Welsh Protestants who had no idea of the significance of certain words and phrases. It is an example of the conservation of ancient material by an illiterate peasantry. The provenance of these verses is Glamorgan, the vehicle of their preservation is the 'Triban Morgannwg', and in its haunting lilt medieval Catholicism lives again. I have italicised words which contain relics of the old beliefs :

Golch dy lygaid wrth y Felin
Ar y cyntaf o Fehefin
Yf o'r Ffynnon dan Rhiw Trapa
A'r manwyno a fadawa.[101]

(Wash your eyes by the Mill on the 1st of June, drink of the well below Trapa Hill, and the King's evil will leave you.)

Mi wela Ffynnon Baclan
A'r ferch fonheddig ddiddan
Yn plethu llaw mewn *dwfr byw*
Ei gwallt 'run lliw â'r arian[102]

(I see Ffynnon Baglan, and the contented lady wreathing her hand in living water, her fair is the colour of silver.)

I am indebted to the generosity of Mr. Myrddin Lloyd,

[100] HM, 372-4. [101] *Cymru Fu*, 5 Nov., 1887. [102] HVN, 200.

M.A., of Edinburgh, for permission to publish the following tribannau from his manuscript collection :

1. To the well of St. Helen, Swansea ; this triban can be traced back to circa 1850 :

> I gyrrau Abertawa
> Aeth Wiliam fardd mewn dagra ;
> Wrth wthio'i glun i *ddyfroedd byw*
> Fe gafodd fyw hyd Clama.

(To the environs of Swansea, in tears, came William the bard ; by thrusting his leg into the living waters, he was enabled to live until May-day.)

2. To the well near Cors Crymlyn (near to the modern Skewen oil works) :

> Mi es at Ffynnon Farged
> Gan ofni am *fy nhynged*
> Nid oes mo'r eglwys ar y twyn
> Na *dwfwr swyn* yn cerdded.
>
> Ysgubwyd yr hen *greirfa,*
> Mae'n agos iawn i'r tonna,
> A'r ffynnon ? Dagrau'r *santes bur*
> Sy'n treiglo i'r rhigola.

(I went to Ffynnon Farged, fearing as to my fate : there is no church on the knoll and there is no holy water walking : the old place of relics has been brushed away—it is very near the sea : and the well ? The tears of the pure saintess now flow into the furrows.)

3. To Ffynnon y Fflamwyddan, Llancarfan :

> Mi euthum yn lled egwan
> At ffynnon y Fflamwyddan,
> Gan synnu pam os dyna'r gwir
> Ceir lles o dir Llancarfan.
>
> Pam na wnai Ffynnon Beti
> Neu bistyll mawr Corneli,
> Neu Lygad Lai a dwr Wernfraith
> Llawn cystal gwaith a hynny
>
> Ond at y dŵr mi etho
> Gan yfed cawg ohono
> A chasglu llaid at blastar cro'n—
> Mae'r po'n yn ddistaw heno'

Mi ddeuaf felli drwyddi,
Caf hongian ar y perthi
Ryw ddarn o racsyn, fel bo'r Llan
Yn gwybod am y miri.

(I went, feebly, to the well of the erysipelas, wondering, if true, how benefit was obtained from Llancarfan land. Why was it that Ffynnon Beti, the great pistyll Corneli, or the source of Llai, or the water of Wernfraith, could not do equally well ? But I went to the water and drank a bowlful, and then gathered mud to make a plaster—my pain is silent to-night. And so I shall recover, and I shall hang a piece of rag on the bushes, so that the village will know about the merriment.)

The significance of these verses will be analysed in the following chapters on belief and ritual. Other counties had verses to the wells, and a Cardiganshire rhyme runs:

Llangammarch a Llanwrtyd,
Llandrindod, Ffynnon Hyfryd,
Yr unig ffynnon sy'n iachau
Yw ffynnon fach Llanrystyd.[103]

At the close of the nineteenth century, and in the first half of the twentieth, the well-cult had survived all attempts to destroy it. In his evaluation of survivals, Spengler wrote, 'The present-day piety of the peasant is older than Christianity : his gods are more ancient than those of any higher religion.' It seems that the old religions never die nor fade away.

[103] ex inf. Mr. Elwyn Evans, M.A. of NLW.

Chapter V

BELIEF AND RITUAL

Times of visitations—summer—November—New Year's eve—offerings—general—pins—rags—stones—hair—healing wells—bathing and drinking—healing of animals—divination—health—fish and eels—matrimonial—detection of thieves—weather prognostication—good luck—drinking from skulls—punishment for pollution—cursing wells.

THE classification as given in this chapter is not hard and fast, and it will be seen that there is a certain overlapping of divisions. Further sub-division could have been made, but this has been avoided as much as possible. Although discussion in detail is extremely important to a study of this kind, it is apt to lead to a 'fragmentation' that may obscure the general pattern and unity of the well-cult as such. Belief and ritual are too intimately connected to be discussed separately, so we shall sub-divide the beliefs for convenience and include the appropriate ritual under each sub-division. Certain ritual is common to a number of wells, and a brief initial review will save repetition later on.

(*a*) *Times of visitations*

Wells were visited at all times of the year, but there were some very special occasions confined to particular seasons and dates. The Celtic calendar was based on the seasons, the most important dates being *Calan Mai* (Beltane, 1 May) and *Calan Gaeaf* (Samhain, 1 November). This gave way to the Roman calendar, which, with minor adjustments, has lasted to our times. It is believed that the Church introduced feasts to correspond in point of time with the earlier pagan festivities which were assimilated almost imperceptibly into the Christian year. There is evidence that well-visitations took place in pre-Christian days (see Ch. 2 above, and p. 96 below), but we have no direct proof that such visitations were made during the seasons which we shall consider here. The difficulty is that the Christian calendar with its saints' days has been so thoroughly established for so long that it is impossible now to say with certainty whether the times of the visitations are sanctified survivals of the earlier faith or whether they owe their origin to the Christian feasts.

The pagan *Calan Mai* (1 May, old 12 May, Beltane) was the festival of summer, the period of rebirth and growth. All forms of water were said to be especially potent in May and June, and in Pembrokeshire it was believed that young women would retain the beauty of their complexions by bathing their faces in dew before sunrise on May Day. In the 17th century, Llangynwyd Well (Glam.) 'was a great resort in the month of May,'[1] and Baglan Well (Glam.) cured ricketty children only on the first three Thursdays in May, of which Ascension Day (an extension of the Christian Easter) had to be one.[2] On May Day, Priest's Well, near Narberth (Pem.) was dressed with mountain-ash,[3] dancing took place on the banks of Llyn Ffynnon Llyffant (Caern.)[4] and bonfires were lit beside St. John's Well (Glam.)[5]. Generally speaking, spring and summer was the most popular period for well-visits in Wales where it was believed that the waters were then most potent.[6] Many of these were associated with Easter and are probably of Christian origin. The following[7] are some visitation dates within this period—*4th Sunday in Lent*—Ffynnon y Foel (Mont.) ; *Ash Wednesday*—Ffynnon Rhigos (Mont.); *Palm Sunday*—Ffynnon Stockwell (Carm.);

[1] Lhuyd, Par, iii, 11. [2] *ib*, iii, 29. [3] see p. 129 below.
[4] LW, 125. Early on the morning of 1 August, crowds visited Llyn y Fan Fach to greet the expected appearance of the Lady of the Lake.
[5] Trevelyan 22 : HWG, iii, 106. In Beltane fires and bonfires on Celtic lands we find the clearest traces of human sacrifice—ERE, II, p. 10. See EEE, 164.
[6] e.g. in the 16th century, healing wells in Europe were regarded as being at the peak of their power in May, less potent in June and July, and finally became very weak after August—DM *passim*.
[7] Authorities for these will be found under the wells so-named in Part II below.

Easter Day—Ffynnon Garon (Card.) also visited on Low Sunday and Easter Monday, Ffynnon Saint (Criccieth, Caern.), and Gumfreston Well (Pem.) where the visitors threw bent pins into the water, a practice they called 'throwing Lent away'; *Easter Monday*—Ffynnon Erfyl (Mont.), St. Caradoc's Well (Pem.), Penylan Well (Cardiff); *Ascension Day*—Ffynnon Barruc (Glam.), Ffynnon Gybi (Card.), Ffynnon Sant (Mynydd y Rhiw, Caern.), Ffynnon Ddeier (Flint), St. George's Well (Denb.); *Whit Sunday*—Ffynnon Erfyl (Mont.); *Trinity Sunday*—Ffynnon Myllin, Trinity Well (in all counties), Pistyll Canpwll, Ffynnon Ceiliog, Ffynnon Dila, Ffynnon Garth Fawr, New Well, Clawdd Llesg Well (all in Mont.).

The following wells were visited *throughout summer*, without any special dates—Summer Well (Pem.), Ffynnon y Saint (Llanddulas, Denb.), St. Helen's Well (Swansea), Holy Well (Gower) and Taff's Well (Glam.). St. Govan's Well (Pem.) was visited throughout summer also, *July* being the favourite month. *July* was also the season of Ffynnon Lochwyd (Angl.). Crowds congregated to play games at Ffynnon Dduw (Caern.) on *three successive Sundays in July*. Ffynnon Newydd (Rad.) was visited in *June, July, and August*; Ffynnon Bedr (Denb.) in *June and July*; Ffynnon Oerog (Denb.) in *June*. Ffynnon Ddewi (Henfynyw, Card.) was visited on *Midsummer Eve* (21 *June*), and Ffynnon Geler (Carm.) was visited from 21 *June to the feast of St. Peter*.

Many folk-customs are associated with the period of Samhain (1 November, old 12 November, Calan-gaeaf, Christian All Saints),[8] but I have found only one well reference. This is Ffynnon Gynfran (Caern.) which, in the 17th century, was visited on 12 *November and on the Sunday following*.

There is more evidence available concerning New Year's Day (1 January, old 12 January). It was believed in Wales that water drawn from wells between 11 and 12 p.m., on New Year's Eve (and also on Easter Eve) turned into wine.[9]

[8] see TGJ, ch. ix, 'The Seasons.' [9] Trevelyan, 4.

In South Pembrokeshire the use of what was called 'New Year's Water' was old custom. Children drew the water in cups which they carried to various houses and sprinkled it with sprigs of evergreen or box over the people. These lustrations were said to bring 'good luck' during the ensuing year. The children chanted the following lines :

Here we bring new water from the well so clear,
For to worship God with, this happy new year ;
Sing levy dew, sing levy dew, the water and the wine,
With seven bright gold wires, the bugles that do shine ;
Sing reign of fair maid, with gold upon her toe,
Open you the west door, and turn the old year go ;
Sing reign of fair maid, with gold upon her chin,
Open you the east door, and let the new year in.[10]

These lines have a Christian and a medieval ring. The *fair maid* would seem to represent the Virgin. Without further forms, speculation as to the meaning of the phrase *levy dew* cannot be profitable. A similar custom was observed on the Pembrokeshire-Carmarthenshire border, in the parishes of Llanfyrnach and Eglwys-Fair-a-Churig.[11] There, the water, called *dwr newy*,[12] was drawn from the well early on New Year's Day, carried into the house and sprinkled with holly over people (sometimes while they were still abed), the furniture and rooms. The first-drawn water alone was efficacious. The custom also prevailed in south Carmarthenshire, and Miss Curtis wrote :

> 'The little children of Pendine still keep the old custom of bringing New Year's water to the houses on Old New Year's Day, 12th January, throwing it plentifully about the entrance, and then singing before the houses the following very ancient pieces of poetry . . .'[13]

At the beginning of this century a curious custom was observed at Llanisen (Glam.). A well near The Cross, Llanisen, was dressed on New Year's Eve with sprigs of

[10] LEW, 407. See CAL, 202-3, for a description of the ceremony and the same verse with a few variants.
[11] ex inf Howell E. James, Esq. [12] lit., new water.
[13] CAL, 293. One of the poems consists of 13 verses of 4 lines each, and the other of 7 verses of 6 lines each. They are of Roman Catholic origin.

box, and at midnight there was a race to the well, when the winner received what was called 'the crop of the well,' namely water, with which tea was then made.[14] This term was mentioned at the end of the 17th century by Lhuyd who stated that a well in Diserth parish (Rad.) was visited by women on New Year's Day, who, after drawing the water, dressed the well with mistletoe ; the first woman to draw this water received 'crop y fynnawn' which made her like 'a queen'.[15] There was a similar custom in Herefordshire[16] where the water was called 'the cream of the well,' and in Northumberland where it was called 'the flower of the well.' It was generally believed that wells could bestow beauty on women. The Gunning sisters were said to owe their matchless complexions to St. Brigid's Well at Holywell, Ireland. Wells in Llantilio Pertholey (Mon.) were said to cure freckles.[17] The foregoing may be compared with the Beltane celebrations in Ireland, where the first water drawn after midnight on 1 May, was called 'the purity of the well': the water so drawn was kept carefully during the year and was regarded as a powerful charm against witchcraft.[18] The custom was also known in Scotland.[19]

Apart from the days mentioned above, and saints' days, the most favoured days for well visits were Sundays (especially in July), Thursdays in May, and Fridays. The most popular hours were night and morning, midnight, before sunrise, dawn, and while the dew was still on the ground.

(*b*) *Offerings*

Amongst the things offered at Welsh wells were clothes, rags, pins, buttons, buckles, coins (particularly groats, pennies and farthings in later days), thorn-points, flowers,

[14] *South Wales Argus*, 10 March 1928. cf. rhyme sung by boys on New Years' morning in the Llwchwr Valley: Codwch yn fore a chynnwch y tân. A cerwch i'r ffynnon i mofyn dŵr glân.

[15] Lhuyd Par. ii, 93. [16] FLH, 91.

[17] Lhuyd Par. iii, 39. Rivers possessed similar powers. In 1171, Henry I passed through Caerleon on his Irish journey, and bathed his face at a ford on the Ebbw, with the result that he was cured of his freckles.

[18] WMEF, i, 280-1. [19] AOSC, 133.

stones, and fowls.[20] There is one example of eggs (Ffynnon Digwg, Caern.), and one example of horses (St. George's Well Well, Denb.) being offered. Usually, the offerings were cast into the wells, but the money was sometimes handed to the parish clerk, parish priest, or the persons who dwelt near the well or who owned the land around it, or else placed in a special receptacle in a niche at the well or in a box or chest in the church. Rags were hung from the branches of trees and on bushes and briars, and occasionally placed under stones near, and sometimes within the well. These offerings were accompanied by ritualistic phrases and ceremonies. The terms 'pin-wells,' 'rag-wells,' and 'wishing-wells,' affected by modern writers, are misleading and unscientific, and should be abandoned. The pin, the rag, and the wish, are but fragmentary survivals of what may have been a more complex ritual and, in any case, they are not mutually exclusive even to-day. It must be emphasized that the 'wishing well' is only a degeneration of the ordinary holy well where the request or prayer has been supplanted by the wish—'a place where religion has been supplanted by superstition.'[21]

Pins were used as offerings at British wells in Roman times, and are found in all parts of Britain.[22] They were widely used in Lhuyd's day, as also were groats and other coins, and, as far as these are concerned, it can be concluded that they represent offerings to the deity of the well for the favour the vortary hoped to receive, and, possibly also, as offerings to propitiate the presiding power. Some 51 wells where pins were offered have been noticed in Wales (see above p. 10, and Map 5) where their distribution is general. Once an offering had been thrown into the well it was considered a sacrilege to remove it. At some wells, the behaviour of such offerings indicated whether or not the votary would be favoured. It was said of Ffynnon Fair

[20] The names of all the wells at which these offerings were made, are not given in this section, as they will appear later throughout this chapter in connection with the ritual and ceremonies carried out under certain conditions. To include them here would mean repetition.
[21] SHW, 9. [22] See FL, 1893, 451-470.

Penrhys that if the pin became discoloured in the water, it was a sign that the votary's wish would be granted,[23] and in the 19th century the well was often 'half-full' of pins.[24] The pins already in Ffynnon Fair on Cefn Bryn, Gower, were said to rise from the bottom to greet a new pin if it were offered in 'fervent faith.'[25] Pins were sometimes bent before being offered.

Rags are found at wells in all parts of the British Isles, in Europe, Asia, Africa, and South America.[26] The significance of the disposal of rags at wells has given rise to considerable discussion, the results of which are inconclusive and indeterminate. The following suggestions have been put forward :

1. That rags represent the survival of the custom of leaving the whole of the garment of a diseased person, whereby the disease will be carried away in the discarded clothes, i.e. the rags represent riddances.
2. That rags are the survival of the custom of leaving the whole of the garment as an offering, and so represent offerings.
3. That rags were a preservative against 'the sorceries of the druids.'[27]
4. That rags are the signs of expiation and an expression of penance.

Although much has been written about this question, nothing can be gained by a recapitulation of the evidence here. All we can say today is that we do not know the exact significance of the rag custom. I have been unable to establish its antiquity in Wales. No early references exist in bardic or other texts, and Lhuyd does not refer to it—a significant silence in one who so assiduously collected such data. The earliest reference to rags in connection with Welsh wells that I have found is in the late 18th century. In Scotland it was established custom in

[23] Arch. Cam., 1914, 357-406. [24] D Hanes, 31. [25] NQ, vi, 497.
[26] See Gomme, discussion on articles left at wells in FL, 1892, 89 : Hartland, 'Pin Wells and Rag Bushes,' in FL, 1893, 451-470 : and Rhŷs CF, ch. vi.
[27] See HWI, 55.

1618 when Christ's Well, Mentieth, was described as 'all tapestried about with old rags,'[28] which is the earliest British reference known to me. Only ten wells in Wales have been noticed where this custom obtained (see above, p. 10) but it is likely that there are more. Rags were not 'offered' at the majority of Welsh wells so far as the evidence goes. At Ffynnon Cae Moch (Glam.), the visitor stood in the well, bathed the wound with the rag that formerly bound it, then applied a fresh bandage, and hung the discarded rag on a nearby thorn tree.[29] Pieces of material torn from underclothing worn next to the skin were hung on bushes after bathing and drinking at Llancarfan Well (Glam.).[30] At Ffynnon Cefn Lleithfan (Caern.) a person wishing to be rid of warts had to approach the well without speaking to anyone and without looking backwards; he was then to wash the warts with a rag and grease, hide the rag under a stone near the well, and return home without uttering a word.[31] Rags were tied to bushes at Ffynnon Myllin (Mont.). Wool, gathered from bushes and hedges, seems to have taken the place of rags at some wells. Thus at Ffynnon Awen (Denb.) patients having washed their wounds, hid the wool under a stone at the well.[32]

Offerings of white or quartz stones were made at some wells, such as Ffynnon Degla (Denb.) and Ffynnon Gwenfaen (Angl.). Pebbles (colour not specified) were dropped into the Trelleck Well (Mon.), and if many bubbles appeared the wish would be granted, if moderately few then the wish would be delayed, but if none the wish would not be gratified.[33] Mr. Alwyn D. Rees discussed the significance of white stones in Celtic archaeology and folklore after his excavation of Ffynnon Degla in 1935.[34] White or quartz stones are found in tumuli and old Christian churches in all Celtic lands, especially on the sites and altars of Manx keeills.[35] Mr. Rees observed that the association of white

[28] Hebrides, 212. [29] Rhŷs CF, 335 : T, 1893, 216.
[30] See below s.n. Llancarfan, p. 186.
[31] Rhŷs CF, 362 : Bygones, 25 July 1900 : M Fardd, 186.
[32] Mont. Coll., 1893, 283. [33] Arch. Cam., 1909, 70-1.
[34] BBCS, Nov. 1935, 87-90. [35] IH, 20.

stones with curative wells was reminiscent of the Welsh and Scots custom of using charms of quartz and rock crystal to give water a magical potency.

Human hair was also offered. Among primitive peoples throughout the world, there is a belief that hair possesses supernatural power. In ancient Greece, youths dedicated their locks to a river-god, and locks of hair have been found at the Late Bronze level in Jutish bogs which may have been votive offerings.[36] I know of only two examples of hair featuring in connection with Welsh wells. Before drinking from Ffynnon Ddegfel (Pem.) a single strand of hair was thrown into the well, and it was believed that a certain cure would ensue. St. Lludd was martyred at Penginger Well near Slwch farmhouse (Breck.), and William of Worcester wrote :

> 'as often as anyone in honour of God and the said saint shall say the Lord's Prayer or shall drink of the water of the said fountain, he shall find at his will a woman's hair of the said saint upon the stone[37] by a huge miracle.'

The Revd. S. Baring Gould made merry over this tale, and wrote, '. . . the well is there, but nearly choked with mud and stones. The woman's hair is on the head of the farmer's wife at Slwch.'[38] It is possible, however, that the retention of the hair circumstance in this ecclesiastical legend is a dim echo of a very primitive well-custom.

(*c*) *Healing Wells*

Wells primarily concerned with healing are the most numerous of all our wells. This is probably because many of them are, in fact, curative in the modern sense of the word. Indeed, curative springs were venerated in prehistoric days, and there is evidence of this from the Bronze Age. Votive offerings of bronzes have been found in medicinal springs and wells in Denmark, Switzerland, France, and Italy.[39] Although no such evidence has been found hitherto in Welsh wells, it is likely that this veneration was

[36] ARS, 173. [37] There was a megalith near the well. [38] BGSW, 292.
[39] ARS, 173.

known in Britain during the Bronze Age, particularly as the well-cult was not localised but widespread and general (see above Ch. 2). As some wells did cure certain illnesses and relieved wounds, the Celt probably attributed this power to all wells and it was not unnatural that he should attribute the cure to the benevolence of the pagan deity of the well, and later, of the Christian saint.

In Wales, some 370 wells are described exclusively as healing wells. In addition, nearly all saints' wells (437), and those associated with churches and chapels (66) and megaliths (62), are also credited with healing powers. In fact over two-thirds of the wells that have been examined by me are alleged to be curative. In this section we shall discuss only those whose reputation for cures was their main and primary characteristic. These are alleged to cure nearly all the ills to which human flesh is heir. Some are

County	Eyes	Rheumatism	Skin diseases	Warts	Lameness	Fractures & Sprains
Anglesey ..	1	2	3	2	2	—
Caernarvon..	12	12	9	13	—	—
Denbigh ..	2	2	4	2	—	3
Flint ..	2	1	—	2	—	—
Montgomery	5	5	3	1	—	2
Merioneth ..	5	10	3	1	—	1
Brecknock ..	1	—	2	—	1	—
Radnor ..	3	1	2	—	—	1
Cardigan ..	15	3	2	1	4	—
Pembroke ..	12	4	—	3	2	—
Carmarthen	8	6	2	—	2	2
Glamorgan	11	6	13	—	1	3
Monmouth ..	1	—	4	1	—	—
	78	52	47	26	12	12

described as being curative in general terms—'cures diverse diseases,' 'has a great reputation for cures,' 'heals all infirmities.' Many are described as remedies for particular maladies, and the preceding table shows the complaints most generally specified and the number and distribution of wells which, it was believed, would cure them. The figures represent the number of wells.

The disease mostly mentioned concerns the eyes—blindness, weak sight, inflammation, styes, 'sore-eyes'—which was far more prevalent in olden days than now. Eyes were usually bathed with the well-water, and it is not unlikely that many persons secured improvement thereby, when the disease was not serious or far advanced. Rheumatism was almost an heirloom in rural areas, as any general practitioner will testify. In my youth, the majority of men engaged in agriculture in the Hundred of Dewsland (Pem.) suffered with rheumatism in some form or other. Skin diseases included scrofula, sores, erisypelas, rash, etc. Bathing and drinking formed the basis of these cures, coupled with that strong faith which 'moves mountains.' Wells also charmed away the ubiquitous wart from Welsh hands, but this treatment impinges upon the 'magic' and 'witchcraft' category.

In addition to the wells and ills tabulated above, two wells claimed to cure cancer (Denb., Carm.), two to cure fevers (Angl., Glam.), six to cure agues (Angl., Caern., Breck., Pem., Glam.), eight to cure wounds (Caern., Mont., Card., Glam., Carm., Mon.), seven to cure indigestion and intestinal troubles (Caern., Mer., Card., Pem., Mon.), four to cure piles and gravel (Mont., Card., Carm., Glam.), four to cure coughs (Breck., Card., Pem), four to cure rickets (Caern., Carm., Glam.), three to cure epilepsy (Caern., Denb., Glam.), and two to cure paralysis (Caern. Carm.). Hope for drunkards was found in Ffynnon Barruc (Glam.) into which empty bottles were thrown by repentant sinners driven there by remorse or 'hang-over,' and in the same county two wells claimed to cure that fashionable disease of our ancestors, the gout. Mental disorders received attention of wells in Anglesey, Caernarvonshire, and

Pembrokeshire, and nervous debility was cured by a Flintshire well. In addition, some wells were visited for the cure of consumption, deafness, toothache, fits and melancholy. The powers of Marcross well (Glam.) inspired the following doggerel :

For the itch and the stitch,
Rheumatic and the gout,
If the devil isn't in you
The well will take them out.

The same well was the last (or first) resort of bald Welshmen, for it was also reputed to restore hair. Feminine complaints were cured at some wells. Holywell (Flint), Ffynnon y Filast (Caern.) and Ffynnon y Brenin (Caern.) were said to cure sterility,[40] and Ffynnon Elwad (Card.) was said to relieve sore breasts. The cure of sterility is a relic of the belief in water as a fructifying agent, and many examples abound in the Celtic lands.[41] British and European spas were widely visited by sterile women, which often gave rise to scandal and gossip. An Italian woman in charge of such a spa recited the following couplet to Montaigne in 1581 :

Chi vuol che la sua donna impregni
Mandila al bagno, e non ci vegni.[42]

So far, we have noticed the times of visitations, the offerings, the illnesses that were cured, and the distribution of healing wells—that is, their 'rationalistic' side. When we turn to the ritual observed we immediately find ourselves re-entering the portals of the religious world of our ancestors. In the early stages of human history there has been an intimate association between religion and medicine, and so long as religion maintained its influence over the intellectual development of a people so long did medicine continue to bear the impress of the religious power. This is clearly defined in the history of the Babylonians, Egyptians, Greeks,

[40] See above p. 65.
[41] For an extraordinary ritual carried out by sterile women in Scotland during the last century, see McPherson, *Primitive Belief of North East Scotland*, 50-1.
[42] DM, 224. 'If you want your wife to have a child, send her to the bath, and stay at home yourself.'

Romans, and the Teutonic and Celtic nations. Among all those peoples medicine was associated with healing wells. Ceremonial, magic, and religion in relation to disease and its cure was universal. Medicine among the medieval Welshmen consisted partly in charms, sorcery, and exorcism, and partly in a real knowledge of the virtues of sulphurous and hot wells and certain herbs. But much of it derives ultimately from the religious lore of the pre-Christian Celts. In modern times, religion and medicine are divorced, but rural Wales refused to allow the decree nisi. In the following sections we shall note the continued combination of religion (prayer, vow, offering) with the rational (or rationalised) remedies (bathing and drinking at medicinal springs).

Bathing and drinking were general. The former took the form of total or partial immersion, while in some cases the water was drawn from the well and the afflicted parts bathed with it. When the patient was unable to visit the well, the water was carried to his bedside in pails, casks, or bottles, and the journey was usually attended by special conditions. The water was to be carried in silence, by night, and the container was not to be placed down until it reached the bedside, e.g. St. Nicholas Well (Breck),. Ffynnon Gynfelin (Card.), and Ffynnon Elian (Denb.). Such was the faith in the power of some of the wells (e.g Ffynnon Llechid, Caern.) that water was carried to the bedside of a dying man in the belief that it would prolong his life.[43] Those who were able to visit the well also observed special conditions. At Ffynnon Aaron (Pemb.) the water had to be drunk out of the palm of the hand ; at Ffynnon Govan (Pem.) it was lifted in a limpet shell ; at Ffynnon Stockwell (Carm.) special cups were used. At some Welsh wells the water had to be drunk out of skulls (see below, p. 115). Visitors to Ffynnon Fair (Aberdovey)

[43] cf. a recent writer on Manx history, 'The writer knows of more than one case in which old dying men had appealed for " a drink of the water from *Farrane Fing*," and another for a draught from *Chibbyr yn Noe* in Lezayre, before their peaceful passing. It was looked upon as a blessed sacrament.'—IH, 24.

and Ffynnon Lochwyd (Angl.) were subjected to some physical stress, for a difficult climb had to be negotiated carrying a mouthful of water without spilling or swallowing a single drop. At the latter the water had to be expectora-ated finally on 'Lochwyd's altar,' while at the former a nearby chapel had to be circumambulated. A plaster, made from moss, clay and mud, was mixed at some wells and applied to the afflicted part of the patient, e.g., at Ffynnon Enddwyn (Mer.), St. Govans (Pem.), Ffynnon Nathan (Carm.), Llancarfan (Glam.) and St. Winifred's (Flint).

Bathing and drinking (in themselves a ritual) was sometimes followed by sleeping on a nearly megalith or tombstone (see above p. 14-18), and the well-megalith connection is sometimes recalled only in the names. Thus, near the healing well of Coed y Ffynnon (Penmachno) is a stone called Carreg y Ddefod (Stone of the rite). In some cases, people, after bathing, went into the well-chapel (Ffynnon Bedr, Caern.) or the parish church (Ffynnon Degla, Denb.). This gave way in some districts to sleeping in relative comfort in a bed at the nearest farmhouse. Infirm children, bathed in the early morning in Ffynnon Gelynin (Caern.), were carried in blankets to the nearby Cae Ial farmhouse, where a spare bed was always kept for such callers.[44] After bathing at Ffynnon Ffos Ana (Carm.), the patient slept at the nearby farm, where, in the case of cripples, the crutches had to be left.[45] At other places crutches were left hanging on trees (e.g. at Ffynnon y Gwaenydd, Caern, and Ffynnon Llancarfan, Glam.), by the well (Ffynnon Gybi, Holyhead), on the chapel altar (St. Govans, Pem.), or in the parish church.

At Ffynnon Barruc (Glam.) no bathing took place. There the votary threw into the well a bent pin or brass buckles, then offered a silent prayer followed by a wish, and finally the journey home had to be made without speaking until first addressed by a stranger. Ffynnon Eilian (Angl.) was visited on the eve of the saint's festival; the visitor drank

[44] Mont. Coll., 1893, 272. [45] TNEW Llanelly, 360.

from the well and afterwards knelt in prayer before the altar of the well-chapel, and finally entered the parish church where offerings, usually groats, were made, in order to obtain a blessing upon cattle and corn and for the cure of agues, fits, scrofula and other ills.[46] This practice at Ffynnon Eilian only ceased after the middle of the 19th century. Those who *bathed* at Ffynnon Eilian made their offerings in Cyff Eilian, otherwise no benefit would be derived from the visit.[47] Visitors came there from all parts of North Wales, and the offerings amounted to a very large sum.

Sick pilgrims carried candles when visiting St. Dwynwen's Well (Angl.) during the Middle Ages. The Lord's Prayer was recited at Penginger Well (Breck.). One visitor to St. Winifred's Well 'washed thrice in the well, and finished the third watch of the night in church with prayer.'[48] A memorandum made in 1586 says that a sick man was cured at St. Winifred's after he had first expressed repentance, craved forgiveness for his sins, and then bathed.[49] Sir George Peckham, a very sick man, was immersed in St. Winifred's where he recited the Pater Noster and Sancta Winifreda ora pro nobis. Those who visited Ffynnon y Groes (Card.) made a sign of the Cross. The incantations and prayers used at the wells have often degenerated into a meaningless babble, and it is almost impossible to salvage any relic from it. Thus, when seeking the solace of Ffynnon Fair (Rhaeadr) the following 'words' were uttered :

Frimpanfroo, Frimpanfroo,
Sali bwli la
Iri a.[50]

A special ritual was carried out at the Eye Well, Llandrindod when seeking a cure for sore eyes. It was as

[46] Carlisle TDW : LBS, ii, 439.
[47] A large trunk still in the parish church, carved with the date 1667.
[48] CBS, 524. [49] BM Add. MS. 14866.
[50] ex inf. Mrs. R. M. Morgan, London. The term 'frimpanfro' was used in S. Wales, e.g. 'Cer oddiyma y frimpanfro'—ex inf. Sir B. Bowen Thomas. It had clearly lost its earlier meaning.

follows[51] : 1. The visitor started to walk to the well taking a certain number of paces. 2. He uttered an incantation[52] in a low voice. 3. He then dipped the fingers of his right hand in the well and applied the water to one eye. 4. He did the same to the other eye with the other hand. 5. It was forbidden to wipe the eyes after this bathing, and if they smarted and produced tears this was to the good. There is a local tradition that the Romans used this well.

In the period 1690-1725, before it acquired a sinister reputation, Ffynnon Elian (Denb.), was emptied three times by the visitor, who afterwards offered a groat or its value in bread, in order to obtain a cure for sick children.[53] This is a known pagan ritual and has a long history.

Generally speaking, survivals suggest that the ritual for cures was simple, and the offerings small or symbolic. Ritual differed in various places. The wart-cure was normally accompanied by a very simple ritual, being merely pricked with a pin which was afterwards offered, and then bathed, but sometimes it was elaborate. The ritual at Ffynnon Cefn Lleithfan (Caern.) has already been described (see above p. 95). Another wart-ritual in North Wales took the following form : 1. A scrap of sheep's wool was found on the way to the well. 2. Each wart was pricked with a pin. 3. The warts were then rubbed with the wool. 4. The pin was bent and thrown into the well. 5. The wool was placed on the first whitethorn tree the visitor saw. It was believed that as the wind disintegrated the wool on the tree, so would the warts break up and vanish. One man claimed to have had thirty-three warts removed from his hand after carrying out this ritual.[54]

The foregoing are comparatively straightforward complaints, but more serious and complicated cases were also

[51] ex inf. Mrs. Arthur Webb, London.

[52] Unfortunately my informant could not recall the words. I found it very difficult to obtain ritualistic phrases and words from the people. Even Mr. Bob Owen, who has very kindly helped me, could not remember the words he had used at wells when a boy. These phrases are extremely important, and it is possible that many may yet be recorded if local societies took the matter in hand—now.

[53] Lhuyd Par., i, 37 : RWJ, 97. [54] T, 219-220.

brought to the wells, such as epileptics and those suffering from mental disorders. At Ffynnon Degla (Denb.) the following ritual was observed by epileptic patients[55]: 1. He visited the well after sunset on a Friday. 2. He washed his hands and feet in the well. 3. He walked around the well three times, repeating the Lord's Prayer three times, and carrying a cock in a handbasket. 4. He then pricked the cock with a pin which was thrown into the well. 5. He gave a groat at the well to the parish clerk. 6. He then repeated (3) supra, but around Llandegla church. 7. He entered the church and placed another groat in the Poor Box. 8. He lay under the Communion Table, with the Church Bible as a pillow, and, covered by a carpet, remained there till daybreak. 9. He then placed the cock's beak into his mouth and blew into it before letting the bird go (this was supposed to transfer the disease). 10. He then offered a piece of silver in the Poor Box. 11. He left the cock behind in the church: if it died in the church the patient would be cured. 12. He again visited the well and repeated (3) supra.

Lhuyd knew of a man who had been cured, when a child, after carrying out this ceremony.[56] In 1749 the Rural Dean made a determined effort to suppress 'that superstitious practice,' but about 1813 the epileptic son of the parish sexton went through the ceremony,[57] and about 1850 a man said he had seen cocks "staggering" about after such a visitation. It is clear that at Ffynnon Degla we are in the presence of stark paganism. Transmission of the disease to the cock finds a parallel in a Babylonian text where Marduk is commanded to take to the king a scapegoat, and to place its head against his own as an act of atonement so that 'his poisonous tabu into his mouth may be cast.'[58] The cock has been associated with epilepsy, and was killed or buried alive as a preservative against the sickness in early

[55] Described by Lhuyd, Bishop Maddox(LBS, iv, 220-2) and Pennant (*Tours*, ii, 15).

[56] A man carried a cock, a boy carried a young cock, a woman carried a hen, and a girl a pullet.

[57] LBS, IV, 220-2. [58] Langdon, *Expository Times*, XXIV, 1912, 11 ff.

times, and the ceremonial sacrifice of a cock against the disease was carried out in Scotland in the 20th century.[59] At Ffynnon Ddeier (Flint) it was customary in the 17th and 18th centuries for the poorest parishioners to offer chickens after circumambulating the well nine times,[60] a cockerel being offered for a boy and a pullet for a girl; they also immersed children up to their necks in three corners of this well to prevent them crying at night; and processions visited it on Ascension Day when the Litany, Ten Commandments, an Epistle, and other parts of the gospel were read.[61] At Ffynnon Gaffo (Angl.) cocks were offered to prevent children from crying and being peevish, but the rite was ineffective unless the 'priest' ate the sacrifice.[62] At Llanrhystyd church (Card.) absolution was granted in pre-Reformation days between 12 o'clock on All Saint's Eve and 12 o'clock on All Saint's Day, and cocks were offered to St. Cynddylig for the cure of whooping cough.[63] In 1853, Welsh people still believed that a newly killed cock placed, while it was still warm, against the feet of a sick person would lead to recovery.[64] With these may be compared the Greek and Roman custom of sacrificing a cock to Æsculapius for the restoration of health, and the Irish custom of propitiating Brigid by burying alive a cock or pullet near the junction of three streams.[65]

Some wells were reputed to cure mental disorders. The ancient well in the churchyard of St. Edrins (Pem.) cured madness, but the ritual attached to it has been forgotten. Tradition relates that this well dried up because a woman washed clothes in it on a Sunday, and a variant says it became dry because a farmer brought a mad dog to drink from it—the dog recovered but the master died.[66] However, the virtue of the water was miraculously transferred

[59] LBS, IV, 220-2.
[60] Circumambulation with a right-hand turn—*deisul*—was carried out at many wells in Man, Scotland and Ireland. Apart from such ceremony at Ffynnon Degla and Ffynnon Deier, there are few examples of it being practised at Welsh wells. For its practice in Wales in other connections see TGJ, 29.
[61] Lhuyd Par., i, 70. LBS, ii, 342. [62] LBS, ii, 50.
[63] Camb. Reg. III, 1818, 220. [64] COT, 131, n. [65] FLBI, 54.
[66] For a precise Scottish parallel see *Hebrides*, 190. cf B. Britt., 235.

to the grass that grows around the base of the church walls, still called *porfa'r cynddeiriog* (the grass of the mad). This grass was eaten between bread, in the form of a sandwich and a money offering was placed in a stone trough in the church wall, the perquisite of the parish clerk.[67]

There is a tradition that Taff's Well (Glam.) was famous for its healing powers in Roman times. A flood in 1799 is said to have bared some 'Roman masonry' adjoining the well, but there are no such traces today. This well was reputed to cure rheumatism and lameness within one month of bathing there. A corrugated iron structure was erected over it to preserve the modesty of the bathers. When a man bathed it was customary to hang a pair of breeches outside to indicate the sex of the bather within; women hung up an essentially feminine garment. It was also called Ffynnon Dwym, and visitors paid annual subscriptions to keep it in repair. During the last century, young people assembled at Taff's Well on the eighth Sunday after Easter, dipped their hands in the well, and scattered drops of water over one another, and then repaired to the nearest green space to spend the remainder of the day in dancing and merriment.[68]

(*d*) *Healing of animals*

Healing at wells was not confined to human beings. Jacket's Well (Rad.) cured mangy dogs[69] Ffynnon y Cythraul (Caern.) removed warts from animals,[70] and Pin y Wig (Caern.) removed warts from the udders of cows.[71] At Ffynnon Beuno near Capel Aelhaiarn (Mer.) cattle were sprinkled with a yew bough that had been dipped in the well.[72] Sick horses were brought to St. George's Well (Denb.) whose waters were sprinkled over their backs and the prayer '*Rhad Duw a Sant Sior arnat*' was uttered, and

67 JCD, 306. WWHR, iii, 287. My grandmother, the late Mrs. Elizabeth Francis of Clawddcam, remembered a boy who had been bitten by a dog being given such a sandwich to eat.

68 Trevelyan, 195. 69 Howse, *Rad.*, 211. 70 M Fardd, 174. 71 *ib*, 192.

72 Lhuyd Par., ii, 49.

afterwards a groat was offered in the Poor Box.[73] At this well, it would seem that horses were actually sacrificed, one being given to the parson.[74] On 12 November, and on the Sunday following, people offered at Ffynnon Gynfran (Caern.) to ensure the health of their horned cattle, and the prayer '*Rhad Duw a Chynfran Lwyd ar y dâ*' was uttered.[75] At Llansantffraid church (Denb.) about a quarter of a mile from Ffynnon Sant Ffraid, it was customary in the latter half of the 17th century to make offerings to St. Ffraid to invoke a blessing on cattle and sheep,[76] and a similar custom prevailed at St. Eilian's Well (Angl.)[77] A sick pig was cured after being physicked with water from Ffynnon Cegin Arthur (Caern.)[78]

(*e*) *Divination*

Divination formed a prominent and important part of pre-Christian religion. Originally, divine kings, pagan priests and priestesses, and later wise men and wise women, warlocks and witches, read future events in natural phenomena such as water, weather, and solar, lunar and astral movements. Well-divination was popular among the Teutons, and in 731 Pope Gregory, addressing German chieftains, prohibited well-augury. In Gervase of Tilbury's *Otia Imperalia* it is said that when Edward the Confessor came to Wales he discovered in a dark wood a well 'which foretold many strange things.'[79] Examples of wells casting the shadows of future events are numerous in Britain. Some wells foretold national disasters, others were consulted as oracles and informed people of marriage prospects, whether lovers and husbands were faithful, whether the sick would recover, how long people would live, what the weather would be like. Others detected thieves, and some foretold the prices of agricultural commodities during

[73] Lhuyd Par., i, 46: iii, 101. In 1550 the parishioners of an Essex parish placed cattle in St. George's charge (Addison, *The English Country Parson*, 1947, 18). In Russia, cattle were sprinkled with holy water on St. George's Day (Walsh, *Readings in Russian History*, 1948, 297).
[74] Lhuyd Par., i, 46. [75] *ib*, i, 40. [76] *ib*, i, 35.
[77] ex inf. Mrs. Myfanwy Howell. [78] A. Wynn Williams, *King Arthur's Well*.
[79] For early Irish examples see FLBI, 176 ff.

the forthcoming year. Much of the divination was carried out in May. The ritual, despite variations, is basically the same, and an especial feature is that the ritual must be carried out correctly to the most minute, and even trivial detail, otherwise, the divination will not be effective.

Wells were consulted as to the fate of a sick person. The ritual invariably took the form of placing an article of the invalid's clothing on the surface of the well. If it floated, recovery would ensue, if it sank death would follow. If the garment floated to any particular part of the well, auguries of a similar nature were drawn. This method was employed at Ffynnon Gwynedd, Ffynnon Gybi and Ffynnon Gelynin (all in Caern.), Ffynnon Myllin (Mont.), etc. At a well in Llanllwni (Carm.) the invalid held his arms in the water, and if they reddened the omen was favourable, but if they remained white the prospects were gloomy.[80] Ffynnon Elwoc (Denb.) was visited on Easter Monday, and after drinking, a pin was offered: if bubbles arose, the visitor would live for at least another twelvemonth: the non-appearance of bubbles heralded death.[81] Sometimes a healing well gave a sign that the omens were propitious for the ritual to be carried out. At Ffynnon Aelhaiarn (Caern.) patients sat on a stone seat waiting for the 'troubling of the waters' as they called the periodic bubbles that suddenly arise from the bottom of the well; after which, they entered the well and bathed.[82]

Fish and eels in wells were regarded with considerable awe and respect. Some were used for divination, and others were regarded as health-giving. Such beliefs and customs are assuredly pagan. There were sacred fish in the temples of Apollo and Aphrodite at Myra and Hierapolis, and they were kept in special tanks in North Africa and India. Fish and eels in wells are found in all Celtic lands, and appear in the *Lives of the Saints*.[83] Invariably holy trees grew over such wells. That this belief existed in

[80] JCD, 304. [81] NLW MS. 8379. [82] LBS, i, 112. OCS, 283.
[83] For Irish evidence see WMEF, ii, 108-113, and cf AMB, ch xv. For Irish and Scottish evidence see EF, 92-3, 101-103.

very recent times in Wales is a significant example of the survival of a pagan creed after the vicissitudes of some two thousand years. Fish and eels foretold the future by their behaviour and also imparted a cure by contact with the flesh of a sick person. The trout in Ffynnon Beris (Caern.) were far-famed.[84] There were two trout in this well, but some writers mention only one. It was regarded as a good omen if one or both appeared when the patient was bathing, but non-appearance was regarded as an ill omen.[85] Bingley, like Pennant, mentions one fish, and he adds that its appearance, after bread had been thrown on the water, foretold good or ill fortune. After consulting the well and the fish, a piece of silver was given to the woman who lived in the nearby cottage, and offerings were also made in Cyff Beris which stood in the parish church. Rhŷs mentions the fish as being 'jealously guarded by the inhabitants' who forced a vandal who once removed it, to restore it to the well.[86] One writer states that there was a large eel in 'Llanberis well,' which if it coiled around the bather would cause a cure: when this happened to one young girl she died of fright.[87] But this story probably concerns Ffynnon Gybi (Caern.). Lhuyd mentions trout in Ffynnon Gwyfan near Disserth church, and he says that Ffynnon Wennog (Card.) once contained trout which bore around their necks something resembling a golden chain, but these fish were destroyed during the Civil War.[88] The keeper of the Department of Zoology at the Natural History Museum, South Kensington, has stated that it was not unsuual in medieval times, for rings to be fitted around fish in ponds and wells, and that the practice continued 'until comparatively modern times.'[89] At Versailles and Fontainebleau, silver rings were attached to fish to record the birth of French princes and princesses. A fish with a golden chain around its body was once caught in the river Dore

[84] Pennant T, ii, 320. J Evans, *Tour through North Wales in* 1798. edn. 1804 180-1. Cathrall, *North Wales*, 1828, ii, 140. Bingley, *North Wales*, edn. 1810, p. 157.
[85] Arch. Cam., 1895, 209. [86] Rhŷs CF, 366. [87] Trevelyan, 17.
[88] Lhuyd iii, 89. [89] LW, 139.

and afterwards kept in the Golden Well (Herefordshire), which is the source of that river.[90] Unusual fish also appeared in streams. In the Dwyfach and Dwyfor (Mer.) salmon came regularly to the banks on the morning of Christmas Day when they permitted people to tickle them and to lift them out of the water. However, when the New Style (1753) altered the calendar, the salmon took offence, and discontinued the practice. Fish in the sacred stream Alun (Pem.) came occasionally to the banks and regarded human beings without fear, and it was said that the more mature of them winked at married women.

In Ffynnon Gybi (Caern.) the patient stood barelegged in the well, and it was believed that a cure would follow if the large eel coiled itself around the patient's legs. A man once removed this eel and the local people believed that much of the well's virtue was lost as a result.[91] Auguries were drawn from the movements of the eel in Ffynnon Elaeth (Angl.) where visitors would wait for many days until the eel made its appearance; a person who lived nearby interpreted its movements.[92] Ffynnon Gybi (Holyhead) and the churchyard well at Llandeloy (Pem.) once contained sacred eels.

Divination in connection with matrimony was observed at wells to which young women yearning for husbands went in mingled desperation and hope. In the Tir Iarll district (Glam.) it was customary for the woman (or man) to take an undergarment secretly from the house, and then dip it in the well. It was carried home as secretly, held in the teeth, and untouched by hands, draped over the back of a chair near the fire—again without using the hands. The woman then retired to a corner of the room and waited. If the oracle was favourable, the wraith of the future partner would appear, turn the garment round, and depart.[93] One woman, having done all this, and waiting expectantly, saw, instead of a swain, a coffin appear on the hearth. The shock was so great that she eventually died.[94] The ceremony

[90] HWE, 78. FLH, 12. [91] Rhŷs CF, 365. [92] Jones, *Cymru*, 1875, i, 92.
[93] TI, 178. [94] *ib.*

at St. Caradog's Well (Pem.) was simpler. On the morning of Easter Monday, the woman offered three pins, then gazed intently into the well, believing that the face of the future husband would appear in the water. A tale relates how one woman was scared out of her wits by the appearance of the evil face of a hairy monster. At Ffynnon Saethon (Caern.) the visitor, already in possession of a lover, threw blackthorn points on the water. If they floated the lover was faithful, but if they sank, matters were doubtful.[95] A similar practice was observed at the Silver Well at Llanblethian (Glam.); if the blackthorn point floated, the lover was faithful; if it whirled round, he had a cheerful disposition; if it sank a little, he was stubborn and sulky; but it if sank out of sight he was downright unfaithful. If a number of thorn points slipped into the well from the visitor's hand, then the lover was a great flirt.[96] At Ffynnon Gybi (Caern.) the lover's 'intentions' were divined by watching the movements of a rag or a feather placed on the water. At Ffynnon Gybi (Holyhead) a rag, handkerchief or feather was used, and if it floated to the south it indicated true love, but if to the north matters boded ill.[97] A more drastic custom obtained in Montgomeryshire. The visitor carried a frog to a well in Llanfair Caereinion parish at midnight, and then, reciting a doggerel rhyme, stuck pins into the wretched creature. It was believed that the true lover would then appear.[98] Fish and eels were also used to help the love-lorn maidens. The movements of a sacred fish or eel in Ffynnon Ddwynwen (Angl.)[99] indicated matrimonial prospects. Prior to 1800 an old woman from Newborough attended at this well to read the omens by watching the movements of small eels when lovers' handkerchiefs were placed on the water. One wife related that she had consulted the well and after spreading her handkerchief two eels appeared, one from the north side and the

[95] M Fardd, 182. T, 1893, 220. [96] Trevelyan, 16.
[97] M Fardd, 176. Arch Cam, 1904, 113-114. [98] Cymru, VIII, 160.
[99] Dwynwen was the patron of lovers in Wales, see *Barddoniaeth Dafydd ab Gwilym*, 1789, 220: Ashton, *Iolo Goch*, 234. *Gwyneddon* 3, 80. WFB, 249. For her association with Glamorgan see Trevelyan, 243-4.

other from the south side of the well, and met in the bottom. The woman in charge said that the visitor's husband would be a stranger from south Caernarvonshire, which came to pass.[100] Lovesick folk also drank from the well, and if the results were not favourable, they returned and immersed themselves completely in its waters.[101] After the omens had been read, visitors placed offerings in Cyff Dwynwen in the local church. Crochan Llanddwyn (Angl.) is still frequented for a similar purpose, and it is believed that if the water 'boils' or bubbles while the ceremony is being performed, it is a sign that the visitor's lover is true. If the ceremony at Ffynnon Lochwyd (Angl.) was concluded successfully, marriage would take place within a month. This well was visited on St. Cybi's day, after the local church had been entered. The visitor had to carry a mouthful of the water and handfuls of sand, without spilling a drop or grain, to the stone 'altar of Llochwyd.' There is no record of such a personal name in Wales, and there is no doubt that this well-name preserves in its mutated form the old Welsh word 'golochwyd,' meaning 'prayer,' 'retiring to pray,' 'a secluded place.' An old chapel once stood near it.[102] Since the well was visited on Cybi's day, it may have been associated with his life. A similar condition attended Ffynnon Fair (Aberdaron)[103] where the water was sometimes carried in the mouth, and sometimes in a pail filled to the brim. The love-sick visited St. Anthony's well (Carm.) where they wished for luck in their tender transactions and offered a pin.[104] Maen Du Well (Breck.) was used by lovers who first offered pins and then wished very earnestly. Young couples visited Ffynnon Fair (Rad.) who believed that the well could bring them 'luck.' An oft-practised form of divination was for a young woman to wash clothing at a *pistyll*. She knelt, washed the article which she beat with two pieces of wood, declaiming '*Am gyd-fydio i gyd-ffatio*'

[100] LBS, ii, 389-391. [101] NLW Meurig Wyn's MS., p. 131-2.
[102] *Life and Works of Lewis Morris*, 1951, 160, 323. [103] T, 1893, 220.
[104] TNEW, 1895 (1898), 359.

(we will live together to strike together). It was believed that the wraith of her future husband would then appear, take one of the sticks and join her in the washing. Marriage was supposed to take place within six months of this occurrence.

As wells were invoked during the pre-marital state, so, also, were they invoked during the wedding period and the married life. In South Wales 'it was customary for a newly-married wife to drop a pin or pins into the house-well immediately after entering her new home. If she neglected to do so, the first year of her married life would be unlucky.'[105] Brides visited the Bride Well (Mon.) on their wedding day, and there is a possibility here that the name has given rise to the custom since the well was probably dedicated to St. Bride, who appears as the patron of Monmouthshire churches.[106] The first of a newly-married couple to drink from Ffynnon Gynon (Glam.) and Ffynnon Geneu (Breck.) would 'wear the trousers' throughout their married life. Although the evidence is slight, it may be that we have here an echo of a very early marriage custom when drinking at a sacred well was included in the ceremony. We know that clandestine marriages took place at wells (e.g. Ffynnon Fair (Wigfair) and Ffynnon Dudwen (Caern.) but I am not entirely satisfied that such marriages did not take place at the well-*chapels* whose remoteness rendered them suitable for Gretna Green tactics.[107]

Divination at wells was employed to detect thieves. In the Life of St. Winifred we read that a man who had stolen (and eaten) a goat, was brought to Winifred's well which proclaimed him to be guilty. He denied his guilt,

> 'Whereupon the goat already eaten gave forth a bleating in the belly of the thief, and so it was clear that he was guilty.

[105] Trevelyan, 18.

[106] Brides bathed in the Brides Well, Aberdeen, on their wedding eve, in order to ensure a family. It is likely that the Christian St. Brigit (Breid, Ffreid) has inherited the popular attributes of her pagan predecessor Bride. There are seven of her wells in Wales, besides a number of church dedications. Mackenzie, writing about the pagan goddess Bride, goes so far as to say 'The Bride-wells were taken over by St. Bride'—AMB, 187-188.

[107] For marriage rites involving wells, see HM, 202-4.

> What a dreadful thing! This which is denied by a rational creature with an oath, is revealed by a brute, and, what is more unusual, by one already eaten.'[108]

At Ffynnon Bedrog and Ffynnon Fair (both in Caern.) the injured party knelt and expressed his faith in the well, and then threw pieces of brown bread into the water, calling out the names of the suspects. When the name of the actual thief was uttered, the bread sank. About 1860-63, a farmer who had lost grain went to Ffynnon Elian (Denb.) to discover the thief. When he returned home he found that the sow had suddenly gone mad. She was the culprit!

The belief that wells could control or influence the weather is undoubtedly pre-Christian in origin, and here the deity of the well is in question. The practices involved divination and propitiation. During the 19th century, Ffynnon Gellionen (Glam.) was visited during periods of drought, when its waters were sprinkled about, to induce the rain to fall. The people then danced on a green near the well, threw flowers and herbs at each other, sang, 'old Welsh ballads,' and played the game of 'kiss in the ring.' The leader of the company then proceeded to the well again crying out three times 'Bring us rain.' His companions then filled containers at the well and scattered the water, either in the vicinity or in their gardens. We are solemnly told, 'Rain always followed.'[109] A well in Cadoxton-juxta-Barry (Glam.) flowed abundantly in an unfruitful year, but if the water was slow in coming it was said to indicate an abundance of crops, grain, and sheep. The same was said of a spring near Plynlimon, and when its waters ran quickly it was believed that everything would be very expensive during the ensuing year.[110]

(*f*) '*Good Luck*'

'Cultured people to-day say that luck is meaningless; men of science declare that there is no such thing as chance, but to many people Luck is almost a personal deity.'[111]

[108] WEVS, s.n. Winifred. [109] Trevelyan, 14. [110] Trevelyan, 4-5.
[111] OHR, 356.

Good luck of a general nature was believed to follow certain well-practices. It was the custom, particularly in Glamorgan and Carmarthenshire, in the early 19th century, for young folk to visit the nearest important spring on Easter Monday, to draw water in jugs, and to strew with flowers the grass, stones, and bushes around or near the well. This ceremony was believed to bring them ' good luck ' during the year.[112] Welsh girls told their ' fortune' in well-water on the morning of May Day, but this probably belongs to divination, although it involves the general idea of luck.

(*g*) *Drinking from skulls*

Sometimes water was drunk out of human skulls. This custom may have arisen from the fact that it was believed that the drinker would thereby acquire the former owner's qualities. It may also indicate that there was a cult of heads of kings, heroes, and ancestors. In olden times, skulls were widely used in magical and curative rites.[113]. Skulls, kept as relics, occur in medieval Wales. Bishop Barlow destroyed ancient silver-encased skulls at St. Davids. There is a tradition that a skull, said to be St. Mark's, was kept in Penmark churchyard (Glam.), but this was probably an onomastic inspiration. An example of the skull of a Welsh *uchelwr*, used as a drinking-cup by those who sought health, is contained in a note to a poem by Dafydd ab Gwilym. The poem was addressed to the 14th century Gruffydd ap Adda ap Dafydd, who was slain at Dolgelley, and the note, translated, reads, ' His skull is kept at Dolgelley and some folk, as I have heard, in this century misuse this skull by drinking from it, to cure the whooping cough and other ailments.'[114] David Jones, parson of Llanfair Dyffryn Clwyd, wrote about 1580-90, that he had seen this skull which bore the mark of a blow, and that people used it for healing. At Ffynnon Llandyfaen (formerly Gwyddfaen, Carm.) water was drunk out of a human skull, but by 1815,

[112] Trevelyan, 4.
[113] See SWO, ch vi, 'Skull and Cap' pp. 91-7 : A. Lods, *Israel*, 1932, 106: ERE, vi, 535. WMEF, ii, 99 : TMH, 169.
[114] *Gwyneddon* 3, 235.

the reputation of this skull was 'in a great degree lost.'[115] This custom continued at one Pembrokeshire well down to the present century. The waters of Ffynnon Deilo (also called Ffynnon yr Ychen) were drunk from 'Penglog Teilo,' of which the heads of the family of Melchior were the hereditary keepers.[116] This is a brain-pan, which must be filled to the brim at the well, and then handed to the visitor by the senior member of the Melchior family. Legend says that Teilo, when dying, instructed his servant to take his skull from the Carmarthenshire Llandilo where he then lay, to Llandilo Llwydiarth, adding that thereby God would be glorified and man benefitted. About 1840, a consumptive youth from Glamorgan drank direct from the well and departed without benefit. His father brought him there a second time, when the boy drank the water from the skull and was completely cured. The earliest reference that I have found to this relic is dated 1811.[117] *Mor iached a dwr ffynnon Deilo* is still a Pembrokeshire saying.

(*h*) *Punishment for well-pollution*

Some tales show that if wells were polluted or desecrated, punishment befell the offenders. In these instances we may perhaps see the traces of a tabu, or, alternatively, the deliberate invention of tales by Christian priests to augment or safeguard the prestige of certain holy wells. One story relates that Ffynnon Drillo (Mer.) ceased to flow because a dead cat or dog was thrown into it. A man threw similar dead animals[118] into Ffynnon Fyw (Caern.), with the result that the 'spirit' of the well took offence, and the water afterwards appeared only on alternate years.[119] Children polluted Wenvoe well (Glam.) with the result

[115] T. Rees, *Beauties of South Wales*, 321.

[116] Hereditary custodians of relics are found frequently in the history of the Celtic church. The Melchiors were descended from Melchior ap Ieuan ap Howell (ob. 3 April, 1591) of Newport. They came to Llandilo Llwydiarth by marriage in the latter half of the 17th century. The skull is that of a young person, perhaps that of a female—Anc. Mon. Pem. I regret to have to say that this relic has now disappeared.

[117] Carlisle TDW.

[118] A variant says because a boy was drowned in it.

[119] M Fardd, 183.

that the water became parti-coloured, brown and red: the parents quarrelled over the matter, and it was only after the families had left the district that the well-water resumed its normal state.[120] Pollution tales of a similar pattern are told in Llangynwyd parish (Glam.) about Ffynnon Rhydhalog[121] and Ffynnon Ffos,[122] and the St. Edrins churchyard well (Pem.) Ffynnon Gurig (Caern.) was closed by a man with the result that a curse fell on him and a malignant ulcer followed his descendants unto the third generation.[123] A farmer once closed the wells at Trelleck (Mon.), and 'an old little man' who appeared on the edge of one well informed him that, as a punishment, no water would flow on his farm. He reopened the wells, and water was plentiful again.[124]

Another example of well-sensitiveness is the belief that if stones were thrown at or into a well, a storm would follow.[125] In these cases the offended well deity is in question, but some may be concerned with rain-bringing wells.

(*i*) *Cursing wells*

A find in a well at Bath shows that commination was practised in Britain during Roman times. A piece of metal was found bearing the words 'May he who carried off Vilbia waste away like that dumb water, save only he who [. . . rusted out] her'[126] I have been unable to establish the antiquity of such wells in Wales, but of their existence in modern times there can be no doubt.

Some Welsh wells possessed a dual character and combined pagan malevolence and Christian charity. The usual explanation offered is that the saints had declared that the wells would grant *any wish* desired. They, evidently, had not bargained for those whose wishes were likely to be evil. Some wells have no sinister traditions or customs, but their names suggest unhappy associations.

[120] Trevelyan, 19. [121] TCE, 151. [122] *ib*, 152. [123] See below p. 150.
[124] Arch. Cam, 1909, 70-1. [125] Trevelyan, 6. [126] LFLC, 91.

Such is Ffynnon y Cythraul (Devil's Well) (Caern.)[127] which, despite its forbidding name owned the reputation of a normal healing well. Ffynnon Pechod (Well of Sin) (Angl.) and Ffynnon Angau (Well of Death) (Carm.), may have had some sinister history. On the other hand, Ffynnon y Pasg (Denb.) suggests a truly Christian well, but, according to one source, it was put to un-Christian use. To 'un-Christianize' oneself to become an expert in the Black Art, one had to take a mouthful of water three times from Ffynnon y Pasg, and to eject each mouthful with evident loathing. After the third performance the operator was qualified to contract with the Devil.[128] St. George's Well (Denb.) had a dual personality, for, apart from healing man and beast, it possessed power for evil and was used as a cursing well.[129] The same was true of Ffynnon Eilian (Angl.), a holy and healing well (see above p. 101), to which people also resorted to lay curses on enemies. At this well, a frog was impaled with a skewer, and two corks were stuck into the protruding ends. It was then placed to float in the well, and so long as the unfortunate frog remained alive so long would the enemy suffer ill-fortune.[130] Names were 'put' in Ffynnon Eilian, to invoke a curse on their possessors. A piece of slate, three inches by two inches, was found in this well, and on it had been scratched an oblong panel with a border of spaced cross-lines, and the initials RF, OAM, MEM, AGM, and M. Pinned through the centre of the slate was a wax figure.[131] Another Anglesey well, Ffynnon Gybi near Holyhead, had a three-fold character—it was used for healing, divination, and cursing; the names of the would-be victims were written on paper, which was concealed under one of the banks of the well.[132]

People who wished to curse their enemies threw bent pins into the holy well just outside Llanllawer churchyard (Pem.), the offering of straight pins being reserved for good

[127] cf. Nant y Cythraul, SW of Flint.
[128] Arch. Cam., 1891, 11. [129] NLW MS 8379. [130] LOC, 223, [131] *ib.*
[132] NLW Meurig Wyn MS., p. 131.

intentions.[133] At Ffynnon y Gaer (Mer.) it was customary to offer a pin when cursing enemies.[134] Ffynnon Estyn (Angl.) had a strange reputation. Formerly its water was carried to the font for baptism. Nowadays local people do not like to drink from it averring that it was once a 'cursing well.' Pennies that had been used to close the eyes of a dead person were thrown into Ffynnon Estyn, and were called *ceiniogau corff* (corpse pennies).[135] There was a belief that anyone drinking from Ffynnon Fach (Mont.) would surely die, but that bathing alone was efficacious.[136]

Among evil wells, Ffynnon Elian (Denb.) holds the blue ribbon.[137] The suggestion that it was the pre-Christian well of one Malaen[138] cannot be sustained. Originally a healing well (see above pp. 70, 103) Ffynnon Elian acquired in the latter part of the 18th century, a reputation for the power to punish people and even to cause them to die (see above p. 71). At the beginning of the 19th century its owner was said to have netted nearly £300 per annum from those who would curse their enemies, and from the cursed ones who would pay to be released from its effects. In the period 1800-1816, an old woman who lived nearby entered the name of the victim in a book, and then threw a pin into the well in the victim's name. For a suitable fee she would take the name 'out of the well.' An account written in 1816 states that the well was emptied before she commenced the cursing ritual.

Prior to 1816, the magistrates, particularly Sir Watkin Williams Wynn, took an active part in trying to suppress the infamous practices at Ffynnon Elian, but to no avail. In 1820, John Edwards of Northop was gaoled for twelve months at the Flintshire Sessions for defrauding Edward Pierce of Llandyrnog of fifteen shillings under pretence of 'pulling him out of Ffynnon Elian.' Its most famous 'priest' was a renegade tailor, John Evans, better known as

[133] Anc. Mon. Pem. [134] Davies LGM, 226. [135] NLW MS. 3290-D.
[136] See below p. 219.
[137] Footnote references to this well are not given in detail here. The sources are listed under Ffynnon Elian on p. 173 below.
[138] YHC, 172-3.

Jac Ffynnon Elian, who was gaoled shortly after 1823 for cursing people at the well. On his release he reverted to his lucrative practice, and was again tried at the Ruthin Assizes on 3 August, 1831 at the suit of Elizabeth Davies, who had paid Jac the sum of nineteen shillings for 'lifting a curse' on her ailing husband. Jac's gallant offer to curse the man who had been initially responsible was declined by prosecutrix. For these activities Jac was awarded six months in gaol. He then abandoned his habits, became a devout Christian and died very penitently in the odour of sanctity on 14 August, 1858. Before he died he contributed to an interesting and illuminating book on his former practices at Ffynnon Elian.[139] An attempt to discourage visitors had been made in 1828 when the parishioners published a letter disavowing belief in the magic of the well. This had no effect. In January, 1829, the well was destroyed and the masonry around it used to make a drain to conduct the water to the river. But it was not easy to stop the springs and the ingenuity of Jac caused them to reappear. In 1845 it was 'still visited by hundreds of people annually, for the purpose of venting malediction against enemies.'[140] In 1860-63, it was still being used for cursing. In 1864 we are told that the original well was closed 'but another well of the same spring is open.'[141] In 1871 it 'was not yet closed, although the belief in its destructive powers is considerably lessened.'[142]

The ritual varied but basically it was the same. The Bible was generally used, and it is said that the famous Jac also used a copy of the Apocrypha written 'in the language of the Caldees,' which Dic Aberdaron had presented to him. The ritual at this well is summarised as follows:

i. *Fees*. One shilling was charged for cursing a man, and ten shillings for lifting the curse. In 1820, five shillings was paid for a curse and fifteen shillings for lifting it, and in 1831, nineteen shillings was paid for lifting it. Perhaps the

[139] *Hanes Troion Rhyfedd cyssylltiol â Ffynnon Elian, ac offeiriad y Ffynnon.* ed. H. Humphreys, Caernarfon, n.d.
[140] Lewis TDW. [141] Williams, *Complete Guide to Llandudno*, 1864, p. 23.
[142] NQ, July-Dec. 1871, 398.

cost of living index was responsible for these rises. That such a large sum could be charged for removing the curse is most significant, since it shows how strong the belief was in the power of the well (cf. above p.71).

ii. *Ritual.*(*a*) *To lay the curse.* The name of the victim was written in a book: his initials were scratched on a slate, or written on parchment which was folded in lead to which a piece of slate was tied, and placed in the well, to the accompaniment of verbal imprecations. Corks were also used. A pin was dropped in the well in the name of the victim, or stuck through his name in the book. The guardian then read a few Biblical passages while the applicant listened. He then handed to the applicant a cup of water, part of which was drunk and the remainder thrown over applicant's head. This was repeated three times, the applicant uttering the form he wished the curse to take. Sometimes a wax effigy was made, pins stuck into it, and a lump of copper attached, while the guardian uttered 'secret words of cursing.' The effigy was then dipped three times and finally left in the bottom of the well. At other times water was carried away for use against enemies. There is a record of a Breconshire farmer taking the water away in two small barrels for this purpose.

(*b*) *To lift the curse* (*dad-offrwm*). The victim (or his representative) appeared and entered the cottage near the well. There he read the Psalms, or listened to them being read. He walked three times around the well. He read portions of the Bible. The guardian emptied the well and handed to the applicant the lead and slate bearing his name or initials. The applicant returned home to read on three successive Fridays considerable portions of the Book of Job and the Psalms. The curse would then be defeated. Sometimes the visitor took the slate home, ground it into dust which was then mixed with salt and thrown on the fire. He was also to take home a bottle of well water, drink it on three successive nights, and to read the 38th Psalm. We are told that the guardian muttered 'something in Latin' and about 'ab Elian' during the ceremony.

iii. *Results*. The person cursed became increasingly ill or met misfortune with 'every new moon.' One woman from Dolanog (Mont.) was doomed to remain in bed until the person who had cursed her should die. She was actually ill for many years and recovered only after the death of her enemy. A rich farmer from Nantglyn (Denb.) deceived a young woman who retaliated by 'putting him in the well,' with the result that he died miserably poor a few years later. Another woman who had been deceived by a farmer from Trefeglwys (Mont.) put him 'in the well', and he was told that the curse would be inoperative so long as he remained within the bounds of his farm. It is a fact that he never left his land until his death shortly before 1882. The Revd. Elias Owen, who knew the details, buried him. Animals also felt the malevolent powers of Ffynnon Elian. A dog's name was put 'in the well' and shortly afterwards it was killed in an accident. A pig was also cursed with disastrous results for the porker.

Large numbers of other cases are on record relating to the evil influence of this well. One can imagine the effect on the mind of a superstitious peasant when he was told that he had been cursed at Ffynnon Elian. But its effect was not confined to the ignorant or uneducated. There is one case of a well-known Nonconformist minister who, believing himself to have been cursed at Ffynnon Elian, took to his bed and became seriously ill. The Revd. D. R. Thomas of St. Asaph wrote, 'I have myself known a man in my own parish who lost £80 rather than ask for it back again, for fear of being put in the well, and have met with a person in England pining away under the belief that she had been so cursed.'[143] We have the testimony of the late Professor T. Gwynn Jones, who said that when a child (1872-1880) the fear of this well was still alive, and the threat 'I'll put you in Ffynnon Elian' was quite common.[144]

[143] *Bygones*, 12 May, 1875. [144] TGJ, 110.

The well was later finally destroyed. A volume could be written on this well alone.

One curse at Ffynnon Elian had an ultimate good. A woman, who had reason to suspect that her husband was unfaithful, made a figure from marl, inserted pins in the region where the heart would be, and then placed it in Ffynnon Elian. For a week the erring husband suffered with heart trouble. The wife then revisited the well and inserted pins in the figure's head and elsewhere, with the result that the husband suffered the pains of the damned. After several weeks of torture, he repented of his past conduct and was forgiven. Another wife, tormented by a quarrelling husband, procured a bottle of water from Ffynnon Elian. Whenever her husband was in a tantrum, she sipped, but did not swallow, the water. The quarrelling ceased and henceforth only a gentle cooing was heard from this robust Welsh peasant in whose heart the tender passion had been miraculously rekindled. These practices are far from being extinct. As late as 1947 invultuation was observed at an Anglesey well in which an effigy with pins stuck into it had been placed by a young woman 'crossed in love.'

Some wells counteracted wickedness, such as Ffynnon Fair (Llanfairfechan) in whose waters articles that were believed to have been bewitched or cursed were bathed. An example also exists of a curse in the right direction. Sykes mentions a well 'near Penrhos' which could cure cancer. The patient washed in the well, uttering curses on the disease. He then dropped pins 'around the well.' This well was visited by many people but by 1880 it had been drained by an unsympathetic farmer on account of the serious damage done to his crops by the visitors.[145]

[145] BG, 356.

Chapter VI

BELIEF AND RITUAL—*Continued*

Fairies—The Ladi Wen and other ladies—witches and wizards—the Devil—Ghosts and spirits—the Negligent Guardian—Treasure—Gwenhudw—Games at wells.

THE difficulties that attend the division of belief and ritual in connection with wells have been noted on page 88 above. Nevertheless such division has to be made in order to facilitate convenience of analysis and discussion. In this chapter we shall discuss the supernatural at the wells, involving fairies, ghosts, witches, wizards, etc.—popular manifestations in folklore generally. There is agreement that the early Church ‘ outlawed ’ certain wells, and it is believed that the deities associated with them were converted into evil spirits, demons, ghosts, and fairies. The Devil of the Christians appears at some wells, but it is possible that, in some instances, he represents a deity of the pagan Celts. Some may represent early guardian spirits. That later trends of thought and modern literary influences have affected tales relating to the supernatural is clear, and the difficulties of distinguishing between a genuine survival and a comparatively modern ‘ ghost ’ are formidable. This renders the interpretation of supernatural phenomena a matter of difficulty, and it behoves the reader to be extremely careful when forming conclusions based on such material.

(*a*) *Fairies at wells*

There are early references to fairies,[1] fays, beautiful women, and elves, at wells, and they feature prominently in

[1] For Welsh fairies see TGJ, ch. iv. The modern assumption that fairies represent a conquered pre-Celtic population can no longer be accepted. Such belief was inspired by Gomme's unhappy intrusion into ethnological bypaths, propounded in his *Ethnology in Folklore*, 1892.

the Arthurian tales. They may represent the lesser deities which were rejected by Christianity. Generally, there is ground for accepting the belief that the fairies were, in the main, benevolent, although examples will be given of some malevolent fairies. An example of pagan survival exists at Newcastle, about five miles south of Llanfair (Mon.). A tumulus there was said, in 1810, to be haunted by spirits of people who wished to atone for the evil they had done in the days of the flesh. Near this tumulus was an ancient oak said to be the rendezvous of fairies and elves, and a sacred well with healing powers under miraculous protection.[2] Fairies were said to dance at the Trelleck wells (Mon.) on Midsummer Eve and to drink the water from harebells which were found strewn around the wells on Midsummer morning.[3] Fairies haunted wells at Llwyn y Ffynnon (Glam.), [4] and the well at New Walk Cottage, Laugharne.[5]

Fairies were believed to live beneath wells, and this is said of a well in Llanreithan (Pem.)—a clear example of ancient belief in the well as an entrance to a subterranean land. A man in the Bala district washed his face in a 'fairy well' and was carried away by fairies, but eventually returned home bringing with him a beautiful fairy wife.[6] It is possible that the 'old woman,' described in a Gower tale, was a well-fairy. This 'old woman' emerged from a well in the garden of Lagadranta farm (Llanmadog), and borrowed a sieve from the housewife. On returning it, she remarked that the biggest barrel in the farmhouse would never be empty of beer so long as the wife told no one about its new peculiarity. She then left and was seen to disappear into the well. The wife, however, could not hold her counsel and the beer ended.[7]

A Pembrokeshire tale mentions a well in fairyland itself. A shepherd boy on Frenni Fawr chanced upon fairies who carried him away to a magnificent fairy palace where he was kindly treated, but strictly ordered not to drink from a

[2] Evans and Britton, *Beauties etc.*, 1810, xi, 68. [3] Arch. Cam., 1909, 70-1.
[4] VN, 200. [5] CAL, 13. [6] Rhŷs CF, 150. [7] HWG, ii, 1879 82-3.

fountain in the palace garden. This fountain contained fish of beautiful colours. One day he plunged his hand into the water. The fish disappeared instantly. He then put the water to his mouth, and a shriek rang through the garden. The meddlesome boy then drank the water, whereupon the palace vanished and he found himself back on the hillside.[8]

(*b*) *The Ladi Wen and other ladies at wells*

It has been variously suggested that the Ladi Wen may represent an ancient deity, a sorceress, and an ordinary ghost doomed to haunt wells. The fact is, that in the great majority of these cases she represents the Virgin Mary in another form (see p. 45 above).[9] The name Gladys adds a complication to the Welsh material. Thus, Lady's Well in Tredegar Park (Mon.) is said to have been the well of Gladys, mother of St. Cadoc, and she was certainly a saint as 'the church of St. Gladewis' was standing 'upon the river Eboth' in the diocese of Llandaff, before 1146.[10] The Ladi Wen is a common ghostly phenomenon, being found at crossroads, ruined houses, dark lanes, hillsides, churches, gateways, fords, hedges, etc.[11] She is rarely represented as a malevolent being, but appears as a mournful and sorrowful figure inviting sympathy rather than condemnation. I have found no reference to the *term* 'Ladi Wen' prior to the 19th century in Wales. In Caernarvonshire tales the Ladi Wen is sometimes represented as a young woman of rank and fashion, in Cardiganshire as a shepherd's wife, and as an old lady, and in Glamorganshire as the ghost of a high-born Norman lady.

She is not always clad in a white garment. A Green Lady haunted Marcross Well (Glam.) and closely watched

[8] WFB, 117.

[9] See CO. Parsons, 'Association of the White Lady with Wells,' in FL, 1933, pp. 295-305.

[10] *Hist. and Cart. Mon. Gloucester*, ii, 55. cf. the waterfall called Sgwd Gladys alias The Lady's Cascade in the Vale of Neath, and Ffynnon Wladus, Card. Capel Gwladys and Fforest Gwladys are marked on 1″ OS maps, on high ground West of Bargoed.

[11] TGJ, 38-39, 148-150.

people as they tied rags to the nearby thornbushes.[12] A woman in 'sombre garments' haunted Penylan Well (Cardiff) in the twilight when her wailing could be heard; she once told a man that she would be released from 'bondage' if he held her firmly by the waist and remained silent while doing so. He tried, but failed to keep silent, and she fled wailing, 'Two hundred years before I shall be free.'[13] An almost identical story is told of a Lady in Grey at Taff's Well (Glam.).[14] A lady in 'old-fashioned clothes' who was attended by forked lightning, haunted the well near the ruins of Bryncethin (Glam.) and once revealed treasure to a servant maid.[15] At St. Denis' Well (Glam.) a Grey Lady was held in bondage for her evil deeds while on earth; she was seen often in the Llanishen district and appeared fascinated by drovers whom she followed for some distance.[16] A 'water woman' is said to be imprisoned in a deep well near Nantlle (Glam.) as a punishment for her misdeeds, and her sorrowful wailing, when heard, presaged death.[17] A farmwife used to ride from Grasswell to Hay, and her journey took her past the Boiling Well (Rad.); on one occasion a 'spirit in white' jumped behind her on the horse as she passed this well, and rode with her until she reached home. The 'spirit' then vanished.[18]

(*c*) *Witches and Wizards at wells*

In witches we may perhaps recognise the priestesses of pagan days, the guardians of the tribal beliefs, who became later the accursed witches, the *gwrach*, the wise woman. The pagan priests lived on as wizards, as the *dewin* and *gwr hysbys*. But what is true of the witch and wizard in the form of ghosts is not necessarily true of human beings who resided at the wells. Sir John Rhŷs has erred, when, describing a woman living near Ffynnon Elian, he wrote, 'Here there is, I think, very little doubt that the owner or guardian of the well was, so to say, the representative of an

[12] Trevelyan, 204. [13] *ib*, 203. [14] *ib*, 195. A familiar folklore motif.
[15] Trevelyan, 145. [16] *ib*, 196. [17] *ib*, 20.
[18] FL, 1913, 515-6.

ancient priesthood of the well.'[19] This very tentative remark was sufficient to inspire Gould and Fisher to say of the same well, that it 'always had a recognised priest, or guardian, or owner, who lived near it, and no doubt represented the ancient pre-Christian priesthood.'[20] There is, of course, no justification whatsoever for such a conclusion and they are guilty of reading in normal or accidental phenomena some 'evidence' to support a preconceived theory.[21] Old women living in cottages near wells, in modern times, were usually very poor people who were only too ready to accept 'tips' from tourists in search of the picturesque, or 'fees' from others who visited the well to carry out customary rites. They cannot be regarded as 'representatives' of a priestess, pagan or Christian. The modern association is accidental, not traditional. No evidence has yet been found to prove that these old dames regarded themselves, or were regarded by others, as 'guardians' or 'priestesses,' or that they were the successors of people who had been so considered. We know, for instance, on his own confession, that Jac Ffynnon Elian was a conscious deceiver and no 'priest.' Plummer's caveat may be cited,

> 'Again it should be borne in mind that many of the customs and modes of thought . . are in themselves neither pagan nor Christian, but simply human. The heathen rite or formula preceded, and in some places influenced, the corresponding Christian observance or expression. But the attempt to discover heathenism everywhere in Christianity has been carried in some quarters to very uncritical lengths.'[22]

Certain names commemorate the witches. Ffynnon y Wrach in Llanfair Caereinion (Mont.) was originally a holy well that has been degraded, for despite its forbidding name, people assembled there on Trinity Sundays to drink sweetened water,[23] thereby perpetuating the memory of its

[19] Rhŷs CF, 397. [20] LBS, ii, 439 ff.
[21] For a similar unjustifiable handling of a tentative statement relating to Ffynnon yr Ychen (Pem.) see L. Spence, *The Mysteries of Britain*, 3rd edn., London, n.d. page 155.
[22] VSH, p. clxxxviii. [23] Mont. Coll., xxii, 325.

religious origin. Pwll Gwrach (Breck.), Ffrwd y Wrach (Mon. and Card.), Rhyd y Wrach (Carm.), and Llyn y Gwrachïod (Pem.) bear witness to their association with water. When Ffynnon Chwerthin in boggy land near Llanberis (Caern.) is approached the ground tremor causes the well to bubble or to 'laugh.' People attributed this to witches and their servitors, the ' old black men ' (*hen fechgyn duon*), and avoided it as a sinister well.[24] Children decorated Priest's Well (near Narberth) with mountain ash (locally called ' cayer ') and cowslips on May Day, in order to keep ' the witch' away from those families who drew water from the well. While decorating the well, the children sang

Cayer, Cayer
Keep the witch in May Fair.[25]

This was a ritual where the ash and the well were invoked to protect people. This decoration appears elsewhere in Wales only at two wells (in Glam. and Rad.) and may be akin to the well-known English practice of well-dressing.[26]

In 1733, Lewis Morris referred to Ffynnon y Wrach as one of the ' wonders of Cybi.' Unfortunately he gives no details of this Anglesey well, but the name is significant. It is possible that it may be linked with Trevelyan's statement, " In Anglesey they [witches] held their revels near the Druidical stones and beside the Roman watch-tower on Pen Caer Cybi, Holy Island."[27] The witches of Llanddona were notorious. Being expelled from their homeland, together with their husbands, they sailed to Llanddona in Anglesey. The inhabitants opposed them and confined them to the beach. Almost dead with hunger and thirst, the witches commanded a well of pure water to gush forth in the sand. ' This well remains to our days.'[28] Impressed by the miracle the Welsh allowed them to settle. Many tales are told of them. They invoked terrible curses at Ffynnon Oer in Llanddona on those whom they disliked.

[24] M Fardd, 170. [25] *Bygones*, 23 Dec. 1874.
[26] See C. Porteous, *The Beauty and Mystery of Well-Dressing*, Derby, 1949.
[27] Trevelyan, 208. [28] OWFL, 223.

One curse is translated as follows from OWFL, 223, where it is given in Welsh,

> You will roam for many ages ;
> In every step you take, you will encounter a stile
> At every stile you will fall.
> At every fall you will break a bone—
> Not the largest or the smallest bone,
> But the bones of your neck every time.

An old Monmouthshire woman, aged 100 in 1899, said that when a girl, going to Garway church, she had to pass the cottage of the witch 'by the well at the bottom of Hell's Wood,' who frightened passers-by.[29] There is a tradition that there was once a 'convent' in this wood, near the well.

References to wizards at Welsh wells are few. One wizard (*dewin*) who lived at Llwyn Ffynnon is said to have practised sorcery with the waters of the healing well of Ffynnon Fednant (Caern.).[30]

(*d*) *The Devil and Wells*

The appearance of the Devil at wells is due to one of two things—either to the Christian priesthood which degraded certain well deities and represented them as the Devil (or demons), or to the folklore of a comparatively late period. He is said to haunt the well at Gerddi Bach Trewilym (St. Lawrence, Pem.) and also the ford between Trewilym and Castle Villa. Near Llanarth church (Card.) is Ffynnon Gloch, and by it is a spot which is said to be under a spell. People standing on this spot are said to be unable to hear the church bells when they are ringing. The legend relates that the Devil having stolen a bell from Llanbadarn Fawr rested by this well, the spot becoming accursed in consequence.[31] The Cardiganshire example may be an onomastic tale : cf. the tale concerning Ffynnon y Gloch Felen (Mer. p. 193 below).

[29] BD, 71. This wood is now called Ellis Wood in Glen Monnow on the Monmouthshire-Herefordshire border.
[30] M Fardd, 179. [31] Davies, *The Story of New Quay*, 1933, p. 38.

(e) Ghosts and spirits at wells

These, again, may be degraded deities, or possibly have been given a local habitation and a name by folklore.[32] The Monmouthshire Ffynnon Ysbrydion and the Pembrokeshire Ffynnon Ysbryd preserve in their names, the locale of spirits. In the 19th century, a monster, ' very big in the middle and narrow at both ends' was seen near Ffynnon yr Ysbryd in Trevethin parish, a place where ghosts were known to haunt.[33] Ffynnon Ffeirad, in a Cardiganshire valley, is so-named because it is haunted by the ghost of a parson who had lived there some centuries ago.[34] The spirit of the venerable Dafis Castell Hywel (1745-1827) is said to have haunted Pistyll Gwyn in Llandysul parish to the discomfiture of servant maids.[35] Here, it is possible that we have ancient well spirits reappearing as ghosts of once living men. At the healing well of Ffynnon Gwenno (Cynwyl Gaio, Carm.) a woman named Gwenno was induced to explore the recesses of a cavern beyond a crag (afterwards called Clochty Gwenno), which had always been the prescribed limit to the devotees of the well. As she passed under the crag she was seized by spirits, and on stormy nights, when the moon is full, her ghost hovers over the crag like a wreath of mist. Gwenno may have been a deity of the well degraded into a sprite, but it must be noted that Gwynio, according to Lewis Glyn Cothi, was one of the saints of Llanpumpsaint, and it is possible that his name may be the one concerned. The tradition, as we have it, seems to suggest a broken tabu involving women. If this is so, then we have here an echo of pre-Christian belief.

Ffynnon y Bwci, in a valley in the Newcastle Emlyn district, is said to be haunted by a ghost. A spirit called Bwci Bach haunted Llanwddyn well (Mont.) and he has been ' seen ' in the 20th century. Many tales are told in the Llanllugan-Adfa-Cefn Coch districts (Mont.) about the Bwgan, a sprite that lived near a well on the Lower Lliw.

[32] See W. Gregor, 'Guardian Spirits of Wells and Lochs,' in FL, 1892, p. 67 ff.
[33] BG, 178. [34] DHPL, 237. [35] *ib.*

Above this well grows a tree, and the Bwgan lives amongst its roots. When the water subsides the Bwgan is angered and is then up to all kinds of tricks. He seems to be a mischievous rather than a fatal spirit. Montgomeryshire people disposed of evil spirits by capturing them, putting them into bottles, which, securely sealed, were dropped into deep wells, such as at Llanllwchaiarn well, Newtown.[36] Ffynnon Bwbach (Flint) and Goblin's Well (Flint) appear to have been named after sprites. The spirit of a wailing child was believed to haunt the field adjoining Ffynnon Digwg (Caern.).

It is said that when the well at Gerddi Bach Trewilym (Pem.) was approached by night, the hoofbeats of a galloping horse could be heard, becoming clearer the nearer one came to the well. As one moved from the well, the hoofbeats became fainter and fainter until they finally died away. Sometimes cries of its rider could also be heard. Have we here a trace of the rascally *ceffyl-dŵr*, or perhaps of a guardian animal-spirit of the well?[37] Irish and Breton legends associate the horse with wells; in pagan lore it is ridden by a hero, in Christian myth by a saint. St. Asaph's horse is said to have made a miraculous leap, and in 1850-60, a stone in High Street, St. Asaph, was pointed out as bearing the impress of its hoof.[38] The hoof-mark of the horse that carried St. Degan from the tragedy of the Lowland Hundred, is pointed out in Pencaer (Pem.), and the hoofmark of the magical steed ridden by St. Gildas is seen on a rock on the Breton coast. Carreg Carn March Arthur, the name of two stones in North Wales, one near Aberdovey and the other near Mold, may refer to the hero Arthur. The name Ffynnon y ceffyl bal (Glam.) suggests an early origin. Ffynnon Ddôl Erw Llyw, near Abergele, is said to be bottomless,[39] and a local story relates that a young man was once ploughing there when the horse became frightened and plunged into the well dragging with it plough and

[36] ex inf. Mr. H. N. Jerman, M.A.

[37] In Devon, galloping spirit-horses protected prehistoric sepulchral mounds—ABM, 50-1.

[38] DSA, i, 2. [39] Lhuyd Par. i, 44.

ploughman, who were never seen again.[40] One night in the last century the vicar and his son saw a white horse walking on its hind legs along a path and disappearing into the churchyard well of Oxwich (Glam.).[41] The *ceffyl-dŵr* is clearly in question here.

Frogs were also associated with some wells, the 'Frog in the well' cycle being known in most lands. A spirit in the form of a frog appears in the Hepste Pools (Glam.).[42] In Dewsland (Pem.) it is held to be dangerous to drink water without cups from certain wells because a spirit in the form of a small frog would jump down the drinker's throat. At the Frog Well (Salop) the Devil and his imps appear in the form of frogs. Dragons and serpents are mentioned as denizens of wells in antiquity.[43] A strange snake was said to lurk in the Grinston well (Pem.) and 'strange creatures' in Ffynnon Digwg (Mer.). The name Ffynnon Wiber (Adder's well) (Carm.) suggests a similar association.

(*f*) *The Negligent Guardian*

There are indications that the negligent guardian derives from a religious origin, the guardian being the priest or priestess of the sacred well. The tale is widespread but the basic elements are constant, *viz*:

1. That there was a guardian, usually a female, whose duty it was to cover the well at night by placing a stone slab over it.
2. That she neglected to do so with one or more of the following results—a lake was formed, a great river flowed from the well, a town was drowned, a countryside was inundated.

It is possible that there is a trace of a broken tabu in these inundation tales, perhaps involving women. There are many Welsh examples, e.g. Cantre'r Gwaelod, whose flooding involved a woman well-guardian ; Llyn Llambedr-y-moch (Pem.) under which lies the 'original town' of

[40] NLW MS. 8379. This story was recorded in 1866.
[41] HWG, IV, 1894, 157-8. [42] Trevelyan, 21. [43] AMB, ch. V.

Mathry; Llyn Llech Owen (Carm.); Llyn Tegid (Bala Lake); Llyn Glaslyn (Caern.) formed by the overflowing of Ffynnon Grasi where Grasi's ghost is still seen: Llyn y Maes, at the bottom of which lies the 'original' Tregaron (Card.).

(*g*) *Treasure in wells*

The lore concerned with this subject shows the well as the guardian and as the repository of treasure. Giraldus relates the story of a Pembrokeshire well that contained a golden torque guarded by a viper which bit the hand of a treasure-seeker. A modern story from the Dinas Emrys—Nant Gwynant district says that one summer's day, while the people of Hafod y Porth were haymaking, a servant left the field and went to a nearby well. He poked his rake handle into it and was gratified to hear the sound of coins jingling. To get at the money he started to remove some of the stones that lay in the well. As he picked up the first stone a tremendous storm arose. The servant and the other harvesters rushed down the hillside to Maes yr Efail where they found the sun shining and not a drop of rain to be seen on the grass.[44] Stories of great storms rising to protect tumuli, cromlechau and other sacred sites occur in the folklore of all lands. The name of Ffynnon Arian near Foel Gron (Caern.) may have been connected with a treasure tale.

Sometimes it was pre-ordained that treasure would be found only by persons of a special physical description or by those fulfilling certain conditions. It was believed that money hidden in Ffynnon Digwg (Caern.) would be revealed only to a red-haired lass herding sheep.[45]

(*h*) *The goddess Gwenhudw*

If the evidence of well-names can be accepted, one goddess, Gwenhudw, has remained with Welshmen to modern times. She was originally a water deity, and the element—*hudw* (hudwy, hidwy, hidw) in her name indicates

[44] JBG, 225. [45] M Fardd 172.

a connection with primitive magic.[46] The prefix *gwen*, evidently represents an effort in Christian times to disguise the true origin of the goddess. She is connected with two wells and a megalith. Between Dolgelley and Garnedd-wen (Mer.) is Ffynnon Gwenhudw, locally called Ffynnon Gnidiw and Cridiw. Its waters cured rheumatism, and, according to tradition 'a little old man' (*hen ddyn bach*) lived nearby. At the extreme north-eastern end of the county was 'the Gromlech call'd Maen Gwynhidw near Maes Gwyn in ye parish of Gwyddelwern abt a qr of a mile distant from ye Church.'[47] She was also patron of a well near the Cardiganshire coast, and her name has been preserved in the will of a clergyman, dated 1779, who then owned *Tir Ffynnon Ddewi* and *Tir Penheoll alias Tir Ffynnon Gwenhidw* in the parishes of Llanarth and Llan-dissiliogogo. According to the Black Book of Carmarthen, Maes Gwenhidwy, was one of the names given to the sea. Rhys Llwyd ap Rhys ap Riccert describes the waves as 'the sheep of Gwenhidwy':

Haid o ddefaid gwenhidwy
A naw hwrdd yn un a hwy[48]

Lewis Glyn Cothi suggests that she was a hirsute being:

Ni adaf mal gwenhidwy
Ar vy min dyfu barf mwy.[49]

Thomas Prys, in a satire on Thomas Hanmer and Rhys Cain, wrote:

Ail yw Rhys yn ael y rhiw
wan hydol i Wenhidiw.[50]

Myrddin Fardd mentions an 'old Welsh tale' in which a mermaid is called Gwenhidwy,[51] and Mr. Jenkyn Thomas wrote of 'Gwenhudiw the mermaid Shepherdess of Ocean' associated with Cantre'r Gwaelod.[52] Dr. Hartwell Jones

[46] For the use of the word *hud* and its relation to magic in early Welsh texts see TGJ, 119 ff.
[47] Lhuyd Par. ii, 50; on p. 59 he spells the name as Gwanhidiw. He also gives a sketch of the cromlech.
[48] BM Add MS. 15003, f. 63.
[49] *Gwaith Lewis Glyn Cothi*: ed. E. D. Jones, Aberystwyth, 1953, p. 135.
[50] *Cefn Coch MS.* 147. [51] M Fardd, 106. [52] WFB, 29.

stated that the word *gwenhidwy* was formerly commonly used in Cardiganshire and Powys for an insignificant or decrepit individual, and often applied to a sickly lamb; and was pronounced *cnidw* in Powys.[53] About 1911, a Mr. David Williams, J.P., of Carmarthen, said that the king of the fairies was Gwydion ap Don, and 'His queen was Gwenhidw. I have heard my mother call the small fleece-like clouds which appear in fine weather the Sheep of Gwenhidw.'[54]

(i) Games at wells

Games involving wells may contain elements of an eaıly ritual in the same way as dancing or jollities at wells are a debased form of the earlier religious exercises. The following game was popular in many parts of Cardiganshire and Glamorganshire. A girl covered her head with a cloth and hid behind a chair or other furniture, or in the corner of a room. Her playmates advanced towards her, one child saying to another, 'Get water from the well.' 'No, I fear the Ladi Witch in the well' was the reply. The children then advanced very cautiously, one of them raising a lighted candle. The 'witch' in the corner then disclosed herself, blew out the candle, while the children dispersed with shrieks. It is possible that this is a trace of a witch's well and a holy candle.

In the latter part of the 19th century a traditional game was played by the children of Roch parish (Pem.) called 'The Witch in the well,' but it is now forgotten. A game called *Bwci'r ffynnon* was played in the Taf valley district on the Pembrokeshire-Carmarthenshire border. A child was selected to be the bwci of the well. The other children divided his body between them, one taking his nose, another his teeth, an arm, leg, etc., and hid themselves behind hedges and bushes while the bwci covered his eyes and counted up to 50. He then searched, crying out '*Le ma 'nghig a'm gwaed i, fy mhen i,*' etc. When the hidden 'possessor' heard the item he 'held,' he would cry in

[53] CBPM, 367 and n: see also TGJ, 75. [54] FFCC, 152.

answer, '*Yng nghwt y lleuad.*' The bwci then gave chase until he caught him, and so it went on until he had recovered all his dismembered body. Then a new bwci would be appointed.[55] This game appears to contain ritualistic elements, but until many more of these well-games throughout Wales have been collected and analysed we must refrain from attempting interpretation.

[55] ex inf. Mr. Howell E. James.

Part II

LIST OF WELLS

This list of wells has been arranged under counties and subdivided into the following five classes :—

CLASS A.—Wells bearing the names of saints and the following designations—Trinity (Drindod), God (Duw), Holy Innocents (Mil Feibion) and Easter (Pasg).

CLASS B.—Wells associated with churches, chapels, feasts, pilgrimages. Some of these may once have borne the names of saints. This class therefore closely resembles Class A.

CLASS C.—Wells which, in early literature or in surviving tradition, are known to have been primarily reputed to be healing wells, and whose names are not those of saints as in Class A, and are not as closely or obviously connected with churches as those in Class B.

CLASS D.—Wells named, apparently, after secular people and personages. It is possible that some of these names may have been those of minor or local saints.

CLASS E.—Miscellaneous wells. There is a very large number of these, but only those which possess a name of possible significance, or concerning which legends and traditions have survived, are included.

ANGLESEY

CLASS A :

FF. ALLGO. Some 400 yards SW of Llanallgo church : a small pool within a rectangular chamber 10½ feet by 7 feet, with low walls of limestone blocks—Anc. Mon. Angl. ' Ffynnon Gallgof ' is strongly impregnated with sulphate of lime, and is still regarded as highly beneficial : adjoining the W front of the church is Capel Ffynnon, a small edifice anciently appropriated to the use of the votaries of the patron of the spring—Lewis TDW ; Llwyd Angl, 215.

FF. ANNON. ' Kae gweyn ffynon Annon ' in the parish of ' Llanbeylan ' in Malltraeth, 1628—Col. D, p. 278. cf. Llyn Anwn, Llanystumdwy, Caern. St. Annun or Anhun is listed in LBS.

FF. BADRIG. St. Padrig ab Alfryd, Confessor, founded Llanbadrig on the N coast. The well is now neglected and a spring alone remains. It was formerly much frequented, and was celebrated for cures, particularly in the case of children—LBS, IV, 52.

FF. BEUNO. In Malt House Lane near the road leading to the river from Aberffraw : also called 'yr hen ffynnon'—NLW MS. 3290 D.

FF. CERRIG CEINWEN. In 1893 there was a neglected well in Cerrig Ceinwen churchyard which was credited with healing qualities: it probably commemorated St. Ceinwen—Mont. Coll., 1893, 274-5.

FF. DDYGFAEL. So spelt on O.S. Map 11 SE. cf. Llanddogwel.

FF. DDWYNWEN. Near Llanddwyn church ruins on Llanddwyn Is. According to Lewis TDW, and Ashton IG, 234, n 2, this well was also called *Ffynnon Fair*. LBS, IV, 389-91, also calls it *Crochan Llanddwyn*, and says that auguries were favourable to lovers if the well bubbled while they performed the ' ceremonies.' See also Anc. Mon. Angl ; ELM ; Peniarth MS. 112 ; Cardiff MSS. 7 and 26. See above pp. 50, 83, 102, 111.

FF. EILIAN. About one-third of a mile NW of Llaneilian church, on a rocky site near the coast, and adjoining a small stream : the foundations of a small building are visible against a vertical rock face which formed one side of the enclosure : the water passes through a fissure in the rock into a hollow within the square—Anc. Mon Angl. See above pp. 50, 72, 101, 107, 118.

FF. ELAETH. St. Elaeth, King, Confessor, founded the church of Llan Elaeth Frenin now called Amlwch. His holy well there was formerly in high repute for healing and divination—Jones, Cymru, 1875, i, 92. *A Brief Sketch of the Royal Eisteddfod held at Beaumaris, August*, 1832, contains this reference—' There are the ruins of an old chapel called Capel Elaethin [*sic*] in this parish [Amlwch].' The ruins have disappeared—NLW MS. 3290D.

FF. ESTYN. Named after St. Iestyn, the founder of the churches of Llaniestyn in Anglesey and Caernarvonshire. It is in the corner of a field on Tyddyn Ucha farm, a short distance from the church. See above p. 119.

FF. FAIR (?). See Ff. Ddwynwen above and Ff. Seiriol below.

FF. FFRAID. Unlocated. St. Ffraid is commemorated in an Anglesey well—Mont. Coll., 1893, 274-5.

FF. MAELOG. Near Maelog Lake, Rhosneigr. About a hundred years ago some of its water was taken to London for analysis and pronounced to be ' the purest water in the whole of N. Wales ' : it cured rheumatism—Ex inf. Mrs. Myfanwy Howell.

FF. GAFFO. Near Llangaffo : also called Crochan Gaffo. The well has disappeared but the nearby farm is still called Ffynnon Gaffo—LBS, ii, 50 : Llwyd Angl., 269 : Myf. Arch., 420 : Traethodydd, 1862, 314-315. For the element crochan in well-names note Crochan Llanddwyn and Crochan Tynycoed. See above p. 105.

FF. GYBI (2). 1. Two wells at Clorach, Ff. Gybi and Ff. Seiriol, were situated on each side of the road from Llanerchymedd, exactly opposite each other. The former was destroyed about 1840 when a new bridge was built, but the latter still flows. Both were visited for healing purposes—LBS, ii, 209. ' The wells are still held in high estimation '—Llwyd Angl., 228. Skinner gives a sketch of the wells ' whose waters were enclosed in a square reservoir of stone work, ' and also of the megalith ' Lleidr y Frydog,' about a quarter mile away.—J. Skinner. ' Ten Days Tour Through the Isle of Anglesea, Dec. 1802 ', Arch. Cam. Supp. 1908. The megalith, now called Carreg Leidr, is near Clorach farm, and is said to represent a man turned into stone after he had stolen the church Bible—Lewis, TDW. The megalith may have been associated with the wells : it is in Llandyfrydog parish.

2. At Caergybi, and used for healing, divination and cursing—Meurig Wyn MS., p. 131 : it was said to cure scurvy, scrofula, rheumatism, etc., and crutches and wheelbarrows left by cured patients were seen near the well in the early part of the 18th century: it once contained a sacred eel : there was a building over the well—Rhŷs CF, 365-6 : LBS, ii. 209. See above p. 111.

FF. REDIFAEL. St. Gredifael founded Penmynydd church, sometimes called Llanredifael. The well is in Cae Gredifael near the church. Its waters cured warts, which were first pricked with a pin, until they bled, and then washed in the well—LBS, ii, 149.

FF. SEIRIOL (3). 1. This well, surrounded by a wall, is about three miles from Penmon church, but in Llaniestyn parish—LBS, iv, 177, 179. 2. This well and the remains of a cell are some

80 yards NNE of Penmon church—Anc. Mon. Angl., illustr : LBS, iv, 177, 179 : OCS, 18, plan : BGNW, 35, photo. See above p. 27. It is said to have been called sometimes Ff. Fair. According to Carlisle TDW, it was ' formerly in good repute '. 3. Near Llanerchymedd—see Ff. Gybi (1) above. Ff. Seiriol was visited at dead of night about the middle of the 19th century, and its water carried to sick people—Mont. Coll., 1893, 281.

FF. WENFAEN. Close to the cliff, about 300 yards W of the Look-out Station on Holyhead Is., and about 1000 yards ESE of Rhoscolyn parish church : there is a well-chamber with stone seats across each corner : there is an outer pool with steps leading down to it—Anc. Mon. Angl. St. Gwenfaen, Virgin, is patron of Rhoscolyn church, formerly Llanwenfaen. Lewis Morris mentions this well in a poem, and says that its water was used as a charm against mental disorders, and that two white spar pebbles were cast into the well as an oblation. It is possible that these white stones are associated with the saint's name—LBS, iii, 185. See above p. 95.

CLASS B :

FF. BRYN FENDIGAID. Near Bryn Fendigaid, Aberffraw parish. In the 18th century, Sir Arthur Owen of Bodeon built a wall around it, but it became ruined and neglected : it was reopened in 1861—NLW MS. 3290 D. Its waters were efficacious for the cure of all kinds of complaints : a fish was kept in it for purposes of divination —NLW Meurig Wyn MS., p. 133. About 400 yards from this well there are some chalybeate springs, near Croes Ladys : local legend states that a woman named Gladys was martyred in this district —NLW MS. 3290D.

FF. DAFADEN. On the headland where Llanddwyn church stood (Newborough parish)—OS 6″, 1891.

FF. Y GORLLES. In Holyhead parish. It is called locally Ff. Golles or Gollais—NLW. MS. 3290D. ' A famous spring called Ffynnon y Gorlles near a ruined chapel called Capel y Gorlles ' ; the well was in the east end of this chapel—Price, ' Short Account of Holyhead ', *Bibliotheca Topographica Britannica*, V, (1790).

FF. LLUGWY. Near the parish church : it had a high reputation for its curative properties, and cured fevers and other ills—ex inf. Mrs. Myfanwy Howell.

FF. LOCHWYD. Near Holyhead—Mont. Coll. 1893, 280. It was once walled and steps led down to it—NLW MS. 3290D. It was visited on St. Cybi's Day, held on the last Sunday before 25 July, and the feast lasted for two weeks : young people first visited the church, and then the well, and returned with sand and water without spilling either—ELM : Mont. Coll., 1893, 280. See above p. 101, 112.

FF. PECHOD. In Llangaffo parish. Tradition states that 'sinners' were whipped as far as the crossroads called Y Chwipyn, and that their sins were washed away at Ffynnon Pechod—ex inf. Mrs. Myfanwy Howell.

CLASS C :
TROS YR AFON SPRING. On Tros yr Afon land, Penmon parish : 'the waters of which hold in solution a sulphite of lime, and contains a considerable portion of fixed air' ; much visited and held in high estimation for its efficacy in chronic diseases—Llwyd Angl, 313-4.

CLASS D :
FF. Y WRACH. Between Caergybi and Ynys Lawd.—ELM.

CLASS E :
FF. HALOG. OS 22 NE. of Pont Rhyd *Alawg*.

BRECKNOCKSHIRE

CLASS A :
FF. AFAN. In Llanafan Fawr—Lhuyd Par., iii, 47.

FF. DDEWI (2). 1. In Llangamarch : Tir ffynnon thewy 1629 —Col. D, p. 6. 2. Near Llanddewi Abergwesin Church—Lhuyd Par., iii, 51.

FF. EIGION. In Llanigon parish—Carlisle TDW. Perhaps identical with the Boiling Well. See above p. 127.

FF. FAIR. In Patrishow parish. Blaen Nant Mair is to the E of Patrishow, and Nant Ffos Mair is a rill flowing from Bryn Du to the Chwefri.

FF. FILO. In Llanfilo parish, whose church is dedicated to St. Milburg—Morgan PN, 70.

FF. GATWG. Just NW of Llangatwg church, which is dedicated to St. Catwg—Rees Map.

FF. GENEU. Or St. Geney's Well, in Llangeneu parish, was near an old building said to have been an oratory of the saint. When the building was taken down about 1790, a farmer found a very ancient iron bell of curious form, which was exhibited to the Society of Antiquaries of London on 2 Feb. 1809—Carlisle TDW. The first of a newly-wed couple to drink from this well would be 'master' throughout the married life—Jones, Geir. Cenedl. Cymru, ii, 131. Its water was said to be good for sore eyes—Lewis TDW. See above p. 35, 113.

FF. GYNGAR. St. Cyngar, Virgin, was a daughter of Brychan. She dwelt on a hillock at the foot of a high Brecknockshire mountain. Unlocated. See above p. 36. cf. Ff. Gyngar, Flint. cf. Penginger Well, below.

FF. GYNOG. St. Cynog lived in a cell under a steep cliff near the top of the hill called Van, about 4 miles from Brecon. There was no water near, and Cynog had to carry it from the river at the foot of the hill. So God gave him water 'upon the top of the rock over the cell'—BM Harl MS. 4181, f. 71. See above pp. 36, 37.

ST. ISHO'S WELL. In Patrishow parish, whose church is dedicated to Isho or Issu. 'Below the Church saw the Sainted Well of [Isho], being a very scanty oozing of water, to which, however, was formerly attributed great Virtue, as within the buildng that encloses it are little Niches to hold the Vessels drank out of and the offerings they left behind'—Fenton TW, 26. For illustr. see Glynne OWC: LBS, iii, 322. The church stands on a knoll above a small stream called Nant Mair. See Carlisle TDW. It seems to have lost its ancient esteem (1903)—Trans. Cardiff Nat. Soc., 36, 1903, 56-7.

ST. NICHOLAS WELL. Near St. Nicholas Chapel, Brecon: regarded as a cure for the whooping cough and nausea: 'resorted to by people living 60 miles off': when its water was carried to the patient, the vessel holding it was not, under any circumstances, to be placed on the ground before it reached the patient: the water from the spout 'will not make broth', and so, for domestic purposes, people drew the water below the spout.—Fenton TW., 340. This holy well is now 'lost.' See above p. 100.

PENGINGER WELL. St. Lludd, also called Alud and Almedha, was a daughter of Brychan, and was martyred by a stone near a mound. This mound is at Pencefngaer, above one mile E of Brecon, and near Slwch farmhouse. To the N of the mound the sanctuary of the saint once stood. One tale states that her pursuer was a pagan Saxon chief, that she hid at this mound, but was discovered and beheaded. She was buried at Usk. Cf. the name Penginger with the Cornish Treginegar, derived from Tre + OW Cynidr, from O Celtic Cuno—setros 'bold-chief' (Gover MS.). See above pp. 96, 102. cf. Ff. Gyngar, Flint.

CLASS B :

MAEN DU WELL. N of the cemetery outside Brecon : accounted holy, pins were offered—Bygones, 8 Apr. 1896. A quaint old well covered by a small stone building : pins were offered by love-lorn maids—*Brecon and its Scenery* (Tourist Handbook), p. 23. See p. 112.

PRIORY WELL. Just N of the Priory Church, Brecon : pins were offered.

CLASS C :

DINAS WELL. To the E of Castell Dinas, in Rhiangoll valley : curative.

FF. DDUW. In Llanavan Vawr parish. 'Much resorted unto by the country people for the cure of Divers diseases'—Lhuyd Par. iii, 47.

FF. Y GWRLODAU. In Llanfihangel Cwm Du parish. 'Of no medicinal virtue excepting in the idea of the Vulgar'—Carlisle TDW. Once regarded as a cure for tertian agues : in 1800 a person was completely cured by drinking the water for a few days—Jones, *Hist. of Brec.*, iii, 179.

CLASS D :

FF. DYCLID. Ff. Dyclid and Ff. y drewi in Llanwrtyd—Lhuyd Par. iii, 50.

FF. GADFERTH. A small spring by the road at the ascent from Camarch to Cefn Treflis in Llangamarch parish (church ded. to St. Cadfarch)—Lhuyd Par. iii, 45-6.

CLASS E :
FF. FERFOR YR HALEN. In Llynwene.

FF. WENALLT. Near Twyn Wenallt, Llanelly parish : to the S is Bedd y Gwr Hir.

CAERNARVONSHIRE

CLASS A :
FF. AELHAIARN. About 300 yards N of Llanaelhaiarn church : an oblong trough by the roadside : the well was roofed by the parish council in 1900 and now supplies the village—LBS, i, 112 : OCS, 283 : see above p. 108.

FF. AELRHIW. Near the church of Rhiw : it is about 10 feet square with seats around it, and was said to cure scrofulous disorders beng particularly efficacious in the cure of a skin disease called, '*Man Aeliw*' (the mark or spot of Aeliw)— M Fardd 185, cf. LBS, i, 113 : Cathrall, *History of N Wales*, 1828, ii, 120.

FF. ARMON. About a mile W of Betws Garmon church, and on the slope of Moel Smythan : it cured rheumatism, and skin diseases —M Fardd 171. About 200-300 yards away are the remains of an old chapel—OCS, 229, plan.

FF. BEDR. About a quarter mile S of Llanbedrycennin : it is overshadowed by a yew: it was once covered by a building 10 feet 9 inches by 6 feet : up to about 1844 children were bathed there and afterwards taken to a little chapel outside the cottage garden— OCS, 98, plan. See above p. 101.

FF. BEDROG. On Bryn Du near Pigstryd village, Llanbedrog. In the 16th and 17th centuries it was considered to be 'beneficial to offer to Pedrog for gangrenes '—Evans, *Report on Welsh MSS*. i, 913. It was said in 1908 that 'lately' a round vessel of black stone was found at its bottom, which was nearly full of pins—M Fardd, 189 : LBS, iv, 102. It also detected thieves. See above p. 114.

FF. BERIS. About a quarter mile NE of Llanberis church. It was reputed to cure ricketty children, who were immersed in it, scrofula and rheumatism—Carlisle TDW. Sacred fish were kept in it—Evans, *Tour through North Wales in 1798*, edn. 1804, 180-1 : Cathrall, *North Wales*, 1828, ii, 140 : Pennant, *Tours in Wales*, ii,

320 : LBS, IV, 92-3 : CF, 366 : Bingley, *North Wales*, edn. 1810, 157 : CLMS, 18 : Arch. Cam., 1895, 209. For a description and plan see OCS, 217-8. According to Trevelyan, p. 17, an eel was kept in it. The Llanberis Terriers record in 1776 that the parish clerk was paid 6s. 4d. ' from a box made in a Timber in the Body of the Church, which are put in by strangers that now and then come to a virtuous well that is in this Parish, and when the Box is too short the wages is made up by an addition from the Parish . . . ' The entry for 1814 shows that his pay was still the same, and states ' There is an Alms Box in the Church, the key of which is kept by the Wardens, and into which 6d. and 4d. pieces were formerly put very frequently by persons who either bathed their children, or came themselves for that purpose, in St. Peris's Well, within a quarter of a mile of the Church, and celebrated in former days for the Cure of Wens, Warts, Rickets, Rheumatism, etc. These small offerings to the Saint amounted at the end of the year to a considerable sum, but at present they are very trifling '—LBS, iv, 92-3. This box was called Cyff Beris. See above p. 72, 109.

FF. BEUNO. About 200 yards from Clynnog church, surrounded by a wall some 6 feet high, with seats, and steps leading to the well : the masonry is ruined—*Cyff Beuno*, 35 : M Fardd, 171 : Pennant, *Tours in Wales*, ii., 385. A short distance away there is a cromlech—Bingley, *North Wales*, edn. 1810, 275 : see also Arch. Cam., 1895, 145. The chapel was dedicated to Beuno, ' to which attaches the popular belief that the powdered scrapings of the stone columns that support the chapel are efficacious as a sovereign cure for sore eyes' ; a collyrium was made by adding a pinch to a bottle of the spring water ; the columns were scored by scrapes, but the church has been restored—Bygones, 29 Dec. 1875. ' Superstitious practices prevailing in Wales in 1589 ', printed in the new edition of Leland's *Collectanea*, II, 684 mentions offering heifers to St. Beuno at ' Clynocgvaur.' For a description and plan of the well see OCS, 278. It is noticed in Camden, *Brit.* (Gough), p. 554. See above p. 16.

FF. CAWRDAF. On Tanygraig land, Aber-erch parish : reputed to cure all ills—M Fardd, 189. This saint is said to be the brother of St. Cadfarch who also had a well in the same parish. There is a megalith called Cader Cawrdaf—NLW MS. 3290D.

DANIEL'S WELL. In Bangor parish. There are two ancient chapels in the parish dedicated to St. Daniel.

FF. DDEINIOLEN. About half a mile S of Llanddeiniolen church; said to cure scorbutic diseases, rheumatism, and warts—Carlisle TDW, Lewis TDW, M Fardd 169. The well, now completely covered with stone slabs, is at the SE corner of the garden of Hen Gapel, where the Methodists once held services—OCS, 207.

FF. DUDNO. About 100 yards from Llandudno church, and once in high repute—OCS, 31 : OCA, 6. Near by, on Gogarth, was a rocking stone called *Crud Tudno*—P Tours, iii, 143.

FF. DUDWEN. In the corner of a field near Llandudwen church : the well has disappeared—LBS, iv, 275. Its waters were especially good for the cure of epilepsy, rheumatism, numbness, sore eyes, etc. Coins and pins were offered : people were baptised in it, and secret marriages solemnised near the well—'*priodasau dirgel mynych a gymerent le gerllaw iddi, yn ystod y canrifoedd aethant heibio*'—M Fardd, 190.

FF. DUNAWD. About 1 mile N of Cae'r Dyni farm, Criccieth—Arch. Cam., 1924, 331.

FF. DWRDAN. In a remote spot at Nant, Bodwrda parish.—Rees CBS, 224 : M Fardd, 187.

FF. ELAN. Near Gelli'r Pentref, Dolwyddelan : also called Ff. Gwythelan—M Fardd, 168. It is about a quarter mile from the church, and was once covered by a building 9 feet 6 inches by 8 feet, with a seat around the walls : the water has tonic qualities and is said to steam slightly in frosty weather—OCS, 134, plan : OCA, 138-9 : *Y Brython*, Jan., 1861 : O. Gethin Jones, *History of Dolwyddelan, Penmachno and Ysbytty Ivan.* Fenton (TW, 189) states that near Dolwyddelan Castle there was a Ffynnon Elen where Roman legionaries 'used to dine'. Its waters were considered good, especially for weakly children and paralyzed limbs—LBS, iii, 218.

FF. FAGLAN. Near Llanfaglan church : famous for curing sore eyes, warts, and rheumatism. Warts were pricked with a pin which was then bent and thrown into the well. About 1840, two basinfulls of bent pins were recovered from the well—*Bygones*, 24 May 1893. It is surrounded by a wide stone seat enclosed within walls—OCS, 250, plan. There is a megalith in its vicinity—Rhs CF, 362.

FF. FAIR (5). 1. On the shore near Ogo Fair below Mynydd Mawr, Aberdaron parish. The tide covers it at the flow, but it is uncovered at the ebb when its waters are clear and pure—M Fardd, 187. A folk-tale concerning its origin relates that a beautiful lady once desired to obtain a very important ' wish ' : after sunset she was visited by ' a strange lady ' who told her that her wish would be gratified if she descended to the well, ascended the steps carrying the water, and walked around the church once without losing a single drop—Trevelyan, 17. The ancient chapel was called Capel Mair or Tŷ Fair, and is said to have been ' erected for the use of the mariners' —Lewis TDW. In its vicinity was Cae Mair. See above pp. 47 2. A three-cornered well on the slope of Moel Fawr, Llanbedrog. Local tradition attributed to it power to heal all human and animal ills provided the visitor knelt by the well and declared his faith in it : it was also used to detect thieves—M Fardd. 183. See above p. 114. 3. In a field called Cae Ffynnon in Llanfairfechan : once a potent well, it has been filled up since about 1874 : the site is in a plantation by the remains of some yews : its water was used for baptism at the church : children were baptised in the well, and articles believed to have been bewitched were bathed in it : bent pins were offered—OCS, 160 : OCA, 177. 4. Near Dinas y Moch, Beddgelert parish, not far from the site of St. Mary's Priory : it is now filled in—OCS, 227. To this well, tradition attributed ' *lawer o rinweddau swyngyfareddol*'—M Fardd, 170. 5. In Botwnnog parish, near Bryncroes : it is near the church where stood formerly a chapel called Tŷ Fair.

FF. GADFARCH. Near the site of an old chapel called Llangedwydd at the northern end of Aber-erch parish : its water was carried to the parish church for baptism—Mont. Coll., 1893, 271. See above p. 82.

FF. GELYNIN. In the corner of Llangelynin churchyard : its water was taken to the church for baptism—Mont. Coll., 1893, 272 : LBS, ii, 104-5. It was used for divination : clothes of sickly children were placed on the water ; if they floated there would be a recovery, if not, death would occur. There are remains of a building around the well : a terrier, dated 1739, says, ' There is also in the South West of the Churchyard, a fine Spring-well, and ye House above it is about four yards in breadth and five in length, and in good repair ' : a terrier, dated 1742, refers to its ' slated roof '—OCS, 85, plan : OCA, 64-5, sketch. See above p. 101.

FF. GURIG. On the land of Gelli'r Monach, Llandegai parish. It cured warts. For a curse that befell a man who closed this well see Hughes, *Hynafiaethau Llanllechid a Llandegai*, p. 86. See above p. 4, 117.

FF. GWYFAN. Below Tudweilog village : cured sore eyes, ague, and warts for which pins were offered—M Fardd, 181. The parish church is dedicated to SS. Cwyfan and Brigit.

FF. GWYNWY. About a quarter mile from Llangelynin church : for the cure of warts a bent pin was dropped into the well *before* bathing : if this was not done, it was believed that, not only would the bathing be ineffective, but that the neglectful visitor would ' catch ' the warts of which previous bathers had got rid—OCS, 86 : OCA, 65 : M Fardd, 169.

FF. GYBI. Near Llangybi church. Its waters were said to cure warts, lameness, blindness, scrofula, scurvy, rheumatism. Crutches and wheelbarrows were seen about the well in the early 18th century. A box, Cyff Gybi, for offerings, stood in the church. In 1750, the Revd. Mr. Williams of Llanystumdwy impressed its virtues upon the owner, William Price of Rhiwlas, who built a bath and a bath-house at the well. A description of the well, printed in 1904, showed that it was then surrounded by masonry with five niches in the walls—Arch. Cam., 1904, 107, ff, illustr. Near the well was Tynyffynnon, and the incoming tenant to it always paid £3 5s. 0d. to the outgoing tenant : of this sum, 10s. paid for Llain y ffynnon, the strip of land close to the well, and the remainder went towards ' llawr y ffynnon.' Water from the well was carried away in casks and bottles for use as medicine. In the 19th century the lasses of Llangybi and Llanhaiarn resorted to the well on the eve of the gwylmabsant. It was also used to divine a lover's ' intentions '. An eel living in it gave it much virtue—CF, 365. Fenton mentions the well as curative but does not refer to the eel (TW, 236). See above pp. 27, 74, 110, 111.

FF. GYNFRAN. Near the church of Llysfaen parish formerly called Llangynfran. Bishop Maddox wrote (1736-43), ' 12 Nov., on which day & the Sunday following the Common People formerly offer'd here for their horned cattle. Another Montpellier '—LBS, ii, 246 ; M Fardd, 168. See above p. 107.

FF. HELEN. On the outskirts of Llanbeblig village, near the river Seiont. The ground has been raised round the well, which is now approached by a flight of modern steps : the water is still taken away in bottles for use as medicine : there is said to have been a chapel called Capel Helen near the well—OCS, 236. St. Helen is listed in LBS.

FF. LLECHID. Near an old chapel called Yr Hen Eglwys or Capel Llechid, near Cae Ffynnon farm, of which the only remains are the foundations of one wall by the E side of the well : apart from the roof the chapel was fairly intact in 1780—OCS, 148 : OCA, 155. It was visited by sufferers from skin diseases. See above p. 100.

FF. LLEUDDAD. On the land of Carrog, Bryncroes parish : a walled well formerly in high repute for curing all kinds of diseases in both man and beast—M Fardd, 187 : LBS iii, 374. The memory of St. Lleuddad ab Dingad is further perpetuated in Gerddi Lleuddad on Bardsey Is., and by Ogof Lleuddad in Aberdaron. He is said to have been a 6th century abbot of Bardsey. M Fardd calls the well Ff. *Leudad.*

FF. OWEN. In Llysfaen parish—Lhuyd Par. i, 40.

FF. RHEDYW. Near the river about a quarter mile NW from Llanllyfni church, which is dedicated to St. Rhedyw : some stone slabs around it suggest that it was once enclosed by a wall : water for church baptisms was formerly obtained from it : a megalith, Eisteddfa Rhedyw, is on the slope of Mynydd Llanllyfni, on the old road to Dolbenmaen—OCS, 261, plan : Lewis TDW. Bedd Rhedyw and Tyddyn Rhedyw are near by.

FF. SEIRIOL. Between two summits on Penmaen-mawr—Carlisle TDW.

FF. TRILLO. In Llandrillo parish. In Fenton's day it was covered by a low vaulted building of quite elaborate proportions (TW, 201). Evans, wrote in 1802, ' Inside St. Trillo's Chappel is a well, formerly much esteemed for the virtues of its waters ; it was supposed to have been the constant residence of the Saint.' Jenkinson wrote, ' St. Trillo's Chapel is a very small, plain building, which covers a spring of water, and the monks of old used to pray for a good haul of fish '—HNW, i, 368.

FF. TYDWAL. On the land of Penrhyn in Llanengan parish : it cured wounds and illnesses.—M Fardd, 185.

FF. DDUW. Near Llanbedrog village : it was about 3 feet square and enclosed with a wall from four to five feet high : it cured rheumatism : adjoining it was another well about 1 foot square where invalids drank the waters, and around this well it was customary for people to assemble for rustic sports, but this custom has been neglected for many years—Lewis TDW. ' . . . Wakes were regularly kept in honour of it, when vast crowds of People met round the spot for three successive Sundays in July, where playing at Ball, and other country gambols were in great vogue. This Custom has ceased nearly Forty years, and the Well is now holden in no estimation ; it [the wall] is about three yards square ; and a small Well about a yard square is attached to it, from which they used to drink the water '—Carlisle TDW, who places it in Llanengan parish. See *Ffynnon Fyw* below.

CLASS B :

FF. FYW. In Llanengan parish : said to be dedicated to Curig whose chapel stood nearby—LBS, ii, 199. Blind people are said to have been cured there—Daniel, *Arch. Lleyn.* 118. A smaller well rose alongside the main well : visitors bathed in the larger well and drank from the smaller one—M Fardd, 183.

HOLY WELL. On a farm so-named in Llangian parish, on the SW slopes of Mynydd Mynytho.

LLANBEDRYCENNIN WELL. Near the church : curative : a yew grew above it : it was covered by a little building, now ruined, some 10 feet by 9½ feet, the well itself being 6 feet by 4 feet and 3 feet deep. About 60 years ago sick children were bathed there and afterwards carried to a little chapel nearby, which had disappeared before 1906—OCA, 90, sketch.

FF. LLANGYSTENIN. Near Llandudno Junction : associated with nearby Llangystenin.

FF. SANCTAIDD. On Gallt Isel on Tyddyn Bach in Carnguwch. See above p. 82.

FF. SAINT (3). 1. Near Criccieth church : visited on Easter Sundays when pins were offered—M Fardd, 174. Keys as well as pins were thrown into it on Easter mornings to solace St. Catherine, its patron, to whom the parish church is dedicated—T, 220. 2. NE of Mynydd y Rhiw on Bron Llwyd : women visited it on Dydd Iau Dyrchafael to wash their eyes and to offer pins—M Fardd, 186. 3. Near the road leading from Aberdaron : medicinal : its protective masonry was removed to build a nearby hedge.—M Fardd, 178.

CLASS C :

FF. YR ALLT. On Yr Allt farm : reputed to cure sore eyes, scrofula, etc : there are some large stones around it, and a strong earth rampart.—M Fardd, 174.

FF. CAE GARW. In Carnguwch parish : cured rheumatism and warts : a pin was offered for each wart—M Fardd, 180 : Rhys CF, 361.

FF. CEFN LLEITHFAN. In Bryncroes parish : within a walled enclosure : famous for curing warts. See above p. 95.

FF. Y CEFNYDD. Near Pennant : believed to cure rheumatism. —M Fardd, 181.

FF. CEGIN ARTHUR. In Llanddeiniolen parish : curative— Carlisle TDW : M Fardd, 169. See above p. 3, 107.

FF. DALAR. On Bryn Baglan : cured rheumatism : after bathing patients left crutches near the well—M Fardd, 188.

FF. DDEFAID. In Llanystumdwy parish : curative.

FF. DWR LLYGAD. In Llanfihangel y Pennant parish—M Fardd, 174.

FF. FEDNANT. Near Nantypistyll : said to ebb and flow with the tide—M Fardd, 179. See above p. 130.

FF. Y FILAST. In Llaniestyn parish : cured sterility in women and other feminine complaints, sore eyes, melancholy—M Fardd, 181. See above p. 99.

FF. Y GWAENYDD. In Llanystumdwy parish : said to be medicinal and miraculous, especially in the cure of lameness : pins were offered—M Fardd, 176. See above p. 101.

FF. GWYNEDD. In Aber-erch parish : divination was practised— M Fardd, 180 : T, 1893, 221. See above p. 108.

FF. NANTCALL. In Clynnog parish : cured melancholy, indigestion, etc.—M Fardd, 171.

PIN Y WIG. A rill in Nevin parish : cured knuckles and hands.— M Fardd, 192. See above p. 106.

FF. PISTYLL Y GARN. In Llaniestyn parish : cured rheumatism, stomach and bowel complaints.—M Fardd, 18.

TAI BACH SPRING. Near Llyn Ffynnon y Gwas, Llanberis : cured malignant ulcers—Rhys CF, 31.

FF. SAETHON. In Llanfihangel Bachellaeth parish : divination practised : pilgrimages were once made to it : regarded as virtuous in the last century : members of the family of Saethon of Saethon were said to bathe in this well in summer and winter. See above p. 111.

CLASS D :

FF. Y BRENIN. In Llaniestyn parish : cured sterility in women, and melancholy—M Fardd 181. See above p. 99.

FF. Y CYTHRAUL. In Llanfihangel y Pennant parish : it cured eye troubles, removed warts both from human beings and animals.—M Fardd, 174. Cf. Nant y Cythraul, a brook SW of Flint.

FF. DDIGWG. Near Pennarth in Clynnog Fawr. ' Ffynnawn Digiwc '—*Llyvyr Agkyr Llandewibrevi*, 1894, 125. See above p. 19, 38, 134. One old woman said that some things resembling oranges grew at the bottom of the well but that no one had succeeded in drawing one to the surface—NLW MS. 3290D. According to Eben Fardd's MSS., quoted by M Fardd, 172, the well was also called Ffynnon Gwttig or Gyttig, and that pins and eggs were offered there ; that it cured warts ; that some strange creatures resembling hedgehogs without their spikes were once seen in it. See also *Cyff. Beuno*, 59-60. The local pronounciation of the name is Digwg or Digwy. See Arch. Cam., 1930, 336-7.

FF. FYMBYR. The old name for Llyn Cwm-y-ffynnon, within a mile of Troed yr Wyddfa. Mymbyr ap Madog is described as an early king of Britain, but there is nothing to associate him with this district.—CLMS, 46.

FF. GRASI. Near Llyn Glasfryn, Llangybi parish ; associated with the ghost of a woman named Grace, and an inundation tale. See TGJ, 108.

FF. LLEWELYN. In Llangybi parish : said to cure the King's Evil—M Fardd, 178.

FF. OFFEIRIAD. From Dolwyddelan a mountain road leads towards Capel Curig ; crossing a brook are stepping stones called Sarn yr Offeiriad, and Ffynnon Offeiriad is nearby. It is oblong and is formed of rough stones and half-covered.—OCS, 135.

CLASS E :

FF. ARIAN. In Mynytho parish, near Foel Gron : a wishing well.

FF. BETWS FAWR. In a field called Cae'r Simdde near Betws Fawr, Llanystumdwy parish : there is a wall of stones around it, and on the SE side an old ash : it is believed that the Romans used this well.—M Fardd, 192.

FF. CHWERTHIN. Near Llanberis village : formerly there were thousands of pins in it, and many corks with pins in them floated on the surface.—M Fardd, 170. See above p. 129.

FF. ISAF. The traditional site of an old church at Bryn Eglwys near St. Anne's church, Bethesda : near the farm of Ffynnon Isaf—OCS, 139.

FF. SARFF. On Mynydd Mynytho, Llanengan parish, near Gwinllan Sarff : tradition states that a serpent lived in the well.—M Fardd, 182.

CARDIGANSHIRE

CLASS A :

FF. AFAN. In Llanafan parish.

FF. BADARN (2). 1. Near Penuwch, now in Llangeitho parish, but formerly in that of Llanbadarn Odwyn—ex inf. Mr. E. D. Jones. 2. On the side of Llanbadarn Road, Aberystwyth : the field by it was called *Pistyll Padarn* (TM) : medicinal.

FF. BEDR (2). 1. Just W of Lampeter ; SW of Peterwell is a farm called Fron Bedr. 2. In Verwig parish.

FF. DALIS. In Dihewyd. Tradition states that a small chapel stood at the well which now supplies the village : Ffair Dalis fawr was once held there before it was moved to Lampeter—CA, 217. About half a mile S of Dihewyd there was in the 17th century, *Llwyn ffynnon ffidalis* alias *Ter Rhid ffynnon ffidalis* : St. Gwyddalus, Martyr, is said to have been patron of a former church at Dihewyd, and the present church is dedicated to St. Vitalis, the Latin form of the name—LBS, iii, 218. Llwynwyddalis is said to be the old name for Dihewyd—CA, 217. Fidelis was one of Teilo's disciples—Lib Land, 365.

FF. DDEINIOL. In the S of Penbryn parish—Evans CPC, 90. Ff. Ddinol (PR, 19 cent.) : Ff. Ddeinol (TM. 1838).

FF. DDEWI (6). 1. Near the site of Capel Dewi on Gwarcoed Isaf, Llandysul parish. Marked on Eman. Bowen Map. There was a graveyard there, and the last burial is said to have taken place about 1780. A fair was held in the graveyard in March annually, but it was removed to Llanarth because it was considered that the water of Ff. Ddewi, which was used for brewing beer for the fair, was impure owing to the proximity of the graveyard : its waters cured whooping cough—DAPL, 36 : JCD, 305. 2. In Llandygwydd parish. 3. Near the ford of Afon Ffynnon Ddewi on the main road from Llanarth to Wervilbrook : cf. *Llain ffynnon Ddewi*, SW of Wervilbrook. 4. Near Henfynyw church (ded. St. David). An old man visited this well on one Christmas Eve. He heard cries for help issuing from the well : a hand then arose and the voice asked the man to hold it tightly. He did so, but relaxed his hold. The hand then vanished into the well and the voice cried, 'I am bound for another fifty years'—Trevelyan, 14-15. A farm called Ff. Ddewi is marked on the Henfynyw terrier for 1818. 5. About half a mile from Gogoyan, Llanddewibrefi parish. *Llyfr yr Ancr* tells how Dewi was met by a woman who implored his help as her son had just died ; the saint entered the cottage and restored the son to life, whereupon a well gushed forth on the spot to mark the miracle. This well was in the kitchen of the cottage called Ff. Ddewi. 6. In Llandysilio-go-go parish. There is a tradition that Dewi rested here while walking from St. Davids : he prayed to God for water to drink with his bread : the well miraculously appeared : the saint then blessed the well, which never freezes in winter and never dries up in summer. See above p. 34.

FF. DEUDIR. In Penbryn parish.

FF. DYSUL. At the N end of Llandysul village. The saint's name was also preserved in *Tir Lloyn Tyssell* which occurs in the parish in 1573—NLW Cilgwyn Clln.

FF. FADOG (2). 1. In Penbryn parish (TM, 1838). 2. Pistyll Madoc, a farm in Llanilar parish.

FF. FAIR (7). 1. In Cwm Wernddu, Llangynllo parish : cured whooping cough and other common ills ; frequented within living memory—DPLl, 15. 2. About 1½ miles SE of Troed-yr-aur church. 3. About 1 mile SE of Llanwnen village. 4. Near Blaenporth, SE of Ff. Wen. 5. In Lampeter parish. 6. N of Llanfair Treflygen where St. Mary's church is in ruins, on the NE of which is a tumulus : *Tir ffynnon vair,* 1684—NLW Bronwydd Deeds : *Ty'r ffynnon faer*—Lhuyd, Par, iii, 93 : *Ff. Vayre,* 1734, and *Fynnonvair,* 1784—NLW Cilgwyn Deeds. 7. In Llangrannog parish.

FF. FEBWEN/FEBWYN. See above p. 44. cf. Rhyd Nebwen in Trelech ar Betws, Carms. Phillimore thinks it is now represented by Llain y Ffynnon, about 2 miles SW of Llan Llyr in Llanfihangel Ystrad parish—OPem, iv, 499 : if this is so then it would appear that there were two wells so-named, the other being in Lampeter parish. Phillimore thinks that the territorial Mabwynion (Mebwenniaun, AD 1165) is derived from the personal name Mebwyn.

FF. FIHANGEL. In Betws Bledrws parish—Lhuyd Par, iii, 87.

ST. FRIDE'S WELL. SW of Ystradmeurig, near Treffynnon—Rees Map.

FF. GARADOG. Near Rhiw Siôn Saer, between Aberystwyth and Bow Street.

FF. GARON. At Tregaron, near Glanbrenig farm. On Easter eve, children arrived with cups to drink sugared water : on Easter Day or Low Sunday, sweethearts foregathered and presented each other with white bread which they ate and washed down with water from the well—LBS, ii, 136. Large crowds, from a distance of 30 miles, gathered at Ff. Garon, and the village children drank sugared water there on Easter Monday—CM Archives (NLW) MS. 886.

FF. GEITHO. In Llangeitho parish. A farmer told Fenton that he remembered the well ' inclosed by three flags, one on each side, and the other above, inscribed with some characters, which were carried to Peterwell, the mansion of the Landlord '—Fenton TW, 11. Gwynionydd wrote a poem to it in 1867—*Caniadau,* p. 94. See LBS, ii, 102. See above p. 83.

FF. CAPEL GWNDA. In Troed-yr-aur parish, once famous for cures. It cured warts—Lhuyd Par, iii, 90. cf. Capel Gwnda farm in Penbryn parish (TM, 1838).

FF. GYBI. Near Llangybi church. ' It has been much resorted to for complaints in the limbs and eyes : but the faith in such sainted Wells is daily diminishing'—Fenton TW, 236. It was formerly roofed : the water flowed into a bath which had seats around it to accommodate bathers : the structure was in a fair state of repair in 1913. The water possessed mineral properties and relieved scrofula, scurvy, and rheumatism. There is a tradition that Cybi lived nearby at a house called Llety Gybi. Lhuyd calls it Ff. Wen. The tradition of Llech Gybi and its association with the well was still known in 1911. See above p. 15.

FF. GYNFELIN. In Llangynfelin churchyard : people bathed their feet there, and also carried water away in bottles for use as medicine—JCD, 302.

FF. GYNLLO. In Llangoedmor parish : ' extraordinary healing qualities ' were assigned to it formerly—Lewis TDW. Especially good in rheumatic cases—LBS, ii, 263.

FF. HOWEL. In Llanrhystyd parish.

FF. LAWDDOG. E of Blaen-porth. ' Sick people visited it within living memory '—Gruffydd Evans, *Story of Newcastle-Emlyn and Atpar*, 1923, 28.

FF. LEICI. In Llandygwydd parish.

FF. OWEN (3). 1. In Tremain parish. 2. Alias Ff. Wen in Llanerchaeron parish. 3. Near Pont Rhyd Owen, Llandysul parish.

FF. WENNOG. A small fair called ' ffair wenog ' was held near the church on 3 January annually—Lhuyd Par, iii, 89. The well was near the church, and its water was especially beneficial to children with weak backs, who were bathed there before sunrise—JCD, 304 : LBS, iii, 198. See above p. 109.

FF. WERFIL/WYRFIL. In the Rhydlewis district.

FF. WLADUS. *Tir ffynnon Wladus* in Llangynllo parish, near Bronwydd AD. 1562—Bronwydd Deeds.

FF. WNNWS. In Llanwnnws parish : cured eyes—Lhuyd Par. iii, 4.

FF. DRINDOD. Near Llando or Llan Ddwy, a church dedicated to the Trinity, near Cardigan—*OPem*, iii, 320 : iv, 461 : 'The Well of St. Trinity, Cardigan ', 1684—Dineley : *Old Wales* (1905), i, 317.

FF. Y DRINDOD. Mentioned by Meyrick (*Cards*, 226 ; also Arch. Cam., VI, V, 324-5, VI, 74) and is probably the well of that name at Llanilar.

CLASS B :

FF. CALLWEN. Near Cellan church : said to have given name to the church—Lhuyd Par. iii, 67, 86.

FF. CAPEL. On Rhodmad farm, Llanilar parish (TM, 1843).

FF. FENDIGAID. In Penbryn parish (TM, 1838).

FF. GLOCH. Near Llanarth church. See above p. 130.

FF. Y GROES. A short distance from Llangrannog churchyard. *Ff. Groes* (TM, 1840). Tradition states that pilgrims formerly rested at the well where they drank and made the sign of the Cross—JCD, 305. A variant says that St. Caranog made the sign of the Cross after drinking from the well. These are onomastic tales. The most probable explanation is that near the well stood an ancient cross, probably of stone. See above p. 102.

FF. GRÔG. In Verwig parish, near Mwnt. Mwnt parish church is called Eglwys y Grôg.

LLANFIHANGEL GENAU'R-GLYN. The holy well of this parish is close to the E. wall of the churchyard. In 1911 it was described as ' surrounded by a small building ' ; it had been a popular resort of people in search of health : shortly before 1911, a crippled girl from Glamorgan visited it, and was able to walk away without her crutches—JCD, 301.

FF. TRISANT. Near Devil's Bridge. There were three separate springs less than a foot apart, each said to possess a special virtue—one for the eyes, the second for wounds and sores, and the third for general complaints. Crutches left behind by cured cripples were once to be seen at the nearby farm of Dolcoion—ex. inf. Mr. Alwyn D. Rees.

CLASS C :

FF. BLAENGLOWEN FAWR. In Llandisilio gogo parish : cured sore legs, etc., and tradition speaks of cripples being cured.—JCD, 305.

FF. DYFFRYN TAWEL. Near Strata Florida there are wells whose waters contain mineral properties, and were much used by people at the beginning of this century.—CA, 33.

FF. ELWAD. In Caron Uwch Clawdd parish : a healing well, especially good for the sore breasts of women : there was a farm there called Maes Elwad—Camb. Reg., 1796, 387 : Cross D, 121-3. The names suggest a holy man. See above p. 99.

FF. FEDDYG. Near the coast, SW of Llanina.

FF. GRIPIL. Just S of Noyadd Drefawr, Llandygwydd. *Ffynnon Cripil*, 1851. The name suggests that the well cured cripples.

FF. LWLI. On Ffynnon-wen farm, Llangynllo parish : it was believed that the waters cured diarrhoea.—DPLL, 16.

FF. PWLLFFEIN. In Llandysul parish, near the river Clettwr : much visited at the begining of the last century, and pins were thrown into it : it has now been destroyed by the river.—JCD, 304.

FF. PISTYLL CYNWY. On the N of Llangynllo parish : especially noted for curing children's cough : cured ' ye chin cough in children '—Lhuyd Par. iii, 91. Query—is it identical with *Pistyll Cymru* in Cwmbach which cured coughs and lumbago—Davies, HPLl, 15.

FF. RHINWEDDAU. In Llanerchaeron parish.

CLASS D :

FF. BECCA. Between Newcastle Emlyn and Llandysul : cured sore eyes and the gravel.

FF. BLEUDUD. ' the fountain Bleydud . . Bleidud ' . . was a boundary mark in S. Cardiganshire in 1184 and 1426,—probably near Cellan—Williams, *Strata Florida*, App lvii. This OW personal name is given as *Bleidud* in *Brut Dingestow* (ed. Lewis), 1942.

FF. BUSHEL. By Lodge Park, Tre'rddôl. Tradition says that Thomas Bushel (temp. Charles I) pushed the body of his murdered wife into this well—CC, 100-1.

FF. Y CEIS. *Plase ffynnon y keis* in Verwick parish, A.D. 1586—NLW Bronwydd Deeds.

PISTYLL EINON. *Tir Pistyll Eynon* otherwise *Tir Ffynnon Eynon*, in Kellan parish, A.D. 1639—NLW Saundersfoot (Thomas) Deeds. It is SW of Cellan, near Ffrwd Cynon.

FF. ELIN. Marked on Rees Map as being NE of Carrog and S of Llanilar, and, according to Sir John Lloyd, belonging to Llanllur—*Hist. of Cardigan*, 78.

FF. FFEIRAD. In a valley joining Blaen-cwm and Faerdre Fawr, Llandysul parish. Haunted. See above p. 131.

FF. FRANCIS. On Penuchaf farm in Llanfihangel Genau'r-glyn : there is a tradition that it restored the sight of a blind old man named Francis—JCD, 301.

FF. GEINOR. At Pontsian, Llandysul parish. Ceinor was once a popular name for a girl in Cardiganshire : but cf. *Egluskeynor* in Glamorgan, A.D. 1140-48 (NLW Margam Deeds), which suggests a saint.

FF. IWAN. In Llandisilio gogo parish.

FF. LEWELIN. In Llandysul parish (1758).

FF. MEREDITH (2). 1. Between Capel Ficar and Ffwrneithin (1781). Is this the ' ffynnon Dafras alias Meredith ', a medical spring in Llanwenog parish (Lhuyd Par. iii, 89) ? 2. A farm in Llanarth parish (TM, 1837).

FF. RHYDDERCH. S. of Pwll y Bilwg, Llanfair Orllwyn parish. Tir ffynon Rhudderch otherwise Tir y Maen Gwyn, Llanfair Orllwyn parish (A.D. 1684)—NLW Bronwydd Deeds.

CLASS E :

FF. BERW. In Penbryn parish (TM 1838). Ff. y Berw, 1789. berw = cress (cresswell).

FF. DDAFRAS. In Llanwenog parish. Cf. above, Ff. Meredith (1).

FF. DDAWNOL. NW of Betws Evan.

FF. FFYN. *Cae ffynnon ffyn*, Pen-y-gaer farm, Llanrhystyd parish (TM 1839). ffîn (boundary) or ffyn (baglau) (crutches) ?

FF. Y FWYALCH. ffynon y voyalch, Bangor parish (A.D. 1547)—NLW Cilgwyn Deeds.

FF. HAIARN. *Park Fynnon Haiarn* on Panteg in Bronwydd, Llangynllo parish (1775)—NLW Bronwydd Deeds.

FF. LEFRITH (2). 1. Just SW of Brynllefrith, Llanwenog parish. 2. In Llandissilio gogo (*c*. 1700)—Golden Grove MSS.

FF. WAEDOG. Near Llech yr Ochain, Penbryn parish. There is a tradition of a battle fought between the natives and invaders—Meyrick C, 179 ; Lewis TDW. cf. Fuller's *Worthies* (ed. J. Freeman, 1952), p. 561.

FF. WARED. Three-quarters of a mile NW of Elerch village.

FF. WIN. At Aberaeron. cf. Rhyd y gwîn, S of Temple Bar, Cards.

FF. YMENYN. Ff. menin (1797) in Llanllwchaiarn. cf Nantyr-ymenin in S. Cards.

CARMARTHENSHIRE

CLASS A :

ST. ANTHONY'S WELL. In Llanstephan parish : marked on Crutchley's Map : had a great reputation as a healing well, and it is still used as a " wishing" well particularly by love-sick people. It was walled and had a niche over it in 1811, but it was not being much visited at that date—Carlisle TDW. The well chamber has been much restored and contains an arched recess and a narrow stone ledge called 'the offerings shelf'—Anc Mon Carm. : see Arch Cam., 1846, 466. Pins were offered—JCD, 302. In 1895 it was commonly called ' Ffynnon Shon Antwn ' by local people—TNEW, Llanelly, 1895, (1898), 359.

FF. BEDR (2). 1. In Cwmpengraig—HPLP, 11. 2. In Cilymaen-llwyd parish. See above p. 48.

FF. BERWYN. In Llandyfaelog, near Kidwelly. St. Berwyn was a son of Brychan—WCO, 139.

FF. CELER. In Llangeler parish, not far from the church. A little chapel stood over it, and it was visited by ' such a concourse of people that no fair in Wales can equal it in multitude ' ; crutches were left there : after bathing they went to the ' Llech ' in the churchyard on which they lay down, and if they could sleep then a cure was certain, otherwise not—Lhuyd Par. iii, 76. It was visited by the infirm during summer, ' but particularly from ye 21 of June to ye feast of St. Peter '—*ib.* According to Carlisle (TDW) it was on the Glebe near the church and he calls it ' St. Celert's Spring.' The well was probably at the foot of Allt Celer hill, near the house of Plâs Geler : no remains exist now of the well-chapel—Anc. Mon. Carm. See above p. 15.

FF. DEILO (2). 1. In Llandeilo Fawr. Bishop Rudd's will, dated 1614, mentions ' Tyrffynnondilo ' in that parish—Men. Sac, 103. 2. On the way to Mynydd y Graig, Kidwelly, near ' Cappel Tylo ' : it was especially good in cases of rheumatism, sprains, etc.—Carlisle TDW. It was also called Pistyll Teilo—*Y Cymmrodor*, 1915, 109, cf. ' Chappell Tylo ' in Kidwelly parish 1593 : ' a chapel called Chappell Tylo ' and ' Tyr Come Tylo ' in Kidwelly parish, 1622—NLW Muddlescomb Deeds. See above p. 27.

FF. DDEWI (2). 1. On Llwyn Dewi, SE of Whitland : tradition states that Dewi sent sick people to be cured at this well : it was reputed to cure sore eyes—Thomas, *Hynafion Hendygwyn-ar-Dâf*, 1868, 14. 2. Pistyll Dewi, SE of Llanarthney village : mentioned as a boundary mark (*i bistill dewi*)—Lib. Land, 74-5, 322.

FF. DUDUR. Near Drefelyn, Llangeler parish. Ff. Dydyr—Golden Grove MS. Tudur is listed as a saint in LBS. See above p. 5.

FF. DYBIE. In Llandybie parish : marked on Rees Map. Fenton (TW, 60) says it was 'formerly much resorted to.' The poet Job wrote a poem on this well—*Caniadau Job*, 80.

FF. DYSSUL. NE of Pantglas House, Llanfynydd parish.

ST. ELLEN'S WELL. *Saint Elen is Wille* near *Frogmerstret* in Kidwelly, 1445—NLW Muddlescomb Deeds.

FF. ELLI. In Llanelly parish : a healing well—JCD, 304. cf. *Gweine Elli* in Llanelly parish 1578—Muddlescomb Deeds.

FF. FAIR (4). 1. Near Kidwelly castle ; pilgrimages were made to it on Lady Day and pins were offered within living memory. See above p. 46. 2. *Tire y Finnon Vayr*, Pembrey parish, 1558—NLW Muddlescomb Deeds. 3. In 1214, King John confirmed lands to Whitland Abbey, among which was Ff. Fair or Oer—Lloyd, *Hist. of Carm.*, i, 351. 4. On Llwynffynnon land, Llangeler parish : Capel Mair is not far from it—HPLP, 12. It is in Cae Ff. Fair, and was probably associated with Capel Mair, a chapel of ease in the parish—Anc. Mon. Carm.

FF. FAIR (FAGDALEN). In St. Clears parish, ' Ffynnon Fair or Lady Well, and Ffynnon y Cyff supply the town with water '—Lhuyd, Par. iii, 60. See above p. 48.

FF. FIHANGEL. In a small well-chamber on Parc Sion Edward, Kidwelly, St. Mary parish : formerly a popular resort on Palm Sunday : not far away stood the medieval chapel of St. Michael—Anc. Mon. Carm. *Saint Michells Well* in Kidwelly parish, 1575 : *Michaells Well*, 1635—Muddlescomb Deeds. Cf. *Seynt Mighell is Chappell* within the foreignry of Kidwelly, 1505—*ib.*

FF. FIL FEIBION. Near Llandilo. See above p. 3.

FF. FOIDA. S of Llanboidy : believed to be medicinal. Ff. Voida 1780—NLW Llwyngwair Deeds. See above p. 4.

FF. FRYNACH. About half a mile W of Llanboidy church : curative : the well chamber is too small for immersion—Anc. Mon. Carm. In the district was *Pant Brynagh*, 1597—PRO, AD, F 448. See above p. 40.

FF. GARMON. In Llanfihangel Yoreth parish.

FF. GATHEN. In Llangathen parish. *kae ffynnon gathen* 1675, Evans and Williams Deeds. This field still so named is on Allt y Gaer farm but there is now no trace of the well.—Anc Mon Carm.

FF. GWENLAIS. In Llanfihangel Aberbythych parish. ' Gwenlaish springs at Cappel Gwenlais '—Lhuyd. There is no chapel today. See above pp. 2, 44. This well is the source of the river Gwenlais.

FF. GYNOG. S of Pantglas on Park Cynog farm : described as *Canockes well* in 1580—Arch. Cam., 1097, 273 : NCPN, pp. xliii, 109. St. Cynog was a son of Brychan. Llangynog is not far distant.

FF. IAGO (3). 1. In Cilymaenllwyd near the boundary with Llandissilio East (Pem.). 2. W of Mynydd Ystefflau-garn, Llanllawddog. 3. In Llanybyther parish ; on Ff. Iago farm is a field wherein, according to tradition, stood the medieval chapel of Sant Iago : the well is in the next field.—Anc. Mon. Carm.

FF. LAWDDOG. In a wood on Bron Llawddog, near Penboyr church—HPLP, 12. Marked on Rees Map.

FF. NON. In Llannon parish. Tradition says that Non drew water from it.—JCD, 303 : TNEW Llanelly 1898 (1897), 361. See above p. 42.

FF. SAWYL. In Llansawel ; supplies the village. Marked on Rees Map as *Pistyll Sawel*. Cf. the chapel of Pistyllsawil, Talley Charter 1331—*Hist. of Llansawel*, 15. Sawyl Ben Uchel (sometimes Isel) is named in old Welsh pedigrees as a Carmarthenshire prince : see under Ff. Sul below. See above p. 27.

ST. STEPHEN'S WELL. Near Llan-y-bri church.

FF. SUL. A spring that until a few years ago flowed into a well at the foot of the rising ground behind Kidwelly castle : the hill was called *mons Solomonis* in an ancient grant (Dudgale, *Monast.* ed. Ellis, iv, 64) : in a lease, temp Edward VI, the well is called *Saynt Sondaye's Well*, and in 1779 a Kidwelly town record mentions a field called *Park ffynnon Sul* : the water now supplies the town : it has been suggested that the name derives from Selyf—Anc Mon Carm. *Funnon Syell* within the liberty of Kidwelly, 1597 : *Parke Ffynon Syll* in the liberty of Kidwelly, 1669 : *Sondayes Well*, 1624, and *Sundays Well* 1678, in the said liberty—NLW Muddlescomb Deeds. Tradition relates that a prince named Benisel was slain here, and the well rose to mark the spot, and that Sul is a corruption of his name—Lloffwr, 431. Tradition has evidently forgotten that his full name was Sawyl Benisel, but it does seem possible that the name may have been derived from Sawyl, especially as the earliest form is *Syell*. In view of this personal and unusual combination of names appearing in early Carmarthenshire pedigrees, this tradition is extremely interesting. 'St. Sunday's Well' is clearly a translation here, but it should be noted that a 'St. Sunday's Well' existed in Dublin in 1624—B. Ryche, *A New Irish Prognostication*, 1624.

CLASS B :

FF. CAPEL (2). 1. Near Capel Drindod alias Capel Bach, between Dre-fach and Felindre—HPLP, 11. 2. In Llanfihangel Rhos y corn : a yew grew over it and there was a tradition of a chapel.—Carlisle TDW.

FF. CAPEL BEGEWDIN. In Llanddarog parish. See above p. 28.

FF. CAPEL HERBACH/ERBACH. In Llanarthney parish. See above p. 29.

FF. CAPEL PEN ARW. In Llangathen parish : near the side of an old chapel within half a mile from the parish church : was once credited with curing sore eyes and rheumatism—Carlisle TDW. The well is called Ff. y Capel, and is at Allt y Capel. There are no traces of the chapel today, but a fragment of masonry can be traced round the well (1913)—Anc. Mon. Carm.

FF. GWYDDFAEN. Called now Ff. Llandyfaen ' near an old ruined chapel ' in Llandyfaen parish—Rees, *Beauties of S. Wales*, 1815, 321. ' a square stone tank, anciently a baptistry for the use of the early Christian Church at the little chapel of Llanduvaen '—Lewis TDW. ' It is enclosed in a square building with steps going down to it, uncovered . . . Near is a small chapel served once a month '—Fenton TW, 60. It was celebrated for its cure of paralytic affections, numbness and scorbutic humours—Carlisle TDW. See above p. 60, 71, 115. Lluyd calls the well ' Gwydd-vaen.' See D Jones, *Hanes y Bedyddwyr* . . . , 1839, 347.

LLANPUMSAINT WELLS. Near Llanpumsaint. Tradition says that there were five wells there used by five saints : in former days, between 200 and 300 people gathered there on St. Peter's Day : in summer the local people suffering from ' aches ' bathed in the wells—JCD, 301. See above p. 2.

FF. LUAN. Both Ff. Lluan and the chapel of Llanlluan, between Mynydd Mawr and Llanarthney, are marked on Rees Map.

FF. SAINT (2). 1. Close to Tabor chapel, Llan-saint, St. Ishmaels parish : now covered and a pump erected over it.—Anc. Mon. Carm. It was associated with the parish church described in 1115-1147 as *ecclesia omnium sanctorum*, and as *chapel of Saint*, in 30-1 Henry VII. cf. Ff. Saint in Llangyfelach and Saint Well SW of Caerau church, Glam. ; Ff. y Saint, Criccieth, Caern. ; Rhyd Saint just SE of the site of the chapel of St. Mordeyrn, Denb. ; and *Maen*

Sainte, Llangyndeyrn parish, 1620 (NLW. Muddlescomb Deeds). 2. S. of Nantyci, on the border of the Borough of Carmarthen—CN, map opp. p. 26.

FF. SANCTAIDD. Over a mile NE of Llanddarog parish church : within a small enclosure 3 feet square and 2 feet deep : the overflow passes into a stone trough 2 feet by 1½ feet.—Anc. Mon. Carm.

FF. CRAIG CEFFYL. A chalybeate spring S of Llandilo—Carlisle TDW.

FF. FFOS ANA. In Cynwyl parish : of high repute—Carlisle TDW. Cripples are said to have been cured there—JCD, 305. There was a circle of stones around it—Lloffwr, 427. It had a high reputation for healing. See above pp. 16, 101.

FF. FRON LAS. On Bron Las farm, Trelech parish : believed to possess curative virtues : its water was drunk before sunrise—TNEW, Llanelly 1895, (1898), 360.

FF. GAING. In St. Clears parish : accounted medicinal—Lhuyd Par. iii, 60.

FF. GAREDIG. In Llanllwni parish.

PISTYLL GOLEU. On the river Taf : cured rheumatism and weak sinews—Carlisle TDW.

PISTYLL GWYN. In Llandyfaelog parish : formerly well-known for curing sore eyes—Lewis TDW.

FF. LYGAID. In the middle of Llanfynydd Bog : a column of mist, 15 feet high, is seen over it occasionally on frosty mornings : it is said to cure bad eyes—ex inf. Mr. Alwyn D. Rees.

NEW WELL/FF. NEWYDD. In Llangynog parish. Judge Vaughan of Derllys is said to have been cured there—Lewis, TDW. At Ff. Newydd there is ‘ a curious cromlech ’—Arch. Cam., 1907, 273, 369. See p. 171.

FF. Y PENTRE. Near Drysgol, Llandybie : cured sore eyes, and has been used ‘ lately ’ (1939)—HPLl, 287.

FF. Y PISTYLL. On land called Pistyll near Kidwelly : cured sore eyes—TNEW Llanelly 1895 (1898), 360 : JCD, 305.

FF. STOCKWELL. On a slope called Arles, Kidwelly St. Mary parish : it was visited so recently as Palm Sunday 1911 by parents and their children for the purpose of throwing in bent pins, of drinking water sweetened with sugar, and for invoking good wishes : a generation ago, special cups were kept in the homes for this purpose : the water is much prized for its coldness—Anc. Mon. Carm. *Stockewyll* 1533, *Stock Well* 1596, and *Stocke Well Street* 1622—NLW Muddlescomb Deeds.

CLASS D :

FF. BECA. In Park y Beca, near Llwynbedw—HPLP, 11. ' lately (1811) discovered, called Rebecca's Well ', and much resorted to—Carlisle TDW ; cured gravel and sore eyes, much resorted to within ' living memory ' (1911)—JCD, 305. The water was believed to be more efficacious in the morning before sunrise, and many a company travelled all night in order to drink from the well before sunrise—Lloffwr, 425 : TNEW, Llanelly 1895 (1898), 359.

FF. BRODYR (2). 1. Ff. Brodyr, a farm in Cilymaenllwyd parish, 1766—WWHR, xiv, 232. 2. Ff. Frodyr, in Pentre Court.

FF. Y CAWR. NW of Cross Hands.

FF. Y FORWYN. In Ff. y Forwyn Wood, near Llysnewydd—HPLP, 11. cf. the p.n. Bedd y Forwyn in Cellan parish, Cards—Lhuyd Par. iii, 86 : and Maidenwells, Pem.

FF. FRANCIS. At the junction of the Carmarthen-Abergwili roads.

FF. GWENNO. In Cynwyl Gaio : once famous as a healing well : a crag is called Clochty Gwenno : mining operations have resulted in the almost entire disappearance of the well by 1913—Anc. Mon. Carm. Pins were offered there. See above p. 131.

JOB'S WELL. Carmarthen. ' In the lower Franchise there is a large spring called Job's Well wch inhabitants and foreigners finde to be very medicinal in the cure of scabs, ulcers and rickets '—Lhuyd Par. iii, 26. Marked on Eman. Bowen's Map. John Dyer, the poet, when a child, entered in his diary, '1709. Fell into a well—Job's Well, Carm'thens.'

FF. JOSI. On a mountainside between Llannon church and Tumble: a curative well of considerable repute : at one time an effort was made to commercialise its waters : there is a tumulus in the vicinity.

THE KING'S WELL. At Laugharne: also called 'The Fairy Well'—CAL, 13.

FF. NATHAN. On the tope of a hill near Duke's Bottom, Laugharne, are three wells, called Ff. Nathan from the name of the owner: one cured weak and inflamed eyes, the second rheumatism, the third wounds: to cure rheumatism the water was mixed with clay and made into a plaster which was applied to the affected part: during the latter part of the 17th century, a Scots doctor enclosed these wells—CAL, 269. See above p. 5.

STEWARD'S WELL, 'a well called the Stewardes Well' Kidwelly 1600; *Warr Fynnon Steward,* Kidwelly, 1624—NLW Muddlescomb Deeds.

FF. YEROTH. *Fynnon Yeroth,* Llanarthney parish 1625—Badminton Deeds.

CLASS E:

FF. ANGAU. Near Felindre, Llangeler. Ff. yr Angau—HPLP, 11.

FF. YR ARMY. At Pen y Gaer, Llandingat Without, is the site of an ancient camp which was well-defined, until 1833, when it was levelled. Ff. yr Army is not far from the Gaer, and it is said that near the well there were traces of 'charcoal' and other evidences of 'a bivouac'—Arch. Cam., 1873, 136.

CARREG CENNEN CASTLE WELL. Under the castle is a passage and a cave, and at the end of this cave is a well 'still' (1911) used as a 'wishing'-well: many pins were found in it—JCD, 302. The well was 'a singular curiosity'—Carlisle TDW.

FF. DDAGRAU. N of Llangynog church, at the SW of Moelfre Wood.

FF. DDWFACH. In Llanegwad parish, c. 1700—NLW Trewern Deeds.

FF. EIDION. NE of Gelli-deg, Llandyfaelog.

FF. FERGAM. Near river Corrwg, S of Llanpumsaint. Ff. Vergam—Eman. Bowen Map.

FF. FFWLBERT. On W bank of river Taf, just S of Llanglydwen church.

FF. FLOIDDAST. There are fields in Cwmtywyll and Panty-porthman called Cae Ff. Floiddast and Bron Ff. Floiddast.—HPLP, 153.

FF. Y GIACH. In Kilrhedyn parish.

FF. HALOG. In Pembrey parish.

LLANDYFEISANT WELL. An ebb and flow well : the stream flowing from it is called Nant y Rhibo—Carlisle TDW : Gwallter Mechain calls the well " Ffynhon Reibio ' (*General View . . . of S. Wales*, i, 108).

PISTYLL LLWYFEN. Between Llangathen church and Cilsan.

PISTYLL Y MARCH. E of Llanfynydd.

FF. MEHERIN. In Henllan Amgoed parish. Cf. *Castell Meherin*, an earthwork in the neighbouring parish of Ludchurch (Pem.). It seems possible that a personal name is involved.

PISTYLL NEFOL. *Pistyll Nevoll*, Llangeler parish, 1538-40—PRO, Lands of Dissolved Religious Houses, No. 4903.

FF. NEWYDD (2). 1. In Llanpumsaint parish where a standing megalith is called Carreg Ff. Newydd. 2. In Llanegwad parish, where there is also a Carreg Ff. Newydd. See p. 168.

FF. NONNY. At Llanllwnny—Carlisle TDW. Near a tumulus called Y Castell on Maes Nonny farm where a nunnery is reputed to have been—Lewis TDW.

FF. NYNUDD. In St. Ishmaels parish.

FF. OLBRI. Close to Llan-y-bri village.

FF. OLCWM. Near Dyffryn Olcwm, Llan-y-bri.

FF. RADUS. In Cwmpencraig.

FF. ROWYLL. In Llanelly parish 1581—NLW Muddlescomb Deeds.

FF. WIBER. In Newchurch parish. Ff. y wiber 1784.

FF. WICHELL. Near Rhiw Aberlleinau. Cf. Bryn Wichell, Blaenpennal, Cards.

FF. YMENIN. In Llanelly parish.

FF. YNID. Between Tripenhad and Trecor : the element *ynid* may be contained also in Tripenhad.

DENBIGHSHIRE

CLASS A :

FF. ARMON (2). 1. In Llanarmon parish, 'formerly much frequented'—Lhuyd Par. i, 157. It is near a place, called 'The Saint's Crossing', and the field to the N of the site is called Cae'r Saint—Anc. Mon. Denb. It is said to have miraculous properties—Lewis TDW. 2. In Llanrwst Rural parish, about 500 yards NE of the church of St. Garmon : surrounded by rough masonry, but now choked with ferns and has almost disappeared—Anc. Mon. Denb. Capel Garmon is in the parish.

FF. ASA (2). 1. In Llannefydd parish—Lhuyd Par. i, 154 : Anc. Mon. Denb. 2. In Gweirglodd Ffynnon Asa, Eglwysfach parish—Lhuyd Par. i, 34. This meadow adjoins the village street of Eglwysfach, and a pump is installed over the well—Anc. Mon. Denb.

FF. BEDR (2). 1. Near Allington church and about 450 yards NW of St. Peter's Chapel : possessed a reputation for the cure of sore eyes and sprained limbs, and was still being visited at the begining of the present century—Anc. Mon. Denb. 2. In Ruthin parish.

FF. DDEINIOL. In Bangor Monachorum parish. Ff. 'Dheniol' —Lhuyd Par. i, 136. See Palmer, *Ancient Tenures, etc*, 1910, 245-6.

FF. DDEUNO. On Gatewen farm, Broughton parish : a small chapel was said to have stood over Ff. 'Dheyno'—Lhuyd Par. i, 132. The well has ceased to flow, but the ruins remain. Deeds of Gatewen, 1738-1824, name that farm 'Ffynnon Beuno alias Capel Beuno,' and the late Sir E. Anwyl said that 'Ddeuno may be for Feuno by interchange of spirants'—Anc. Mon. Denb.

FF. DDOGED. About 60 yards N of Llanddoged church: protected by an enclosure of masonry—Lhuyd, Par. i, 29: Anc. Mon. Denb. Doged is numbered among Welsh saints—CBS, 209. A King Doged occurs in Culhwch and Olwen—Mab. J, 96.

FF. DDYFNOG. About 200 yards W of Llanrhaeadr-yng-Nghinmeirch parish church. Called by Leland 'Fonnon Dunnoc: S Dunokes Welle a mighty spring' (Itin.): much frequented for the cure of scabs and itch, and some said it cured pox—Lhuyd, i, 110. '... provided with all conveniences of rooms, etc., for bathing, built about it'—Willis, *Bangor*, 327. '... arched over, from which the Water used to fall through a Pipe in the Wall into a Bath, whose bottom was paved with Marble, with a building round it and roofed, but now exhibiting one shapeless ruin ...'—Fenton TW, 157. 'The fountain was inclosed in an angular well, decorated with small human figures, and before the well for the use of pious bathers'—Pennant, *Tours*, ed. Rhys, ii, 180. See above, pp. 35, 50, 62, 66, 70.

FF. DEGLA. In Llandegla parish: the well chamber is about 7 feet by 5 feet, and the well is about 4 feet by 3 feet and about 1 foot deep: said to cure epilepsy (Clwyf Tecla) and offerings of fowls were made and coins thrown into the well—Anc Mon Denb. It was said to cure the King's Evil—T. Frimston, *Ofergoelion yr Hen Gymry*, p. 51. See WFB, 278-81: Thomas, St. Asaph, ii, 90: Arch. Cam. 1891, 14. In 1935 the well was excavated by Mr. Alwyn D. Rees, who found in it coins, pins, small fragments of pottery, and dozens of pieces of quartz and calcite—BBCS, Nov. 1935, pp. 87-90. See above pp. 72, 95, 101, 104.

FF. DIGAUN/DIGAIN. In Coed Digain about a mile from Llangernyw parish church which is dedicated to St. Digain: the well is covered with masonry—Anc Mon Denb.

FF. DRILLO. In Llansannan parish, about a mile and a half from the church.

FF. DUDUR. About one mile SE of Llanelidan.

FF. DYSSILIO. In Bryn Eglwys parish, whose church is dedicated to St. Tyssilio—Lhuyd Par., i, 122.

FF. ELIAN. About 600 yards N of the parish church of Llanelian yn Rhos, and just within the township of Eirias: the well has been filled up and has practically disappeared, but the old cobbled pathway to it was still visible in 1912—Anc. Mon. Denb. YHC : *Cambria Depicta*, 1816 : TGJ : LBS. s.n. See above pp. 71, 72, 103, 119-123.

FF. ELWOC. In the township of Hendregyda in Abergele Rural parish : curative, but now neglected and the name forgotten—Anc. Mon. Denb. The well has disappeared within living memory—LBS, ii, 432. Pins were offered there—Lhuyd Par, i, 44. Lhuyd calls it Elwoc [? Elwoe] : LBS calls it Elwoe : the local pronunciation in 1931 was Eflo : the name is probably from Elfodd—Arch. Cam., 1931, 170. See above p. 108.

FF. FADOG. In Llanddoged parish. '*Fynnon Vadog*'—Lhuyd Par. i, 29.

FF. FAIR (6). 1. In Wigfair, Cefn parish : it flowed within a small well-chapel now in ruins—Anc. Mon. Denb. It was ruined in Lhuyd's time who says that the ' gwyl ' of Mary was held there——Par. i, 47. According to Cwtta Cyfarwydd (MS) clandestine marriages were celebrated there as late as 1640—Arch. Cam., 1887, plan of well and chapel : see *ibid*, 1847, 261, illustr. Fenton mentions the well '*and ruins of its pretty Chapel*'—TW, 147. Mrs. Hemans wrote a poem on the well. 2. In Derwen parish '*just under ye Church*'—Lhuyd Par. i, 120. 3. Near Denbigh—Lhuyd 1, 105. 4. Near Ff. Ddyfnog in Llanrhaiadr yng Nghymeirch parish—Lhuyd Par. i, 110. 5. In Llanfair Dyffryn Clwyd parish—Lhuyd Par. i, 150. 6. In a field belonging to Plasdy, Pen-y-cae parish : it is named in a survey made in 1620—Anc. Mon. Denb.

FF. FAIR FAGDALEN. About 200 yards NE of Cerrigydrudion church : enclosed on three sides by rough masonry, and on the fourth side by two upright stones : three steps at the NW corner lead to the water—Anc. Mon. Denb. According to Lhuyd there was an older well in Cae Tydyr, which is about a mile SW of the church—Par. i, 116. The church is dedicated to St. Mary Magdalene.

FF. FARCHELL. In Denbigh parish about 450 yards from the church : curative : coins were thrown into the well : there is no trace of it now, except the channel which took the water away—Anc. Mon. Denb : Lhuyd Par. i, 108.

FF. ST. FFRAID. Within a quarter mile from Llansanffraid parish church—Lhuyd Par. i, 35.

ST. GEORGE'S WELL. In St. George's parish: also called Ffynnon Gegidog: covered by a chamber of large stones—Anc. Mon. Denb. See above p. 106.

FF. GOLLEN. Near Llangollen: associated with St. Collen. See above p. 39.

FF. GWAS PATRIG. In Cerrigydrudion parish—Lhuyd Par. i, 16

FF. GYNHAFAL. About a quarter mile from Llangynhafal church: in an enclosure 10 feet by 18 feet: reputed to cure warts which were pricked with a pin, which was then thrown into the well—Arch. Cam., 1846, 54: Anc. Mon. Denb. See above p. 62.

FF. ITHEL. A periodic spring in Abergele parish—NLW MS. 8379. '*Ffynnon Ithel tan y maen gwyn*' [in Llanddulas, but now included in Abergele Urban parish]—Lhuyd Par. i, 44.

FF. MORDEYRN. About 250 yards N of Nantglyn parish church: the ruins of Capel Mordeyrn, mentioned by Leland, were near the church—Anc. Mon. Denb.

FF. NEFYDD. About 300 yards from Llannefydd church: called Ff. Yfydd by Lhuyd Par. i, 154.

FF. SADWRN. At Foxhall in Henllan parish—Lhuyd Par. i, 105. The name is forgotten, but the well may be identical with the ancient spring on the side of the road from Denbigh to Bwlch Sadwrn in Henllan, and is protected by some rough walling (1911)—Anc. Mon. Denb. The parish church is dedicated to St. Sadwrn.

FF. SILIN. By the roadside near Tyn Llan in Llansilin parish: the spring is said to have been formerly in the middle of the field behind its present position, and to have been destroyed by the owner of the land who filled up the old well chamber.—Anc. Mon. Denb.

FF. WENFIL. '*In the township of Eryrys, half a mile below ye Church by the river*' (in Llanarmon parish)—Lhuyd Par. i, 157. Now marked on maps as Wenwyl, the well is about 20 yards from the river Alun, and its waters were reputed to relieve sprained limbs——Anc. Mon. Denb.

FF. WNNOD. This well is now called Fron Fach Spring, and is near Melysfan, Llangwm parish. A quarter of a mile from the church—Lhuyd Par. ii, 53. The church, formerly dedicated to SS. Gwnnod and Nathan, is now dedicated to St. Jerome.

FF. Y DRINDOD. In Llanforda parish.

CLASS B :
FF. BRAWD. In Cerrigydruidion parish : cured warts, etc.—Lhuyd, Par. i, 116.

FF. Y CAPEL. In Gresford parish : cured eyes—Lhuyd i, 144.

FF. Y CREIRIWR. On Llywenny Green, Denbigh—Lhuyd Par. i, 105. Earlier forms may determine whether or not the name is connected with *crair* (relic). Cf. Ff. Crair p. 215 below.

HOLY WELL. In Burton parish.

FF. NEWYDD. In Llanrwst Rural parish : enclosed by a large roofed building with a dressing room and other conveniences : doubtless a healing well, but no traditions have survived.—Anc. Mon. Denb.

FF. OEROG. In Llangollen Rural parish : much visited by rheumatic patients : in 1911 a man was seen bathing his sprained shoulder there—Anc. Mon. Denb.

FF. Y PASC. In the upper part of Llanelidan parish. See above p. 118.

FF. Y SAINT (3). 1. In Bangor Monachorum parish—Lhuyd Par. i, 136. 2. Near the church in Gresford parish—Lhuyd Par. i, 144 : Anc. Mon. Denb. 3. In Tre'r Nant Tin, near Bryn Gwyn, Llanddulas parish : it was held in great veneration and had masonry around it which was ruinous in 1866 : on ' a certain Sunday in summer ', multitudes visited the well and practised hydromancy ; after the ceremony the people repaired to a little house called Cefn-y-fedwen where the remainder of the day was spent in revelry and drunkenness : the family of Cefn-y-fedwen always provided the ale and derived great profit therefrom—NLW MS. 8379: mentioned by Lhuyd Par. i, 44.

CLASS C :
FF. AWEN. In the upper part of Llanrhaeadr DC, near Denbigh : a healing well—Mont. Coll., 1893, 283. See above p. 95.

FF. ERDDIG. In Gresford parish : ' *a pur[gative] water much resorted to* '—Lhuyd Par. i, 144.

FF. SARA. Near Pyllau Perl in Derwen : pins were offered there —Cymru, viii, 9 : believed to cure cancers—Carlisle TDW : and rheumatism. Crutches were often left at the cottage near the well which was burned down about 1860—Anc. Mon. Denb. Lhuyd called it *Ffynnon pyllie perl.*

CLASS D :

FF. ARTHUR. In Llangollen parish—Lhuyd Par. i, 113 : Anc. Mon. Denb.

FF. Y BRENIN. Near Ffordd y Saeson, in Llanarmon Dyffryn Ceiriog parish.—Anc. Mon. Denb.

FF. Y DOCTOR. In Ruthin parish—Lhuyd Par. i, 147.

FF. MEIRCHION. Close to Llys Meirchion, E of Henllan village.

CLASS E :

BEDWELL. In Royton. See NCPN, 205. Ff. Daniel was near.

FF. Y CWRW. Near Bwlch Gwyn : now called Ff. Groyw—RJT, 70.

FF. DDOL. In Llanddulas parish : said to be bottomless—Lhuyd Par. i, 44. It was also called Ffynnon y Ddol Erw Llyw. See above p. 132.

FF. Y FIGIN. '*phynnon y Vigin ym mynydh Elian*'—Lhuyd Par. i, 37.

FF. Y FUWCH FRECH. In Henllan parish—Lhuyd Par. i, 105. See above p. 6.

FF. LLAETHOG. NW of Cefn-brith.

FF. Y MEIRCH—W of Ff. Abel in Betws-yn-Rhos parish.

FF. NAID Y MARCH—N of Llyn Bran.

FF. SAEREN. In Llanynys parish—Lhuyd Par. i, 113.

FF. SIDS. In Llanynys parish. '*Ffynnon Sids ym mynydd y Sceibion*'—Lhuyd Par. i, 113.

FF. WEN. In Henllan parish : there are ruins of two buildings nearby, one having been a bath-house fed by water from the well, and the other a dressing room provided with a fireplace—Anc. Mon. Denb : Lhuyd, Par. i, 152.

FF. WRROL. In Llanfair Dyffryn Clwyd parish—Lhuyd Par. i. 150.

FLINTSHIRE

CLASS A

FF. ASA. In Cwm parish : said to ebb and flow : Richard Parry of Pwll-Alog, Esq, 'sett neat pillars about it'—Lhuyd Par. i, 64. Visited by sufferers from rheumatism and nervous complaints—Carlisle TDW. Dr. Johnson states it was covered with a building which had disappeared—*Diary of a Journey into N. Wales in 1774.* p. 77. Pennant says it was enclosed '*with stone in a polygonal form*'—Tours, ii, 113, edn. Rhŷs. See above p. 69.

FF. BEUNO (2). 1. Beneath a tree in a meadow near Castle Hill in Holywell Urban parish—Anc. Mon. Flint. 2. South of Tremeirchion village, enclosed by a wall : the overflow passes through the mouth of a carved stone representing a human head.—Arch. Cam, 1897, 123, sketch.

ST. BRIDE'S WELL. In Disserth parish.

CHADWELL. Near the church (ded. St. Chad.) in Hanmer parish. Noticed by Lhuyd Par. i, 142.

FF. DANIEL. In Bangor Is-y-coed parish. Anc. Mon. Flint.

FF. DDEIER. About 300 yards from Bodfari parish church. See above p. 90, 105.

FF. FAEL Y SULIEN. In Cwm parish : also called Vicarage Spring : reputed to cure ophthalmic cases : the covering of the well chamber bears the date 1772—Anc. Mon. Flint : Lhuyd Par. i, 64.

FF. FAIR (8). 1. In Northop parish—Lhuyd Par. i, 89. 2. In Halkyn parish churchyard—Lhuyd Par. i, 84. 3. In Newmarket parish—Lhuyd Par. i, 60. 4. In Whitford parish where there is also a Llyn Ffynnon Fair—Lhuyd Par. i, 74. 5. About half a mile W of Sceifog parish church—Lhuyd Par. i, 77 : '*now entirely neglected'*—Lewis TDW. 6. In Cwm parish, '*wrth y Vicariaeth'*—Lhuyd Par. i, 64. Cf. Ff. Fael a Sulien above. 7. Near Meliden church which is dedicated to Mary : the well is said to have also been known as St. Melyd's Well—Anc. Mon. Flint. 8. In Rhuddlan parish—Lhuyd Par. i, 52.

FF. FELID. In Gallt Melid township, Meliden parish—Lhuyd Par. i, 55.

FF. FIHANGEL (4). 1. In Bodfari parish : needles were offered for the cure of warts, sore eyes, etc—Lhuyd, Par. i, 70. 2. In Newmarket parish—Lhuyd Par. i, 60. 3. In Cilcain parish—*ib*, i, 80-1. 4. In Caerwys parish : cured sore eyes, warts : Afon Mihangel flows from it—*ib*, i, 67-8.

FF. OSWALLT/OSWALD. In Whitford parish : a field near the well is called Aelod Oswald commemorating the tradition that St. Oswald was dismembered at his martyrdom—HWG, 156. His chief well was at Oswestry.

FF. GWYFAN. A short distance from Disserth church : it once contained trout—Lhuyd i, 153 : it is now drained—LBS, ii, 202. The church is dedicated to St Cwyfan.

FF. GYNGAR. In Eastyn (Queen's Hope) within a field of the church—Lluyd Par. i, 98. cf. Penginger, Breck.

FF. LEUCU. Now called Ffynnon Cilhaul. '*Ffynnon Leiki alias ff Kilhayl'*—Lhuyd Par. i, 64.

ST. WINIFRED'S WELL/FF. GWENFREWI. In Holywell, see above pp. 38, 39, 49-50, 59, 62, 64, 65, 66, 70, 72, 77, 82, 102, 113.

CLASS B :

FF. FEDW. In Caerwys parish. '*Ffynnon vedw y Tervyn lle bydhis ar darllen yn amser Profesfiwn'*—Lhuyd Par. i, 68.

WHITEWELL. Just W of Oak Bank, and SW from Iscoed Park. Alongside the well is Whitewell chapel and graveyard. See NCPN, 212.

CLASS C : None.

CLASS D :

FF. ADDA. SE of Bagillt.

FF. BARIS. In Hope parish near Rhos Estyn—Lhuyd Par. i, 98.

GOBLIN'S WELL. In Mold Rural parish, in Maes Garmon field.

CLASS E :
FF. BWBACH. In Cwm parish. See above p 132.

FF. CRAIG ARTHUR. In Rhydylwfnaid parish. Lhuyd Par. i, 60.

FF. EULO. In Hawarden parish. '*a Well in Ewlo yt had formerly a wooden dish*'—Lhuyd Par. i, 95.

FF. FIGIN. In Llanasa parish, *near ye Church vizt within a stone's cast, above ye Church*—Lhuyd Par. i, 58.

FF. LEFRAITH. In Caerwys parish—Lhuyd Par. i, 68.

FF. LEINW. In Cilcain parish—Lhuyd Par. i, 80-1. *fons non procul a Rudhelan in provincia de Tegengel*—Giraldus, *Works*, vi, 137. Said to ebb and flow. Noticed by Camden and Pennant.

FF. WYRYD. In Caerwys parish.

GLAMORGAN

CLASS A :
ST. ANNE'S WELL. Near Llanfihangel church : it was covered and the water flowed through the breasts of a female bust sculptured upon a stone slab, which was believed to represent St. Anne—Arch. Cam. 1888, 409, illustr.

BAGLAN WELL. Marked near Baglan Hall on Eman Bowen Map. Some equate it with Ff Pant yr Arian, whither in the 19th century, ricketty and other sick children were carried—HVN, 200. See above pp. 66, 85, 89.

FF. BARRUC. On Barry Is., said to cure King's evil, fevers, agues, sore eyes and pains in the head—Lhuyd Par. iii, 45, 73 : visited by women who washed their eyes in it on Holy Thursday and offered pins—Carlisle TDW. See above pp 98, 101.

ST. BLEDDIAN'S WELL. In Llanbleddian parish, 1580—Hopkin James, *Old Cowbridge*, 119.

FF. DEILO (2). 1. On the right side of the old road leading from the E end of Llandaff cathedral to the old ruined palace : once believed to possess miraculous healing powers—EG, 277 : for a photograph of the well, taken about 1903, and a good description see Arch.Cam., 1933, 350. cf. Erw Deilo (A.D.1535), a piece of land belonging to Llandaff Manor. See above p. 17. 2. Half a mile SE of Pendoylan.

ST. DENIS' WELL. In Llanishen parish : considered efficacious in scorbutic complaints—Carlisle TDW. It is probably identical with Ff. Llandenis near Capel Denis, which was visited by people with sore eyes : in 1905 it was described as a shallow pool inside the northernmost enclosure of Roath Park—Matthews, *Cardiff Records*, 368.

FF. DDERFEL. See above p. 56.

FF. DDEWI (3). 1. Near Llangyfelach church : a fair was held at Llangyfelach on St. David's Day—Arch. Cam., 1920, 364. 2. On the coast, just S of Southerndown, St. Bride's Major. 3. In Moor Road, Newton Nottage, Porthcawl : the little valley was called Dewiscumbe in the 12th century : there was once a chapel near the well, and the remains of a roadway called Heol y Capel can still be traced through the Croft leading from the well to the chapel site : nearby is Cwrt Offeiriad. Dewiscwm is now called The Rhyll. It was said in 1938, ' a few years ago there was but a muddy heap of stones by the way-side ; lately a partial restoration has been attempted . . '—HAC, 47, and see p. 50, *ib*, for a sketch of the well and three large trees growing around it. It is marked on Rees Map.

FF. DYDFIL. In Merthyr Tydfil : said to be named after one of Brychan's martyred daughters.

FF. DYFRIG (2). 1. In Llanvithyn parish : a healing spring *Ff. Dyfri*—CBS, 379. 2. Ff. Dyfry in Coed Ff. Dyfrig, near Carnllwyd, Llancarfan parish.

ST. FAGAN'S WELL. See above p. 66.

FF. FAIR (14). 1. Not far from Reynoldston Church ; near a megalith : also called ' Holy Well ' and ' Lady Well '—Carlisle TDW : Lewis TDW : Trevelyan, 131. 2. St. George parish, reputed to possess great restorative powers. 3. In Cwm Nash valley, Monknash parish, near the site of an old chapel. 4. ' Pant y ffynnon vayr ' on the Aberpergwm estate, 1722—VN, 199. 5. On the Corntown coast. 6. Near Ewenny—Fenton TW, 348. 7. 300 yards from Llangynwyd church. 8. In Dyffryn Llynfi, Llangynwyd parish. 9. On Mynydd Penrhys, Ystradyfodwg parish : see above pp. 6, 19, 47, 60, 93-4. In Penard parish—' ad fontem beate Marie de Pennard '—Clarke, ii, 91 : Morgan, *Ant. Sur. East Gower*. AS ST. MARY'S WELL. 11. In a little cove below Lavernock House, Lavernock parish, where the bay is called St. Mary's Well Bay. 12. St. Mary's Well and Eye Well, are close together, just NW of St. Marychurch, Llanfair parish. As LADY'S WELL. 13. In Margam parish. 14. St. Mary's Well, near St. George's Well, Reynoldston parish—Carlisle TDW.

FF. Y FIL FEIBION. Enclosed by four stones, near Llangyfelach Church,—Arch. Camb. 1920, 364.

FF. GARADOG. Near Llanilid : a ' rag-well of less note '—*Trans. Cardiff, N.S.* 1903, 36, 57.

FF. GATTWG (5). 1. Near Gelli-gaer—Fenton TW, 346. 2. Near St. Cattwg church, Pendoylan parish. 3. Near Aberkenfig : *Fynon gattuke* 1518—Birch, *Margam*, 355. 4. Cadoc's Well, just E of Kibwr Castle—Rees Map. 5. W of Court Colman—Rees Map.

ST. GEORGE'S WELL. Near Reynoldston church (ded. St. George)—Carlisle TDW.

FF. GERI. In Llanilid parish—LBS, ii, 199. The church is dedicated to SS. Ilid and Curig.

FF. GRALLO. ' Llangrallo alias Coychurch. Near ye Church & South of it we have many fine springs one of them called Fynnon Grallo & a little westward ffynnon Court Gwilym an ancient & quite demolished place formerly moted round ye mote onely discernible ' —Lhuyd Par. iii, 14.

ST. GWNNO/GWYNNO'S WELL. Adjoining Llanwonno churchyard : curative.

FF. GWYLANGEL. On Gwynfaen Farm, Llandilo Talybont parish : ' Gwyl Fihangel ' is a suggested etymology—ex inf. Mr. Alwyn D. Rees.

FF. GYNON. In Llangynwyd : divination was practised there : the first of a newly married couple to drink from it would be the dominant partner—*Cymru,* viii, 161.

FF. GYNWYD. In Llangynwyd, NE of the church—TCE, 151.

ST. HELEN'S WELL. By St. Helen's chapel, which stood on the S side of what is now St. Helen's Avenue, Swansea : chalybeate, its waters eased wounds and cancer : during 1850-60, some 20-30 people visited it daily throughout summer—Morgan, *Antiq. Soc. of East Gower,* 43. See above p. 86.

FF. HYWEL. On the N edge of Sutton Wood.

FF. IAGO (2). 1. SW of Maesteg. 2. N of Kenfig Hill.

FF. ILLTUD (4). 1. 'Fynnon Illtid ar-dyr-y-ddi-Hewid is a faire spring'—Lhuyd Par. iii, 37. 2. At Craig Ddu, Michaelston-super-Avan. 3. Near Craig Buarthcapel, Llanwynno parish : when a boy, 'Glanffrwd' hurt his ankle and was taken by his father to bathe it in this well—*Llanwynno,* p. 236. 4. '. . .fontem Sancti Iltuti', 1334, near Llansamlet, mentioned as a boundary mark—Glam. Ch. iv, p. 1190.

FF. ILLTUD—unlocated (2). 1. A manorial boundary mark on the W side of Coed-ffranc. 2. Mentioned in a medieval deed as being on the Afan side of Baglan Higher—VH, 200.

FF. JOSE. Near Tondu.

ST. JOHN'S WELL (2). 1. South of Newton church. See above p. 89. 2. At Beggar's Bound, just N of St. Athan village.

MARGARET'S WELL. Coed-ffranc. See above pp. 49, 86.

ST. MICHAEL'S WELL. At the Gnoll, Neath, 1720—VN, 200.

ST. NICHOLAS WELL (2). 1. Near Tai ffynnon, N of St. Nicholas village and church. 2. In Llanwynno parish : also called Ff. y Cyffylogiaid because woodcocks haunted it.

ST. PETER'S WELL (6). 1. In Bishopston parish : remains of a chapel may be seen there—NCPN, 115 : Morgan, *Antiq. Svy of East Gower,* 173-8, illustr. 2. Near Kibwr Castle. 3. In Llantwit Major parish, it once contained 'sacred fish'—Trevelyan 17.

4. NE of Caer Worgan. 5. N of Barry. 6. As Ff. Bedr, in woodland on SW of Graig Fawr, to the W of Margam Abbey.

FF. Y DRINDOD (2). 1. A little to the N of Llandough church (ded. Holy Trinity) : formerly resorted to by cripples and persons suffering from skin diseases but ' now ' (1811) neglected and unfrequented—Carlisle TDW. 2. As Trinity Well, near the church in Ilston parish—NCPN, 118.

CLASS B :

BLESSED WELL. ' Bledsedewille ', 13th century—*Glam. Ch.* 2299. ' blessed or holy well.' Lost. Cf. Ff. Fendigaid elsewhere in Wales.

FF. Y CAPEL. Near a house called Capel, just N of St. Donat's village.

HOLY WELL. In the Resolven district. See above p. 17.

LLANGENNITH WELL. In the village and near the church is a very old well, built around with large stones, and covered by a capstone on which is a rude incised cross within a square—HWG, iii, 145, sketch.

ILSTON WELL. Near a chapel dedicated to St. Cennydd.—See above p. 26.

MURTON WELL. Below the village of Murton is a ruined chapel, and near it, is an ancient well.—EG, 201.

OXWICH CHURCHYARD WELL. It was roofed and there was a large flat stone on its edge in front of the well : it was large enough for immersion. No-one dared visit this well at night. In 1855 and 1872 the nearby cliffs crumbled and fell, destroying Oxwich Rectory, and causing the well to dry up—HWG, iv, 1894, 157-8. See above p. 133.

SAINT WELL. SW of the parish church of Caerau.

SCRADDOCK'S WELL. In Cheriton parish, where there is also a Scraddock's Gutter. ? St. Caradoc—HWG, ii, 1789, 121.

CLASS C :

FF. ABEROGWY. Said to have nine springs (*tarddle*) each of a particular nature—D Hanes, 29.

FF. CAE MOCH. Between Coychurch and Bridgend, enclosed by a circular wall, and over the well, in 1901, was a dying thorn tree, and a little distance away was another thorn on which Sir John Rhys found over a dozen rags—See above pp. 19, 95.

FF. CAERAU. In Llangynwyd parish : cured rheumatism : the patient bathed and dropped a pin into the well—Evans, *Dyffryn Afan*, 61 : Phillips, *Folk Lore of Margam and Afan*, 41.

CEFN BRYN WELLS (3). 1. On the NW end of Cefn Bryn, Gower, is a well under a reputed cromlech called Arthur's Stone : it is curative. 2. Holy Well on Cefn Bryn, curative, and frequented on Sunday evenings in summer, when pins were offered. 3. The Stinking Well, on Llanrhidian Saltmarch. See Lewis TDW : Camden, *Brit.* (Gough) 1789, ii, 503 : *The New Swansea Guide*, 1823, 68-9. Cf. Ff. Fair above.

COEDARHYDYGLYN WELL. St. George-Super-Ely, by the side of the road to Peterston : reputed to cure eye diseases : pins were dropped into it, and rags were tied to branches of the tree that grew over it—Shepherd, *Short History of St. George Super Ely*, 39.

FF. Y CLWYF. On the N bank of Ford Brook in the Llancarfan district : a noted healing well—Arch. Cam., 1913, 99. Also called The Rag Well.

FF. DDREWLLYD (2). 1. So-called owing to its smell : also called Ff. Cwm-twrch owing to its situation : cured skin diseases—D Hanes, 31. 2. Between Gilfach Goch and Nantymoel : sulphurous : still used to cure rheumatism and sore eyes.

ST. DONAT'S CASTLE SPRING. On the cliff below the castle : said to cure erysipelas—A. J. Richards, *Transactions of Afan and Margam Historical Society*, 1929, 71 : Trevelyan, 317.

FF. FYDW. In Llangyfelach parish : medicinal *c.* 1750.

FF. Y FFLAMWYDDEN. On the S side of Moulton brook in the Llancarfan district : noted for healing properties—Arch. Cam., 1913, 99. ' fflamaiddan, = erysipelas. See above p. 86.

FF. GARTH MAELAWG. Between Llantrisant and Llanharan. In 1856, Dr. Herapath analysed it, and afterwards hundreds of people came there to seek relief from piles, gravel, shortness of breath, blood troubles, skin diseases, scurvy, etc.—D Hanes, 30.

FF. GELLI DAWEL. On the Pontypridd-Berw road : a mineral spring with a reputation for curing eye troubles.

FF. GILFACH. On Gilfach mountain : curative, formerly much frequented.

FF. GILFACH ISAF. In Llangynwyd parish : broken and sprained limbs were treated there—TCE, 152.

PISTYLL GOLAU (2). 1. Less than half a mile from Radyr church : cured sprains and weak sinews—Carlisle and Lewis TDW : mentioned in Cadoc's Life—CBS, 61. 2. A late 12th century charter names Pistilcoleu as a boundary mark near the Taf, and it is probably the Pistyll Golau on Nant Clydach near Llanwonno—Birch, Margam, 18.

FF. Y GRAIG. In Llantrisant parish : said to cure King's Evil—Lhuyd Par. iii, 9.

FF. Y GREEN. In St. Athan's parish : cured sore eyes ' before sun rising '—Fenton TW, 347.

FF. GWALA. Between Tyrau and Clyn : fractured limbs were bathed there—VN, 1199.

FF. IFAN. At Llandidawc, Tythegston : said to cure King's evil —Fenton TW, 348.

FF. LYGAD. Near Kenfig Castle : cured eye diseases.

FF. LLANCARFAN. About two fields from the village, said to cure King's Evil ; many rags hung around this well—D Hanes, 29. ' Several wells or springs at Llancarfan . . were renowned as pin and rag wells '—Trevelyan, 18. The ' marl ' of ' certain wells and springs ' at Llancarfan, was made into a paste and applied to parts affected by erysipelas—*ib*, 317. A photograph taken in 1906 shows the well below some trees and bushes, with rags hanging from them—*S. Wales and Mon. Contemporary Biographies*, 1907, 40. It is said that cattle refuse to drink from this well. John Aubrey mentions two crutches hanging from an old oak tree above this well, and says it is reputed to cure King's evil—*Philosophical Trans.*, XIX, 727 (Oct. 1697). One of the Llancarfan wells, called The Breach Well, was inspected by Mr. Alwyn D. Rees on 24 July 1935, when he was told by a woman that she had been cured of erysipelas there after bathing morning and night for one week. Mr. Rees counted 14 rags tied to the surrounding bushes, and he was told that pins were thrown into the well : another well nearby is reputed to cure King's Evil, and is walled around and overgrown with bushes—ex inf. Mr. Rees. See above pp. 95, 101.

LLANGYNWYD WELL. Cured gout and ' all aches ', particularly visited during May—Lhuyd Par. iii, 11. See above p. 89.

PENYLAN WELL. Cardiff. It was a great resort for all classes on Easter Mondays—Lewis TDW : people drank from it, then threw in a pin, and made a wish—Trevelyan 203. Rags were once hung at the well, and in the 19 century ' a sort of fair ' was held at it at Easter—Trans. Cardiff Nat. Soc., 36 (1903), 57. See above pp. 17, 127.

TAFF'S WELL. Also called Ff. Dâf and Ff. Dwym, on the E brink of the river in Eglwysilan parish : cured rheumatism : crutches were left behind—D Hanes, 29-30. See above p. 106, 127.

FF. VYSGAR/WYSGAR. In Llangynwyd parish : curative : bathing and drinking were practised—TCE, 152.

CLASS D :

FF. ARTHUR. A boundary mark near the river Taf, mentioned in a deed dated 1203—BM Harl. Ch. 75, A, 32.

FF. DILIC. On Drymma Hill in the Cilybebyll district. ' . . a spot called Bedh Dilic Gawr, between Lhan Sawel and Baglann, and this grave is over thirty feet long '—Peniarth MS. 118 (*c.* A.D. 1600). There was a St. Dilic to whom a Cornish church is dedicated—AS, 149. See above p. 7.

FF. FANON. ' Aper finnoun Uanon ' on the Ewenny—Lib Land 204 : Rees Map : Glam. Charters, i, 16. For the name Banon see OPem, i, 101, 448, 507 ; iii, 295. Sir Ifor Williams suggests that it is the ' Spring of the queen or fair maid ' (banon)—Arch. Cam., 1945, 246. Banon was also a personal name. cf. Cysteint son of Banon, Isgawyn son of Banon, two of Arthur's warriors—Mab J, pp. xxiv, 102. The ' forest called Moyluannon ' and ' Moylvannan', near Abergavenny, are mentioned in 1348 and 1368 (query vannau). There is a Bryn Banon near Llandderfel, Mer., and a river Banon which rises at Blaen Banon in the Precelly Hills, Pem.

FF. GOLLWYN. Near St. James' Chapel, Pyle. See above p. 62.

GREGORY'S WELL. Near Flemingston. (? saint).

FF. LAWRENCE. SE of Dyffryn House (? saint).

FF. MYNWEN. Near Merthyr Dyvan church.

FF. RHINGYLL. W of St. Helen's church in Eglwysilan parish. Cf. Tre Rhingyll SW of Ystradowain.

FF. WRGAN. Ff. Wrgan or Gwrgan, on Llwyni Farm in Llangynwyd parish—TCE. The name Gwrgan(t) is found in early Glamorgan deeds and pedigrees.

PISTYLL ARIAN (3). 1. N of Bridgend. 2. St. Bride's Major. 3. E of Llanharan House.

FF. Y BLAIDD. On E bank of Nant y Gwyddel, W of Mynydd Aberdâr.

FF. Y BRYCHAU. SW of Llandough village.

BUTTER WELL. 'the gavel of Boterwellemed' (in Rhossili or Landimore) 1399—HWG, 148.

FF. CANTHED. Marked S of Bishopston on Rees Map. It was certainly near the coast at Caswell Bay—Glam. Ch. i, 8 : Arch. Cam., 1950, 26.

FF. Y CEFFYL BAL. N of Abergwynfi village.

FF. DERGUIST. Probably in Senghenydd district—Lib Land., 246.

EAGLE'S WELL. NW of Boverton.

FF. ELY. On Carn y Celyn, E of Gilfach Goch.

FF. Y FAN HALOG. In Llanwynno parish.

FF. GEILLACH. See RJT, 13.

FF. GYFFYR. In Cwm Maelog near Margam Abbey—Arch. Cam., 1914, 406.

FF. LISS. Mentioned as a boundary mark in St. Brides super Ely in a medieval charter.—Glam. Ch. i, 29.

FF. LEFRITH. In Llangyfelach.

FF. Y MAEN. Near Kibwr Castle—Rees Map.

SHEE WELL. See above p. 51.

FF. SWYO. In Llanblethian parish.

WICKED WELL. Near Margam.

MERIONETH

CLASS A :

FF. BADARN. Near Mynydd Ffynnon Badarn, SW of the reservoir at Tŷ Cam.

FF. BADRIG. In Llanenddwyn parish : cured certain diseases in children—Anc. Mon. Mer. It also possessed mysterious and magical properties : its water was carried to the fonts of Llanenddwyn and Llanwywe for baptism several centuries ago—Davies LGM.

FF. BEUNO (2). 1. In Llanycil parish, about 100 yards SW of Bala : '*Ffynnon Veino yn ymil yr Eglwys*'—Lhuyd Par, ii, 68. It was within a sunken rectangular stone enclosure : the parish church was dedicated to Beuno—Anc. Mon. Mer. The hilly district to the SW is called Bronnydd Beuno : in Cae Mawr a field was named Acre Feyno—TM, 1838. 2. '*Cappel AylHayarn in ye borders of Lh. Elidan* [Denb.] *ruinous time out of mind. There's only an ew tree at present,*—Lhuyd Par. ii, 49. '*Fynnon veino*' was near Gwyddelwern church, and the impress of Beuno's horse's shoe was to be seen '*ar Vaen Beino*'—*ib*, ii, 52. Gwyddelwern church is dedicated to Beuno : the well is sometimes called Ffynnon Ucha—Anc. Mon. Mer. See above p. 106.

FF. DDECWYN. By Plas Llandecwyn, not far from Llandecwyn church—Lhuyd Par. ii, 106.

FF. DEGID. 'Fynnon Gower nere the Church [Llangower] & Fynnon Tegid, a qr of a mile off'—Lhuyd Par. ii, 22.

FF. DELAU/DELA. In Llanbedr parish, near Llwyn y Ffynnon Delau, on Hen Bandy farm: now closed.—Anc. Mon. Mer.

FF. DRILLO. About 500 yards N of Llandrillo church: said to cure various diseases—Lhuyd Par. ii, 58: Lewis TDW. It was originally in the corner of a low-lying meadow, but when the tenant farmer objected to 'trespassers' about 1850-60, the well ceased to flow but re-appeared in the field of a neighbouring farm: the incident was regarded as the intervention of the saint: for another account see above p. 116. By 1913 it was dry except during the wet or winter weather—Mont. Coll., 1893, 284: LBS, iv, 263: Bygones, 20 Sep. 1911: Anc. Mon. Mer. See above p. 16.

FF. DDEINIOL/DDANIEL. Within a rough stone enclosure, about 40 yards NW of Llanfor churchyard: its name was known in Lhuyd's day but was forgotten before 1913—Lhuyd Par. ii, 64: Anc. Mon. Mer. The church is dedicated to St. Daniel. See OPem, iv, 470.

FF. DDERFEL. Near Llandderfel church—Lhuyd Par. ii, 60. It is protected by a stone slab and some rude masonry, and there is a small bath some 4 feet wide.

FF. ELEN. In Llanfrothen parish, on the side of Sarn Elen, by Croesor village.

FF. ENDDWYN. Nearly 2 miles from Llanenddwyn church. St. Enddwyn is said to have been cured of a sore disease after bathing in it: later patients left their crutches and threw pins into the well to ward off evil spirits. Some elaborate masonry surrounds the well and bath, and it may once have been covered: its waters were held in high repute in opthalmic cases and glandular affections, and scrofula was cured by drinking the water and then applying some of the moss as a plaster to the afflicted parts—LBS, ii, 452: Anc. Mon. Mer. See above pp. 35, 101.

FF. FAIR (8). 1. Near Betws Gwerful Goch church: called 'Ffynnon y Saint' by Lhuyd (Par. ii, 76) and 'St. Mary's Well' by Lewis (TDW). In a meadow called Gwerglodd y Saint, about

100 yards from the church is an unnamed spring—Anc. Mon. Mer. 2. 'By ye Church' in Llandecwyn parish—Lhuyd Par. ii, 105. 3. Near Llwyn Artro, Llanenddwyn parish: formerly much frequented by sufferers from rheumatism: it dried up in 1909—Anc. Mon. Mer. 4. In Gwyddelwern parish: sometimes called Ffynnon Gwern Beuno, Ffynnon Wen, and Ffynnon Issa—Anc. Mon. Mer. 5. In Llandanwg parish: Ffynnon Fair Harlech is a spring on the E side of Castle Hill, about 10 feet beyond the Castle wall: The neighbouring parish is Llanfair—Anc. Mon. Mer. 6. Close to Dolgelley town: considered effiacious in cases of rheumatism: a few Roman coins have been found there—Lewis TDW. Masonry was built around it in 1837 or 1838, and it was again repaired in 1850: it was 'neglected' in 1890. The well was disused and half-choked with rubbish in 1828—Morris CM, 97; *Bygones*, 20 March 1878: Ellis, *Dolgelley and Llanelltyd*, 8, 60. About 25 yards W of Ff. Fair is a small spring called Ffynnon y llygaid which was visited for ophthalmic disorders—Anc. Mon. Mer. Near Ff. Fair there was another well called Ff. Rhydd, on Brynmair Farm—Morris CM, 97. 7. About 80 yards SE of Maentwrog church: it supplied the neighbouring houses—Anc. Mon. Mer. 8. In Llanfair parish, nearly on top of a hill to the E of the parish church: neglected and overgrown—Anc. Mon. Mer: Arch. Cam., 1936, 283. See above p. 46.

FF. FIHANGEL. Alias Y Ffynnon; in Ffestiniog parish; said to cure rheumatism and other ills, and was visited until the beginning of the 19th century—HPF, 46. It rises beneath the floor of an old ruined house, and flows through an iron pipe from under the ruins: it was 'still' visited (1914) by sufferers from rheumatism, fractured limbs, and other maladies.—Anc. Mon. Mer.

FF. FROTHEN. Near Llanfrothen church—Lhuyd, Par. ii, 108. The name is now lost, but a well situated a few yards from the church and protected by masonry, is called *Hen Ffynnon* and is undoubtedly the one that Lhuyd called '*Fynnon Vrothan*.'

FF. GADFAN. Near Towyn church: cured rheumatism, scrofula, and cutaneous disorders. Before 1850 it was enclosed and made into two baths with four dressing rooms attached, and in charge of a caretaker—Lewis TDW. In 1894, the owners of the baths, finding they did not pay, filled them with stones and converted the buildings into a coach-house and stables—LBS, ii, 6. In 1672-3 it was stated '*in the churchyard of Towyn Parish lyeth a decayed chappell known as St. Cadvan's chappell, or its scite*'—OPem, iv, 545.

FF. GOWER. On the verge of Bala lake, S of Llangower church. '*Ffynnon Gower mewn chwarter milhtir ir Eglwys lle y byddys yn golchi plant rhag y llechin*'—Lhuyd, Par. ii, 70. A megalith called Llech Gower is in the parish. According to legend, Gower had another well in the middle of what is now Bala lake, and that the old town was around it.—Rhys CF, 376, quoting a MS. written between 1750 and 1780. St. Cywair is the patron of Llangower church. See above p. 133.

FF. SANTFFRAID. '*Fynnon Sanfraid a qr of a mile above ye Church*' (of Llansantffraid Glyndyfrdwy)—Lhuyd Par. ii, 47.

FF. SILIAN. By ' Rîg Chappel '—Lhuyd Par. ii, 46. Marked on O.S. maps as Ff. Silin, it is a considerable distance from the parish church.

CLASS B :

FF. Y CAPEL (2). 1. In Llanfachreth parish : possibly a well chapel stood nearby—Carlisle TDW : beneficial for sore eyes and much resorted to until ' a few years ago '—*Bygones*, 21 July 1880 : about 300 yards W of the church, said to have been called Ff. Gwyddno at one time—Anc. Mon. Mer. It was brought into existence through a miracle performed by St. Machreth—Davies LGM. 2. Ff. Capel in a field called Cae Capel on Tyddyn Sion Wyn farm, in Llanfihangel y Traethau parish—Arch. Carm., 1914, 304-6, illustr.

CLASS C :

FF. CAE GWYN. On Cae Gwyn in Mallwyd : noted for eye complaints—Carlisle TDW.

FF. CLEINI. Or Ff. Llwyn Cleini, on Hafodredydd near Dolgelley : said to be medicinal—Davies LGM, 225.

FF. CWM RHWYFOR. In Tal-y-llyn : efficacious in the cure of ' several disorders '—Carlisle TDW.

FF. FFRIDD ARW.—In Brithdir parish : cured rheumatism, etc.

FF. Y FRON. In Llanegryn parish : cured rheumatism, etc.

FF. FYNWS. In Llangar parish : bent pins were offered for the cure of warts.—Lhuyd *Par.* ii, 56.

FF. Y GRO. A medicinal well on Llwyn land near the river Wnion. In 1796, Dafydd Ionawr wrote 10 verses in praise of this well and described how he had derived benefit from its waters—*Gwaith Dafydd Ionawr* quoted in Morris CM, 99.

FF. LYGAID. Near Bwthyn y Graig : said to cure eye complaints —Morris CM, 98.

FF. RHIW'R CAWR. At Mawddwy : cured sore eyes—Davies LGM.

FF. Y TYDDYN MAWR. In Ardudwy : especially efficacious in rheumatic cases.—Davies LGM, 225.

CLASS D :

FF. YR ABAD. In Llanelltyd parish. '*Fynnon yr Abad odhiar y Vynachlog*'—Lhuyd Par. i, 3.

FF. GWENHUDW. Or Gwenhidiw. Near Ty Blaenau between Dolgelley and Garnedd-wen : cured rheumatism. See above p. 134.

FF. Y GWYLLIAID. At Bwlch y Groes near Dinas Mawddwy. It was medicinal and relieved bowel complaints—Davies LGM, 227. See above p. 54.

FF. OLEDD. A walled well in Llanaber parish, which was formerly reputed to cure rheumatism and scorbutic complaints. Also called Ff. Goledd—*Bygones*, 21 July 1880.

CLASS E :

FF. Y GAER. Between Llwyn Cleini and Ffynnon Cnidw, near Dolgelley : it was used for cursing or bewitching (*rheibio*). See above p. 119.

FF. Y GLOCH FELEN. In Corwen parish. '*An old brazen yellow bell found by Fynnawn y Gloch velen at Kraig Korwen.*'—Lhuyd Par. ii, 45. See above p. 130.

FF. LLAWR DOLYSELER. In Llanfachreth parish : a magical well (swyngyfaredd)—Davies LGM, 277.

FF. MAEN Y MILGI. In Llandrillo parish. An ebb and flow well—Lhuyd Par. ii, 59. See above p. 18.

MONMOUTHSHIRE

CLASS A :

ST. ANNE'S WELL. At Trelleck—Arch. Cam., 1909, 70-1.

FF. BEDR. Some 300 yards SE of Bryngwyn church.

FF. FFREID (2). 1. St. Freid's Well near Skenfrith (church ded. to St. Bride)—BD, 71. 2. In Bridewell Wood in Llanvaches parish.

FF. ELICHGUID. Near Mathern : a boundary mark of a grant relating to Mathern—Lib. Land, 142 : OPEM, IV, 455. See above p. 35.

FF. FARGET. In Llanvaches.

FF. GOFOR. In the grounds of Llanofer House : curative, crutches were left there—Bradney, *Hist. of Mon.*, i, 385. See OPem, iii, 301, n 3, where it is suggested that the name involved is Myfor not Gofor.

FF. GYBI. Just outside the S wall of Llangibby churchyard.

ST. JOHN'S WELL. At Caerleon.

LADY'S WELL. In Tredegar Park. Said to be named after Gwladys, mother of St. Cadoc. See above p. 126. A bath-house was erected over it in 1719.

ST. MAUGHAN'S WELL. In St. Maughan parish—Lhuyd Par. iii, 75.

PWLL MEURIG. Some 1½ miles SW of Chepstow. For miracles performed there see *Hist. Britt.* (ed. Mommsen). pp. 216*a*-217*a*. See above p. 53.

ST. MICHAEL'S WELL. In Rockfield parish. In this well there were some stones with red spots which are said to be the bloodstains of ' some Saint ' who was beheaded there—Lhuyd Par. iii, 75. See above p. 39.

ST. NOE'S WELL. ' In Skenfrith, where was her chapel, St. Noe's, also her bridge and holy well '—WCO, 169.

ST. PATRICK'S WELL. At Govilon, near Abergavenny.

FF. SANT SANNAN. Just SE of St. Sannan's church, Bedwellty.

ST. TEWDRIC'S WELL. Tewdric King of Glamorgan died at this well and ordered that a church be built at the spot where he died. The well is near the NE corner of Mathern House. Pwll Meurig is a short distance to the W. Both Tewdric and his son Meurig are listed as saints in LBS.

FF. WENOG. A holy well in Trefethin parish.

FF. WYNHAEL. 'fontem Sancti Gwynhael' in Wolvesnewton parish, 1425: 'ffonnon Wynhayll' 1488: 'fynnon Wynhayle' 1537—Badminton Deeds.

CLASS B:

CHAPEL WELL. A field near Pont y cleifion, Usk, is called Chapel Well field, and belongs to the poor of Usk: a chapel is said to have stood near the well in this field: the water possessed healing properties, being especially good for inflamed eyes—Clark, *Usk*, 1856, 100. The church at Usk is ded. to St. Mary.

FF. Y GARREG. In a meadow in front of the Priory house, Abergavenny, bounded by Holy Well Lane.

HOLY WELL (4). 1. In Holy Well wood near Monmouth. 2. W of a tumulus N of Caldicot. 3. Between Troy and Wonastow—Rees Map. 4. In a wood in Mamhilad, a wishing well at which pins were offered—*Cymru Fu*, 22 Feb. 1890: NCPN, 262.

LAVENWELL. In Lavenwell wood just SE of the ruined St. Keyna's chapel in Runston.

PRIEST'S WELL. In Darran wood: curative: a great oak grew over it: Franciscan friars who lived near Rockfield made annual pilgrimages to it—BD, 81-2, sketch. See above p. 2, 38.

SIMMERY WELL. At Monmouth: said to be derived from 'St. Mary.'

CLASS C:

FF. CROFT HIR. In Llangattock Veibon parish: cured the King's Evil—Lhuyd Par. iii, 19.

NEWCASTLE WELL. Near Newcastle is a well with a great reputation for healing: See above p. 125.

TRELLECK WELLS. According to tradition there were originally nine wells, of which four now remain, all fed by different springs, each supposed to cure different diseases. The 'Three Wonders of Trelleck' were the wells, three great megaliths and a tumulus. For a good description of the wells see WWS, 149-150. See above p. 74, 95, 117, 125.

LLANTILIO PERTHOLEY. 'Many large springs arise on the sides of ye Hills and in meadows, some of which have been found good for curing wounds, ulcers, Inflamations &c and for taking away warts, freckles, &c'—Lhuyd Par. iii, 39.

CLASS D :

FF. ARTHUR. A boundary mark on lands belonging to Tintern—OPem, iv, 680.

FF. BRITROU. In the Gwentllwg district—CBS, 343 : WEVS, 73.

FF. EURDIL. 'finnaun eiurdil,' . . . 'efrdil,' near Monmouth—Lib Land, 252-3, 532-3.

FF. EFA/EVE'S WELL. At Newport.

FF. FEDWYR. See above p. 54.

SWYNSWELL. In Mathern parish, 1535-7.

FF. ANGOERON. Near Llanofer : bent pins, buttons, 'and other small objects' were offered : the wish had to be made silently, for otherwise the spell would be broken—*Trans. Cardiff Nat. Soc.* 36, 1903, 56.

CHEPSTOW WELLS (2). 1. Two wells near Bridge St., Chepstow, said to ebb and flow. 2. Near Chepstow.

FF. GWAED. At Mynyddislwyn.

FF. GWERCHYR. 'Fonon gwerchyr' Wolvesnewton parish, 1428—Badminton Deeds.

FF. Y MARCH. In Aberystruth parish.

THE WISHING WELL (2). 1. Near Croft Hir Brook, W. of St. Maughan's church. 2. Near Mamhilad : pins were thrown in—*Cymru Fu*, 22 Feb. 1890, sketch.

FF. YSBRYDION. In Coed Ysbrydion, W of Pontypool.

MONTGOMERYSHIRE

CLASS A :

FF. ARMON (2). 1. In Llanfechain, about 300 yards SE of the parish church (ded. St. Garmon) ; built around with stone, and covered with stone slabs and earth : its water was formerly used for baptism, and sick people bathed in the well—Anc. Mon. Mont. In the churchyard is a mound called Twmpath Garmon—Arch. Cam., 1923, 443. 2. Called variously Armon's Well and St. Garmon's Well, in Castle Caereinion Urban parish—Anc. Mon. Mont.

BENNION'S WELL (3). 1. In Llanymynech village : used for charms as late as 1878—*Bygones,* 4 Dec. 1878. 2. St. Bennion's Well in Carreghofa parish—Anc. Mon. Mont. 3. Bennion's Well in Llandrinio parish—Anc. Mon. Mont. *Note*—The probable association of St. Beuno with the districts of these wells, and the probability that the form Bennion is derived from the saint's name, has been discussed by Phillimore in OPem, iv, 673-7.

FF. DDOEFAN. In Cwm Doefan, Llanrhaiadr-ym-Mochnant parish. Canon S. J. Evans equates Doefan with Dogfan, the patron saint of the parish—*Hanes Plwyf Llanrhaiadr-ym-Mochnant,* 1940, 30. The well is said to be virtuous.

FF. DDOGFAN. In Llanwddyn parish, close to the NE bank of Llyn Fyrnwy : cured eye complaints. Thomas calls it Ff. Dwgan and suggests that it may represent Dwyfan, patron of the neighbouring parish of Llanrhaiadr—DSA, i, 256.

FF. EILIAN. In Llanrhaiadr-ym-Mochnant : sometimes called Ffynnon Cwm Ffynnon.

FF. ERFYL. About 400 yards NW of Llanerfyl church : baptismal water was drawn from it : visited by young people on Whit Sundays, Trinity Sundays, and Easter Mondays, when dancing followed the drinking of sugared water : the well was arched and the water flowed through a spout—BGNW, 260 : Camb. Reg., 1796, 384 : Lewis TDW ; Mont. Coll. XVI, 77 ; XXVIII, 331 : *Works of Rev. Griffith Edwards,* 1895, 69-70.

FF. FAIR (4). 1. Also called St. Mary's Well and Ff. yr Eglwys, in the churchyard of Llanfair Caereinion : it retains remains of old masonry, and, though neglected, its waters were still believed to possess curative properties in 1910—Anc. Mon. Mont. 2. Lady Well, in Ladywell Court Lane, Newtown : now covered over : formerly a pump drew water from it for domestic purposes, but it was abandoned by 1909—Anc. Mon. Mont. 3. Lady Well, in a field below the road leading from Pant to Colton Farm in Church-Stoke parish—*Bygones*, 22 Nov. 1911. 4. In Berriew parish : destroyed before 1909—Anc. Mon. Mont.

FF. GADFAN. A short distance from Llangadfan church : once covered by a building—Camb. Reg, 1796, 385 : had a high repute for cures. It was proposed to build a road over this well, but the rector, the Revd. Griffith Howell (1839-1863) intervened, and an arch was constructed to take the road over it—LBS, ii, 6 : Anc. Mon. Mont.

FF. GADFARCH. St. Cadfarch is patron of Penegoes church, occasionally called Llangadfarch : of this well, Bishop Maddox wrote—'*St. Gadfarch's Well* is in one field of ye Glebe. Ano[ther] P[ar]cel of ye Glebe is called Erw Gadfarch' : its waters were beneficial in rheumatic cases—LBS, ii, 9-10.

FF. IDLOES. Near an ash tree on the Lower Green (now Hafren Street) in Llanidloes—Bygones, 22 Feb. 1893.

FF. ILLOG. In Hirnant parish (church ded. St. Illog) : cured diverse diseases : pins offered : 'much resorted to for its mineral power'—Carlisle TDW. 'It is now called Ffynnon Hise'—*Bygones* 3 Aug., 1910.

FF. IWAN. Or St. John's Well, on Garn Farm, Hirnant : in great repute for children's ailments. See above p. 48.

FF. MADOC. In Llanfair Caereinion parish. A mineral spring of recent repute and resort—*Bygones*, 21 March, 1894 : Anc. Mon. Mont. See above p. 83.

MICHAEL'S WELL. In Llanfihangel-yng-Ngwynfa : also called Ff. Penisa'r llan : it is about 150 yards SE of the church : its water was formerly used for baptism—Mont. Coll., 1898, 310 : Anc. Mon. Mont.

FF. MYLLIN. About 300 yards W of Llanfyllin church : also called Ff. Coed y Llan : St. Myllin is said to have baptised converts in it. People visited it on Trinity Sunday to drink sugared water, the local maidens 'standing treat' : the men then returned the compliment with cakes and ale in the public-house at Tynllan. Rags were tied to bushes near the well by sick visitors—Bygones 21, March 1894 : Lewis TDW. It was also used for divination—Bygones, 21 March, 1894. See above p. 36, 95.

ST. TYDECHO'S WELL. Near the parish church of Garthbeibio : said to cure rheumatism, but is now filled up and the water diverted into a drain : a stone image of the saint's head, formerly kept in the N side of the well, has been lost : pins were thrown into the well and it was considered a sacrilege to remove them : patients also bathed in the well and drank the water—Camb. Reg., 1796, 385 : Mont. Coll., 1873, 13 : *Bygones*, 1 Feb., 1911 : Lewis, TDW. Ff. Rhigos (q.v.) is near.

ST. TYSSILIO'S SPOUT. On the W side of Rhuallt in Welshpool parish : it is the ' fons Tessiliau ' of Gwenwynwyn's charter (1202) to Strata Marcella—OPem, iv, 635 : Anc. Mon. Mont. Cf. Ffynnon Nant Tyssilio in Oswestry, which was visited on St. Oswald's feast (Lhuyd Par. i, 129).

GOD'S WELL. Posts and rails were 'placed before God's Well in Arthur Street,' Montgomery, in 1690.—Arch. Cam., 1923, 364.

TRINITY WELL (5). 1. In Guilsfield Without parish : still frequented on Trinity Sunday in 1910, when water sweetened with brown sugar (white would not do) was drunk : in olden times people from Welshpool, Meifod, and Llandyssilio, sat around this well on Trinity Sundays and sang hymns—*Bygones*, 21 June, 1899, 7 Oct. 1903 : Anc. Mon. Mont. 2. In Cletterwood parish. 3. On the W slope of Moel y Golfa, Trewern parish : people drank from it on Trinity Sundays. 4. On Boncyn y beddau hill, Tregynon parish : people met there on Trinity Sunday afternoons to drink sugared water—Mont. Coll., 1890, 178. 5. In Llandrinio parish : people drank sugared water there on Trinity Sundays—Anc. Mon. Mont. : *Bygones*, 21 June, 1899.

CLASS B :

PISTYLL CANPWLL. In Tregynon parish : frequented on Trinity Sundays—Anc. Mon. Mont.

FF. GEILIOG. Twenty yards W of a camp on Allt Dolanog, Llanfihangel-yng-Ngwynfa parish : a popular resort on Trinity Sundays—Anc. Mon. Mont.

FF. DILA. In Llanfihangel-yng-Ngwynfa : frequented on Trinity Sundays.—Anc. Mon. Mont.

FF. Y FOEL. At Llansanffraid on the fourth Sunday in Lent, peas or grains of wheat were roasted, and carried to the top of the Foel and eaten with great ceremony with water drawn from the Foel well—Mont. Coll., iv, 134.

GARTH FAWR WELL. Near Guilsfield, in the cleft of a rock on Garth fawr hill : visited on Trinity Sunday when sugared water was drunk—BG, 51.

HALLY WELL. Near Trefnanney in Meifod parish : tradition says that there was a place for worship near the well, and that the well was once covered by a building.—*Bygones*, 1 Feb. 1911.

HOLY WELL (3). 1. In Forden parish (church ded. St. Michael), a 'holy well,' about 250 yards S of the vicarage : pilgrimages were formerly made to it, but only a spring now remains—Anc. Mon. Mont. 2. Near Sarney. 3. In Meifod parish.

NEW WELL. In the township of Dolforwyn : pilgrimages were made to it on Trinity Sundays when sugared water was drunk.

FF. RHIGOS. Near St. Tydecho's Well (qv.) in Garthbeibio parish : cured sore eyes : sugared water was drunk there by Garthbeibio parishioners on Ash Wednesdays and Trinity Sundays —Anc. Mon. Mont : *Bygones*, 15 Nov. 1893 ; 1 Feb. 1911.

CLASS C :

FF. BAICH Y CAWR. At a crag called Baich y Cawr near Llanrhaiadr waterfall : said to cure warts and other excrescences, for which pins were offered : there is a tradition that a giant, his wife, and servant lived nearby—*Bygones*, 3 Aug. 1910.

BLACK WELL/FF. DDU (2). 1. Near Newtown : reputed to cure rheumatism—*Bygones*, 12 Jan. 1887. 2. A medicinal spring in the SE of Aberhavesp parish : said to cure scrofula, once much frequented by local people—Lewis TDW ; *Bygones*, 1 Feb. 1911.

CLAWDD LLESG WELL. Variously called Ff. y Clawdd Llesg, Pistyll y Clawdd, Ff. Spout, and The Spout Well. It is on the border of Meifod and Guilsfield parishes, in the township of Trefedrid : up to the early part of the 19th century it was visited on

Trinity Sundays when sugared water was drunk, and afterwards the people repaired to a nearby alehouse called Yr Hen Dafarn : the custom was stopped by two local ministers—*Bygones*, 5 Feb. 1896. But people continued to visit the well afterwards. 'Till late years' young folk assembled there on the 8th Sunday after Easter to drink the water and afterwards to spend the day in dancing on a green sward—Lewis TDW. An inscription above the spout read, 'Every wound to be held for twenty minutes under the spout three times a day' : another inscription reads, 'I found health here, F.W. Elmore, 1898'—*Bygones*, 26 July 1899. For further details see *Bygones*, 18 March 1896 when the well had been patronised 'recently by a young man from a distance who was suffering from a polypus in the nose.' See Anc. Mon. Mont. : Mont. Coll., 1881, xiv, illust : See above p. 84.

FF. CILYN. In a field called Cae Cilyn, Llanidloes : once considered medicinal, and people washed their eyes there—*Bygones*, 22 Feb. 1893.

FF. FACH. A roadside well in Llanfihangel-yng-Ngwynfa : once noted for its virtues especially in cases of eye diseases : there was a local belief that anyone *drinking* from the well would die— Anc. Mon. Mont. : Mont. Coll., 1898, 310.

FF. Y FFINNANT. On Ffinnant Farm, Llansanffraid Pool parish: the well chamber was approached by several steps and its floor was flagged : a small wooden hut accommodated bathers—Anc. Mon. Mont. It had a great reputation for curing sprains, bruises, and muscular ailments : it is also called 'Ff. Yscibor' from its proximity to an old barn : the original well is now closed and the spring diverted into an adjoining field.—*Bygones*, 16 Feb. 1910.

HAFOD Y GARREG WELL. On Hafod y Garreg farm in Is y Garreg parish : reputed to cure the gravel—*Bygones*, 15 Nov. 1911.

FF. GEDWEN. In Trefeglwys parish : it was famous for its curative properties. 'The water of it of such vertue being boyled and put in milke breaks it into possett'—Lhuyd Par, iii, 42.

FF. Y GROFTYDD. In the township of Teirtref, Meifod parish : sulphurous, cures cutaneous diseases—Lewis TDW.

PISTYLL GWYN. On Penrallt Common, Machynlleth : it cured sprains—*Bygones*, 15 Nov. 1911.

FF. IEWYN. Also called Ff. Cwm Ewyn/Tewyn, about a mile N of Pennant Melangell church, near Craig Cwm Ewyn : said to cure rheumatism, scrofula, and skin diseases—Anc. Mon. Mont. : Arch. Cam., 1894, 148 : *Bygones*, 3 Aug. 1910.

FF. ISEL. On Buches y Foel Ortho, Hirnant parish : people still occasionally visit it, as the water taken directly from 'the eye of the well' is of reputed efficacy in some infantile ailments—Anc. Mon. Mont.

PENEGOES WELLS. At Penegoes are two wells alongside each other, enclosed with low walls : the water of one is said to be of higher temperature than the other : both were in repute for divers complaints : frequent pilgrimages were made to them within living memory—Anc. Mon. Mont.

CLASS D :

FF. ARTHUR. About 1½ miles E of Llanfihangel-yng-Ngwynfa. *Finnoun Arthvr Guinna* [read Guinva], *Funon Arthur villa*—Bridgeman, *Princes of Powys*, 157, quoting IPM dated 1309. It was filled up before 1895 because it constituted a danger to cattle : it was remembered in 1910 when its site was marked only by a damp spot on Cae Dŵr on Cefn Llwyni : in its original state it was 4 feet deep and above 12 feet square, was surrounded by a stone wall, and steps led down to it : the township is called Ffynnon Arthur—Anc. Mon. Mont.

FF. ELIAS. In Llansanffraid Deuddwr : visited by people who suffered from weak eyes : a large yew grew over it, but the well was silted up in 1911—*Bygones*, 25 Aug. 1909, 16 Feb. 1910. Sugared water was drunk there.

FF. MODRYB. On Glanbrogan Hill, Llanfechain : reputed for medicinal properties.—Anc. Mon. Mont.

FF. Y MYNEICH. Immediately S of the site of an old *hospitium* of the Knights of St. John, NE of Bryn Adda, Llanwddyn parish.

NICHOLAS WELL. On Trederwen farm, Llandrinio parish : formerly in much repute—Anc. Mon. Mont.

CLASS E.

FF. Y CAMPIAU. On E slope of Y Disgwylfa hill, Llanfair Caereinion parish : just below the spring is a small plateau where visitors congregated to play games after drinking sweetened water from the well—Anc. Mon. Mont.

FF. DAROGAN. In the township of Teirtref, Meifod parish : it is protected by a cupola 'which has stood for many years' :—Lewis TDW.

GALLT Y MAEN WELL. On Gallt y Maen, Meifod parish : it was visited by young people who drank the water and then went to a fenced green called Bryn y Bowliau where they spent the rest of the day in athletics : 'the practice has for some time been totally discontinued'—Lewis TDW.

LLANFAIR CAEREINION WELL. Unlocated : used for divination. See above p. 111.

LLANLLUGAN WELL. Near the parish church, and near the Lower Lliw river : a tree grows over it.—Ex inf. Rt. Hon. J. Clement Davies, M.P. See above p. 131.

LLANLLWCHAIARN WELL. In Newtown : evil spirits were exorcised here. See above p. 132.

FF. Y WRACH. On NW slope of Moel Pentyrch, Llanfair Caereinion parish. See above p. 128.

PEMBROKESHIRE

CLASS A :

FF. AARON. In Llanreithan parish.

FF. BEDR (2). 1. In Little Newcastle parish. 2. In Newport parish. The local pronounciation is Beder.

THE WELLS OF BRYNACH (4). 1. Bernard's Well/Brynach's Well/Ffynnon Frynach, in Henrysmoat parish : near the old chapel of St. Brynach, about three-quarters of a mile NE of the parish church : it is protected by a modern hood of masonry, and adjoining it are traces of a well-chamber : a small hedge now separates the well from the old chapel site—Anc. Mon. Pem. See above pp. 43-4. 2. In Llanfair Nantgwyn parish. See above p. 40.

3. In Llanfyrnach parish, about 1½ miles S of the church : said to possess healing properties—Anc. Mon. Pem. 4. About 600 yards S of Cernydd Meibion Owen, and within a stone enclosure called Buarth Brynach which was about 5 to 6 feet wide—Fenton TP, 195-6. The wall does not exist today. (With this cf. Buarth Caron (AD 1184) in Caron parish, Card.) *Gavell Pistill Byrnach,* Nevern parish (1603)—NLW Bronwydd Deeds.

CANNA'S WELL. In Llangan West parish : much resorted to, it was reputed to cure the ague and intestinal complaints. The custom at the well was associated with a megalith. See above p. 15. The treatment was continued for some consecutive days, sometimes up to 14 days and more. An old man, aged 78 in 1872, remembered people undergoing treatment, and he had seen hundreds of pins in the well. About 1835-45, the tenant carried off the soil between the well and the watercourse, with the result that the water partly disappeared—Anc. Mon. Pem : Arch. Cam., 1872, iii, 235, illustr : See NCPN, 159.

ST. CARADOG'S WELL. In St. Thomas parish, Haverfordwest. ' The well of St. Caradoc near the well of St. David ' in Haverfordwest (1315)—Corporation Deeds. It was visited by lovers on the morning of the fair held there on Easter Monday. ' . . . the noted Cradock's Well, whose sanctity and supposed virtue were derived from its having been a favourite haunt of that hermit saint, whose cell was at Haroldstone . . . ' Fenton TP, 112. ' . . . a Well there, called *Caradog's Well,* round which, till within these few years, there was a sort of vanity Fair, where cakes were sold, and country Games celebrated '—Carlisle TDW. The well was enclosed in 1838—Anc. Mon. Pem. See above pp. 43, 111.

FF. DDEGFEL. On the borders of Brawdy and St. Elvis parishes. Tradition states that St. Degfel, going on a pilgrimage from Haverfordwest to St. Davids, drank from this well and bathed his eyes there. It has been visited within living memory for the cure of warts. Warts were bathed on Sundays before the dawn, and the treatment was continued on the following seven mornings before the dew had gone. See above pp. 35, 96.

FF. DDEGWEL. Ff. *Degwel* in St. Dogmael's parish—Census 1841. The name occurs several times and the form *Degwel* is consistent : the same documents give the following place-names in the same parish—*Capel Degwel* and *Cwm Degwell.*

FF. DDEWI (18). 1. On the E of St. Davids : a farm of this name existed there in 1765 : the name is now lost. 2. Near St. Lawrence but in Hayscastle parish : the cottage by it was called Ff. Ddewi. 3. In Mathry parish : *park ffynnon Dewy* occurs on Mabws Fach farm in 1842—TM. 4. Near Newhouse, Llanreithan parish. 5. In St. Dogwells parish : the Welsh name for this parish is Llantydewi. 6. A rustic called Terdi beseeched St. David to provide a well as the land was dry : 'starting out, therefore, and opening a little bit of the surface of the soil with the point of his bachall, a most clear fountain gushed forth, which, bubbling up in a continual vein, supplies the coldest water in time of heat'—WESD, 16. Giraldus states that this took place at Brawdy—*Op.*, III, 390. 7. On the land of Meardy farm, but in Whitchurch parish, a few yards from the boundary with Brawdy parish : nearby are the farms of Ffynnonddewi and Ffynnonddewi fach, both in Whitchurch. The bulk of Meardy land is in Brawdy, and its name was Ffynnonddewi until about 1810 when it was altered to the present name : the well is accounted holy, and pilgrims to St. Davids are said to have visited it. 8. Near Fishguard town : it was known in 1894 but is now lost. 9. In Llanychllwydiog parish—Lhuyd Par, iii, 82. 10. In Maenclochog parish—OPem, i, 255 : Census, 1841. 11. To the E of Manordeifi. 12. In Llanddewi Velfrey parish : it has ceased to flow, but is commemorated in the field-name *Park ffynnon ddewi*, which is half a mile W of the parish church. 13. The origin of Pistyll Dewi is assigned to St. David who prayed to God for a new well during a drought : the well immediately arose, and at times ran with wine and milk—Giraldus, *Itin. Kam.*, VI, 109 (Rolls Ser.) : *Book of Llandaff* (ed. Evans) 103 : El, 110, 4-16 : CBS, 408. This well was in the churchyard of St. Davids Cathedral, and the rill from it, called Pistyll Dewi, flowed into the river Alun—LBS, ii, 318. Jones and Freeman (*Hist. of St. Davids*, 232) identify it with 'St. Mary's Well which rises near the east end of the Cathedral, and of which the water runs through the crypt of the College chapel.' In 1866, Sir G. Scott destroyed this Pistyll Dewi—WESD, 101. 14. At Porthclais creek are the ruins of Capel y Pistyll and its holy well called Pistyll Dewi—Willis SD, 53 : Men. Sac,. 2 : Angl. Saer, ii, 631 : Jones and Freeman, St. Davids, 228 : WWHR, vi, 39 : Fenton TP, 64. St. David was baptised in it. See above p. 34. 15. In the field behind Llys Dewi on the Dinas-Newport road, in Newport parish, is Pistyll Dewi. The medieval Capel Dewi was roughly on the site of the present Llys Dewi. *Capel Dewy* is mentioned by George Owen—OPem, ii, 509, and it is mentioned in 1851—Census. The name Cwm Dewi occurs in the neighbouring parish of Dinas as Dewiyscome in 1434, Comdewi in 1594, and Cwm Dewi in the 1841

Census. 16. 'the well of St. David' (1315) in Haverfordwest—Corporation Deeds. In October 1333 and 1461-83 deeds mention *fontem Sancti David'* as being near Barn Street in that town. It stood between that street and Dewi Street, (now Dew Street) nearer the latter at Fountain Row, a little collection of houses destroyed in the 19th century. It supplied part of the town with domestic water, and in 1697 the Corporation leased the 'Fountain' or 'Conduit Head' to William Yearnold, plumber, for 500 years at a peppercorn rent. 17. On a field on Paskeston farm, Cosheston parish, is St. David's Well : pilgrimages were formerly made to it : a few stones, much overgrown, may be the foundations of the well-head—Anc. Mon. Pem. 18. On Harglodd Issa farm, St. Davids parish, 1669—J. H. Davies Deeds in NLW.

FF. DDWYSANT. Two wells at a cottage so-called, about 50 yards SE of Penrith parish church : it is said that the original holy well was not the cottage well, but a spring in a field on the S of the road : the name is said to derive from two holy women who once dwelt there—PAS.

ST. DECUMAN'S WELL. A short distance SW of Rhoscrowther church : —Fenton TP, 219. For the name Decuman (Degyman) see OPem, ii, 304 *n*. See above pp. 37.

FF. DEILO (2). 1. On the boundary of the parishes of Crinow and Lampeter Velfrey, in a field S of Llangwathen farm, a few hundred yards from Crinow church : it was once known for its. healing properties—Arch. Cam., 1896, 265 : Anc. Mon. Pem. 2: In Llandeilo Llwydiarth, near the ruined church : also called Ff: yr Ychen. It is about 100 yards NE of the church, and was protected by a stone enclosure, while the overflow passed into a pond. It still has a reputation for curing tuberculosis, whooping cough, and certain respitory diseases. An old man, alive in 1906, remembered many people coming to the well who 'were cured by faith', and as a boy, he and two other lads were cured of an illness after drinking the water out of Teilo's skull early in the morning—Carlisle TDW : JCD, 299-300 : Timmins, 173 : Pem. Antiq. 752 Arch. Cam., 1898, 276, illustr : Rhys CF, 400 : LBS, iv, 239-40 : Anc. Mon. Pem. See above p. 25, 81, 116.

FF. DEGAN. Near Tai Bach, Llanwnda parish : a stream running from it reaches the sea about half a mile away, near which is the site of Capel Degan, Cnwc Sant Degan, and a field called Park y Capel. In 1720, Goff, mentioning the well and the 'ruined chapel,' said, 'above the said spring a tumulus called St. Degan's knwc or knoll, where people resort to seat themselves on holidays and Sundays.' Fenton (TP, 13), wrote that veneration for Degan ' is hereditary amongst the inhabitants of this district, who tell a thousand miraculous stories of him,' and described one of his relics. Tegan survives as a surname in NW Pembrokeshire.

FF. DOGMAEL. Immediately outside the churchyard of Meline : the water for the font was formerly taken from it : it is too small for total immersion.—Anc. Mon. Pem.

FF. EDRIN/EDREN. In St. Edrins parish, formerly in the churchyard. See above pp. 105, 117.

ELLEN'S WELL (2). 1. On the cliffs, half a mile E of Chapel Bay, Angle parish. 2. A farm in Llawhaden parish : the Welsh name for the neighbouring parish of Bletherston is Tref Elen.

FF. FAEDDOG. Near Porthmawr, St. Davids parish.

FF. FAIR (15). A.1. In Maenclochog parish : cured rheumatism—Carlisle TDW. See above p. 16. 2. Just outside Eglwyswrw village, near the road to Newport. 3. In Llanychllwydog parish : ' Park Ffynnon fair ' on Sychpant farm (TM, 1842). 4. In Ffynnon Fair Wood, Llanfair Nantygof parish, above half a mile NE of the parish church. 5. At the side of the road in the S corner of Henrysmoat parish : it is protected by a few boulders—Anc. Mon. Pem. 6. In Mathry parish : ' Park Ffynnon fair ' on Pencnwc farm in 1842 (TM). 7. Ff. Fair near Ambleston village, Ambleston parish 1830—NLW Deeds. B. As St. Mary's Well. 8. At the E end of St. David's Cathedral—Jones and Freeman, St. Davids, 232. 9. Near the site of St. Mary's Chapel, about half a mile N of Angle : mentioned by G. Owen—OPem, ii, 555 : it has been covered and a pump erected—Anc. Mon. Pem. 10. ' St. Mary's Wellback, a fieldname in Camrose parish. C. As Lady Well. 11. On Cresswell Hill. See above p. 48. 12. By the parish church of Spittal which is dedicated to St. Mary. 13. In Roch parish, whose church is dedicated to St. Mary. 14. On Moysland farm in St. Mary Out Liberty, Tenby : near this well, a white cornelian seal bearing a mitre and a coat of arms was once found—PAS. 15. In the parish of the Hamlet of St. Thomas, Haverfordwest.

PISTYLL SAN FFRAID. *Pistyll San ffred*, near the old chapel of St. Ffraid, near Henllys, Nevern parish, 1418—NLW Bronwydd Deeds. The field on the NW and next to Castell Henllys is called

Pant Sant Fread—TM. The O.S. Map 6″ shows a spring there. *Capel St. Ffredde* is mentioned by G. Owen as a chapel to which pilgrimages were made—OPem, ii, 509.

FF. FIHANGEL. Near Castlebythe church : the water rises in a small stone-built basin—Anc. Mon. Pem.

ST. GOVAN'S WELL. On the cliff side by St. Govan's chapel, Bosherston parish : especially famous in the cure of failing eyesight, lameness, and rheumatism. In 1775 Sir Thomas Gery Cullum saw a man from Carmarthen who had a pain in his hip bathing the afflicted part and drinking the water : some money was placed on a stone altar in the chapel for the ' priestess ' : the water was lifted out with a limpet-shell—Y Cymmr, 1927, 46-7. It is mentioned as a popular resort of sufferers by Fenton (TP 227) and Carlisle (TDW). Towards the middle of the century it was still visited and crutches were seen on the chapel altar—Lewis TDW : BGSW, 196. Near the well is a deposit of red clay formed by rock decomposition, and great virtue was attached to it : a poultice of this was applied to limbs and eyes, and the patients then lay there for several hours in the sun. See above pp. 66, 77, 79, 100.

FF. GURIG. In Newport, where Ffair Gurig was formerly held : Capel Curig was to the SE of the castle.

FF. GWESLAN/GWESTLAN. During a drought, Gweslan and Eluid, disciples of St. David, caused through prayer, Gweslan's Fountain and Eliud's Fountain, to rise in the city of St. Davids, at which wells, the blind, crippled, and diseased persons were cured —El, 110 et. seq. Following the account of Pistyll Dewi, which distilled wine, Rhygyfarch wrote, ' But we know of other sweet waters too, given by the disciples in imitation of the father, serviceable for human use and health '—WESD, 16. The names are long lost and the wells cannot be identified. See LBS, s.n.

PISTYLL HOWEL (2). 1. *Pistyll Howell* in Whitechurch (Cemaes) 1591-95—NLW Bronwydd Deeds. 2. In Llanwnda parish : ' Park ffynnon Howel ' near Rhos Howel—TM 1843.

FF. IAGO. In Bayvil parish.

FF. IASE. In Nevern parish : ' fonon Yease ' 1503—Bronwydd Deeds. Iase was the Welsh form of Joseph.

ST. JOHN'S WELL—In Windpipe Lane, Tenby.

ST. JUSTINIAN'S WELL. On the SE of St. Justinian's chapel, St. David's parish—Willis SD, 54 : Anc Mon Pem. See above pp. 36-7.

FF. LAWDDOG. In Bridell parish.

ST. LEONARD'S CHAPEL WELL. Slight remains may be seen on the NE slope of the Rath in Rudbaxton parish : the chapel is mentioned in 1398 : the well, adjoining the chapel site, was restored a few years before 1915—Anc. Mon. Pem. Its water was especially good for sore eyes—JCD, 301.

ST. LEONARD'S WELL. By the roadside, a short distance from Rosemarket parish church.

ST. MADOC'S WELL. Outside the churchyard wall of Rudbaxton parish church (ded. St. Michael). The saint's name is also preserved in a field called St. Madoc's Park, SW of Trerhos in Hayscastle parish.

MARGARET'S WELL. W of Templeton village.

PISTYLL MEUGAN. This well and its chapel were famous in medieval times. No traces of the chapel now exist. Pistyll Meugan, about half a mile E by N of Llanfair Nantgwyn parish church, still flows strongly in the yard of Pistyll Meugan farm. In *Llyfer Plygain*, 1618, it is called ' Sainct Meigan yng-Hemys', where fairs were said to have been held on Ascension Day, Thursday after Trinity Sunday, and the Monday after St. Martin's Day. Traditions of Ffair Feugan still remain. The Rural Dean of Cemaes wrote to me, " The reason commonly attributed for the building of the church at Meigan is, that there are several streams of water to the south of the church's traditional site, which are said to contain three distinct types of water which will never mix. One is said to be good for the eyes, and the cure of warts, another for rheumatics and crippled joints, and the third for 'clefyd y galon ' . . . " The farm of Pistyll Meugan is partly in Bridell and Llanfairnantgwyn parishes. Cf. the names, Spite Meigan (Eglwyswrw), Llanfeigan and Meigan Hill (Bridell), and Cwm Meugan (Llanfairnantgwyn). Trefeigan, near Croes-goch, is probably named after a layman. See above pp. 26, 59.

ST. NICHOLAS WELL (2). 1. A copious spring now enclosed within a conduit at Watery Lane, Monkton—Anc. Mon. Pem. 2. Ff. Nicholas in Llanychllwydog parish—Lhuyd Par, iii, 82.

ST. NON'S WELL. Near the ruins of Non's chapel, St. Davids. It cured all kinds of complaints, and was reputed to ebb and flow. When it was cleaned in 1825, coins were found in it, bearing out Fenton's statement in 1810 (TP, 63-4). See PAS : JCD, 305-6 : AAW : WWHR, vi, 40. See above pp. 27, 42, 69, 79. The Roman Catholics restored this ancient well, and in July 1951, it was solemnly re-dedicated and a pilgrimage made to it—The Western Telegraph, 12 July 1951.

ST. OWEN'S WELL. In Narberth parish—BM Stowe MS. 1024 (18th cent.). The name is lost. See above p. 17.

ST. PETROX WELL. On the glebe of St. Petrox.—Lhuyd Par, iii, 5.

ST. SALMON'S WELL. The name of part of a field in Steynton parish (TM), but now lost.

FF. SAMSON (3). 1. S of Llangolman. See OPem, i, 255. 2. In Llandeloy parish : 'park Ffynnon Sampson' on Trenichol farm, 1845 (TM). 3. Pistyll Samson, near Bedd Samson, Newport parish. See above pp. 4, 43.

FF. WNDA. 'Park Ffynnon Unda' (Will 1777, and TM, 1843) on Penfeidir farm, Llanwnda parish. See above p. 43.

CLASS B :

BATHESLAND CHURCH HILL. In Roch parish about 500 yards SE of a site marked as that of a church is 'the holy well' ; and midway between the site and the well is a second, unnamed spring : immediately S is Bathesland farm—Anc. Mon. Pem.

BLETHERSTON HOLY WELL (2). 1. Immediately NW of Holywell Cottage, Bletherston parish is 'The Holy Well', formerly of repute in children's ailments—Anc. Mon. Pem. 2. To the north of the church is a 'Holy Well' from which water for baptism used to be drawn—*ib*.

BURTON CHURCHYARD WELL. It has been used occasionally as a baptistry : restored and cemented : the well space is 8½ feet by 3½ feet, and 3½ feet deep—Anc. Mon. Pem.

CARSWELL. In Jeffreston parish : a chapel once stood there—PRO, Patents, 38 Henry VIII.

CASTLE RAG WELL. Near Brimaston, Hayscastle parish. Tradition states that pilgrims used ' to exchange their rags there ', which accounts for the name !

FF. CWMWDIG. In the farmyard of Cwmwdig. There was a chapel over it, described in medieval deeds as Eglwys Cwmwdig. In the 17th century the well was still ' finely arched over '—Fenton TP, 65 : Anc. Mon. Pem. See above p. 76.

GUMFRESTON CHURCHYARD WELLS. Just S of the church is a worn flight of stone steps leading to three wells, two of which are chalybeate : they were visited by many people : crooked pins were thrown into them on Easter Day. See above p. 90.

HOLY LAKE (2). 1. A holy well in a field called Holy Lake on Trerhos farm, Hayscastle parish. 2. A field so named on Bernards Hill farm, Hayscastle parish—TM, 1842.

LLANDDINOG WELL. In Llandeloy parish : said to have been the holy well of a chapel which is traditionally said to have been at this farm.

LLANDELOY CHURCHYARD WELL. At one time enclosed with masonry, and among the remains of this, scattered around the well, a piece was found with a niche carved in it. An eel is said to have lived in the well. Its water is used for domestic purposes.

LLANLLAWER HOLY WELL. Just outside the churchyard wall on the NE side : enclosed by a chamber of rough masonry, 6½ feet from the rudely-vaulted crown to the base : evidently constructed for bodily immersion—Anc. Mon. Pem. ' . . . once had the reputation of most miraculous efficacy in various disorders ' but ' of late years ' visitors and offerings were very few—Fenton TP, 312. It was supposed to be good in cases of sore eyes, and coins and pins were offered. When ill was ' wished ' towards any one, a bent pin was thrown in—PAS. It also seems to have been called Ff. Gapan —WESD, 101.

NINE WELLS/NAWFFYNNON. Near the boundary of St. Davids and Whitchurch parishes. See above p. 26.

FF. PENARTHUR. In St. David's parish. See above pp. 5, 17.

RHYNDASTON HOLY WELL. A fine spring in a field called Holy Well on Rhyndaston farm, next to Park y Twmp : efficacious in eye affections, and was visited by people from great distances—Arch. Cam., 1898, 195.

SAINT'S WELL. In Minwere parish. 'Seynts well'—PRO, Patents, Henry VIII: 'Sayntes well' 1542-53—Haverfordwest Corporation Deeds.

FF. SHAN SHILIN. Near Letterston church. A 'legend,' recorded in 1888, stated that the well was named after an old woman called Shan who had fallen into it, and in whose pocket a shilling was found—*Cymru Fu*, 18 Feb. 1888. It is said that its curative waters were once sold at a shilling a bottle, and hence the name—JCD, 306. St. Silin's name has been suggested as the origin, and the church is dedicated to St. Giles.

FF. UCHAF and ISAF. Two wells near Martell Bridge, Little Newcastle parish. Tradition says that pilgrims refreshed themselves there before starting on their last lap to St. David's—ex inf. Mr. S. G. Howells.

WAKESWELL. In St. Twynells parish.

WARREN HOLY WELL. 'There is a holy well in the churchyard on the west of the tower, on the steps of which once stood a cross, on the south,' 1851—OWC, 124.

FF. WEN. Between Treiva and Hendre Cross, Llandeloy parish: once regarded as a holy well.

WHITEWELL. About a quarter of a mile S of St. David's Cathedral. '. . . the well that gave the name to it retains its arched covering . . .' Fenton TP, 64. Here Bishop Beck (1280-93) formed a hospital, called later the priory of Whitewell. The site of its chapel is by the spring. The spring has been diverted for domestic uses and supplies the deanery—Anc. Mon. Pem: WWHR, VI, 64-5. See NCPN, 32.

CLASS C:

CARNCWN WELL. At the foot of Carn Ingli, on the right of the road leading from Newport to Cilgwyn: in a cleft of an overhanging rock, and is said to rise and fall with the sea tides: reputed to cure warts, a pin being thrown into the well for each wart—Anc. Mon. Pem.

FF. CLAF. On Dyffryn farm, Llampeter Velfrey. 'Sick folk used to drink at this well'—PAS.

HIGGON'S WELL. In Uzmaston parish : said to have been of great repute in medieval times : visited by Banks in 1767 : Norris made two good sketches of it showing a little building with a window, and roof pitched like a church—Anc. Mon. Pem, illustr.

HOTWELLS. In Little Newcastle parish : medicinal.

LLANLLAWER WELL. On the side of Llanllawer mountain, formerly in high repute for agues, etc., but now neglected—Lewis TDW.

FF. LYGAID (2). 1. On the S side of Castell Clegyr Boia, St. Davids parish—Arch. Cam., 1903, 1 ff. It was an 'ebb and flow well,' and G. Owen states that children looked at it in order to learn the state of the seatides—O Pem, i, 245 : see also Willis SD, 64. Its name suggests that it was considered curative in cases of eye trouble. 2. 'Ffynon ligaud,' St. Dogmaels parish—Census 1851.

FF. OLDEN. About 500 yards NW of Little Newcastle village : formerly in repute for infantile ailments : 'Ffynnon Olden' appears as a field name in 1844—TM. Carlisle (TDW) and Lewis (TDW) miscall it *Golden Well,* saying that it was an 'ebb and flow well' and that it was efficacious for coughs and sore eyes.

TRELEWELYN WELL. In Manorowen parish : reputed to cure sore eyes—PAS.

CLASS D :

FF. ADDA (2). 1. In Meline parish. (2) W of Trecwn House.

FF. ARTHUR. 'Park ffynnon Arthur' on Henfedde farm, Clydey parish—TM. 1849. Two fairs were held annually at Henfedde.

BISHOP'S WELL. The name of a field near Houghton schoolhouse, Burton parish : there are several springs near, but none is now called Bishop's Well.—Anc. Mon. Pem.

FF. CEISIED. 'fynnon Ceisied' from which the brook Nant Erwyn flows—Lhuyd, iii, 13 (sub. Llanglydwen, Carms.) Ffynnon Ceisied (near Llain Ceisied) and Rhydyceisied are in Llanfyrnach parish. Cf. Nant y Ceisiad, Mon.

CLERKENWELL. In Newport. 'Clerkynwell in Newport' 1434 —Journal NLW, 1951, p. 4. The clerk's well. See NCPN, 41.

FF. DICI. In Nevern parish, 1851—Census.

FF. DRIDIAN. Near Ffynnondridian farm, St. Nicholas parish, is 'the consecrated well which characterizes and gives its name to the spot'—Fenton TP, 15. See above p. 5.

FF. DUNAWD. Near St. Davids: See above p. 41.

FF. DWGI. In Llanycefn parish.

FF. FRENIN. Near Ambleston village.—TM. 1843.

FF. GADWGAN. In Llanfyrnach parish, 1841.

FF. LEWELYN. E of Mynydd Morfa, just over the border of Mathry parish, in Granston parish.

FF. OFY. In Dinas parish: reputed as a healing well. 'Penrynzovy' (near Ff. Ofy) 1394—PRO, AD: 'Ffynnon ofy' 1585—NLW Bronwydd Deeds. 'ffinnonovey' 1723—NLW Llwyngwair Deeds.

FF. OLWEN. In Llanfair Nantygof parish, 1712—NLW EE & W Deeds.

PRIEST'S WELL. Near Red Cottages, Narberth. 'Preistes will' 547—Cal PR re Pem, iii, 134. See above pp. 89, 129.

CLASS E:

FF. BARCUD. On the borders of St. Davids' and Llanrhian parishes: also called Kite Well.

PISTYLL BLAIDD. In Nevern parish, 'Pistyll y Blaidd', 'Pant y llech', and 'Maen Hir y Bayvill' are mentioned as being in the same neighbourhood in 1603—NLW Bronwydd Deeds.

BRANDY WELL (2). 1. In Amroth. 2. In Lampeter Velfrey.

FF. Y BRAG. Near Llechryd, 1609—NLW, Morgan Richardson Deeds.

BRORGHYS WELL. 'the Brorghys Well' 1492. At St. Davids. Perhaps identical with Ff. y Cwcwll (q.v.).

FF. Y GARREG. Close to a mound called Bedd Samson near the mouth of the river Nevern, in Newport parish. See above p. 14.

FF. CERRIG HIRION. In Park Cerrig Hirion near Cromlech Meibion Owen, Nevern parish : there are remains of a cromlech in the field—Anc. Mon. Pem.

FF. CORANAU/CROWNSWELL. 'Crowneswell' 1633, 1680—NLW, Bronwydd Deeds : 'Fynoncoraney' in Bridell parish—Census 1841.

FF. CRAIR. 'Finnon Crare otherwise Crayre' 1639—NLW Evans and Williams Deeds. Is *crair* (relic) in question here? Cf. Ff. y *Creiriwr*, Denbighshire, p. 176 above.

CROESWELL. In Fishguard parish, 1816—PR. Now lost.

CROSSWELL. In Meline parish, 1851.

FF. Y CWCWLL. On Quickwell Hill, outside the close of St. Davids Cathedral. 'the Cwccwll Well' 1828—PR : WWHR viii, 88, 'the well called Fwnnon y kwckwill,' 1624—NLW Evans and Williams Deeds.

FF. DROYTEN. In Letterston parish, 1790.

FF. FANWYDD. In Newport parish. Ff. fanwidd 1841—Census. Ff. fanwydd 1855—PR. Ff. manwyd 1851—Census.

FF. GAMIL. In Llandilo Llwydiarth parish, 1841—Census.

GRINSTON WELL. On Grinston, Brawdy parish. A flying snake (*gwiber*), covered with scales (*crwgwn*) is said to have flown from St. Edrin church tower to the marshy Rholwm near Grinston, where it lurks, and at nights visits Grinston well and coils up in the bottom of it.

FF. HALOG. In Clydey parish.

PISTYLL HOTCH. In Fishguard. 'Pistyll Hotch' 1772—PRO. Papers of Great Sessions Pembs., 1772.

FF. LICWR. Near Crosswell, N. Pem.

LLANUNWAS WELL. On the seaward side of Llanunwas, Whitchurch parish. 'A long time ago' a man found two circular stones, similar to hand-querns in the well. See above p. 54.

PENCW WELLS. On Pencw headland, above Goodwick : said to ebb and flow—Fenton TP, 11. See above p. 16.

PISTYLL PWG (2). 1. In Nevern parish. 2. In Maenclochog parish.

FF. WAIR. In New Moat parish.

FF. WELL-NA-BUWCH. In Llandewy Velfrey parish : marked on Eman Bowen Map. 'Finnon Gwell Nathan,' 1703—Picton Castle Deeds.

FF. YSBRYD. 'Finnonisprid'—Census 1841. In Little Newcastle parish.

RADNORSHIRE

CLASS A :

ST. ANNE'S WELL. About half a mile from Presteigne, at the side of the river Lugg.

CHADWELL. In the deanery of Clun—Rees Map.

PISTYLL CYNLLO. Near Llanbister church : '*a noted spring*'—Carlisle TDW. The church is dedicated to St. Cynllo.

FF. DDEWI. Or David's Well, in Llanbadarn Fynydd parish : much frequented, highly esteemed—Carlisle TDW.

FF. FAIR. In Rhaeadr parish. Formerly much frequented by young couples to whom it was supposed to bring good luck after drinking sweetened water : was considered (in 1911) to be efficacious in eye complaints—Anc. Mon. Rad. Visited on Sunday evenings by young people during spring and summer, to drink water sweetened with sugar—Williams, Rad., 290 : JCD, 303. See above pp. 81, 102, 112.

FF. GEWYDD. At Disserth.

FF. GYNYDD. About $1\frac{1}{2}$ miles NW of Glasbury, on the N edge of Ff. Gynydd Common. Finnon Kynid 1653—Arch. Cam., 1918, 32. Called Ff. Gynidr, and known locally as a 'wishing well' in 1949—Howse, Rad., 211. See Lhuyd Par, ii, 31. In the period 1900-10 a small open well-house was erected over it, and the earlier well-chamber has been partially covered over.—Anc. Mon. Rad.

JACKET'S WELL. Near Knighton : formerly called St. Edward's Well, its water was applied externally in cases of sprains and rheumatism : —Howse, Rad, 211. It has been suggested that the name is a corruption of Ff. Iechyd, but there are no early forms to establish the etymology. See above p. 106.

PETER'S WELL. Near Cwm Gwalley : known in the 1850s—Howse, Rad, 211.

CLASS B :

BLACK WELL. N of the site of Rhaeadr castle, and traditionally said to have been its water supply : the field is called Waun y Capel—Anc. Mon. Rad.

CAPEL FFYNNON. In Cascob parish, there is a field called *Capel Ffynnon*—Lhuyd Par, ii, 36.

LLANDRINDOD. There is a holy well by the old church at Llandrindod—Howse, Rad., 211. See above p. 102.

PILLETH CHURCHYARD WELL. In the parish churchyard on the N side of the tower is the holy well formerly visited for the cure of eye diseases : an oblong enclosure with steps leading to the water at the south end—Anc. Mon. Rad : Glynne, Arch. Cam., 1897, 56 : Williams, Rad, 313. The well had been allowed to deteriorate, but when it was cleaned about 1910-11, steps leading to it were discovered.—Arch. Cam., 1911, 114. The church is dedicated to St. Mary.

SAINT'S WELL. Near Ffynnon Garreg farm, Abbey Cwmhir : the name is lost—Anc. Mon. Rad.

CLASS C :

CLYRO WELL. Close to Tir y Mynach near Clyro : said to be efficacious in eye complaints—Carlisle TDW ; Anc. Mon. Rad. Also called The Monk's Well.

FF. LLANANNO. By Knighton : medicinal.

LLANBISTER PARISH WELLS. Three 'black sulphurous mineral springs', visited by people suffering from skin diseases.—Williams, Rad., 232.

FF. NEWYDD. At the foot of Rallt Hill, Llanano parish: good for scorbutic and scrofulous complaints: visited in June, July, and August, when the water was supposed to be most efficacious—Williams, Rad, 230.

CLASS D:
SOLDIER'S WELL. In Llanbister parish.

CLASS E:
BUTTER WELL. In Llanbadarn Fynydd.

LLANDEGLA WELL. A sulphurous well on the river Cymaron: it may have been once under the patronage of Tegla.

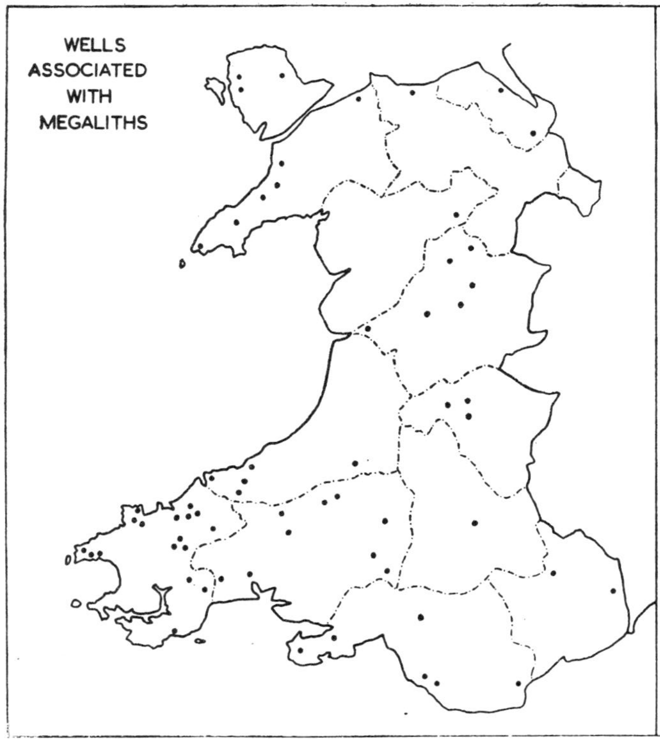
WELLS
ASSOCIATED
WITH
MEGALITHS

Map 1.

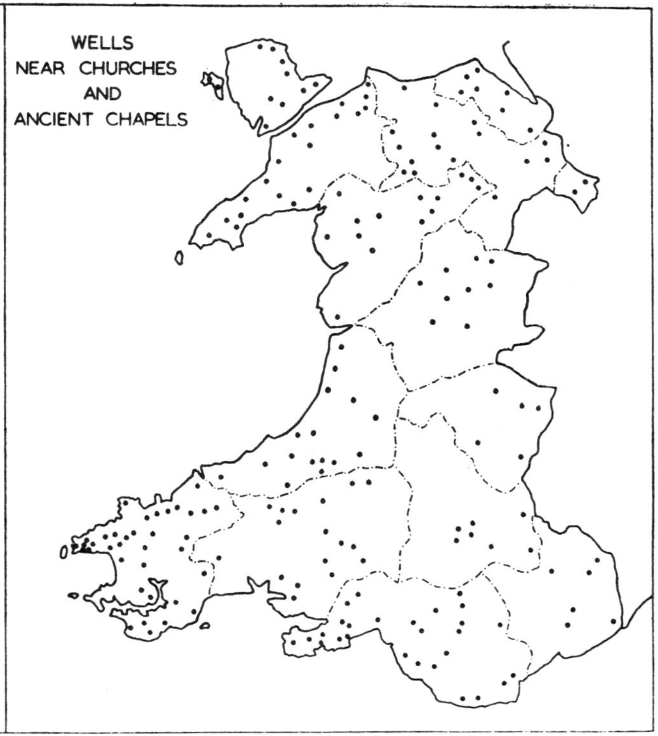
WELLS
NEAR CHURCHES
AND
ANCIENT CHAPELS

Map 2.

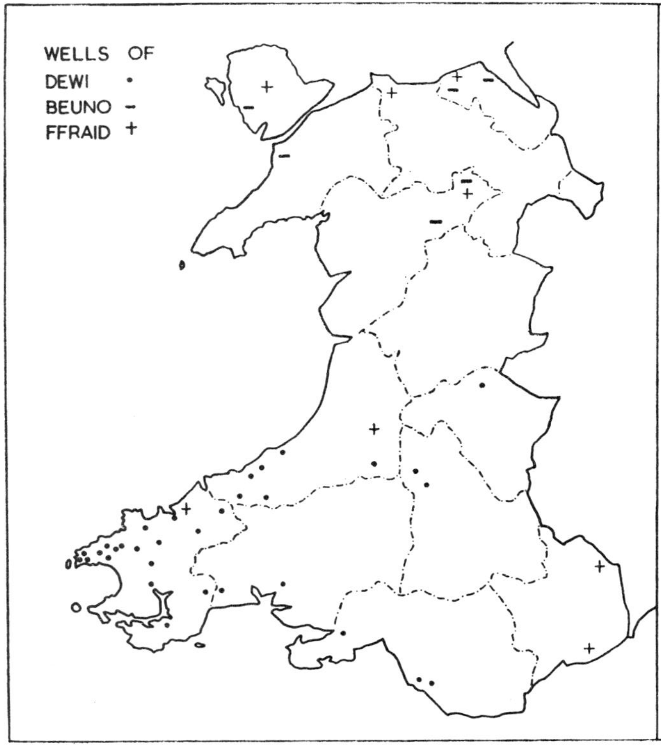
WELLS OF
DEWI •
BEUNO –
FFRAID +

Map 3.

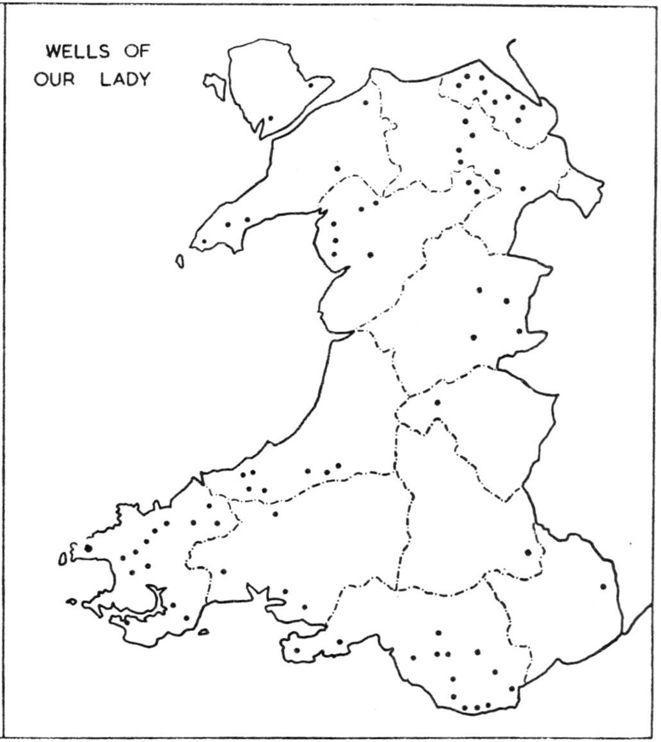
WELLS OF
OUR LADY

Map 4.

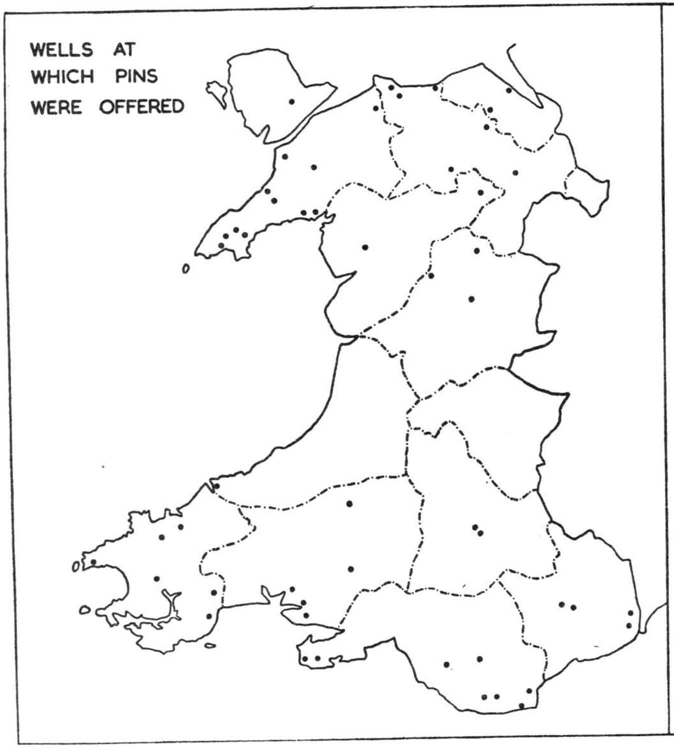
WELLS AT
WHICH PINS
WERE OFFERED

Map 5.

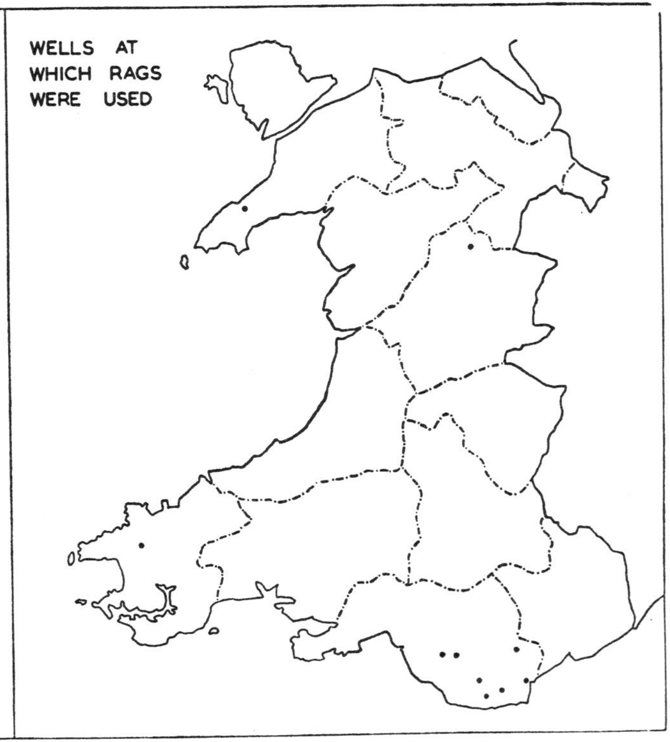
WELLS AT
WHICH RAGS
WERE USED

Map 6.

INDEX

D

E

F

G

H